18.50

SO-ARK-471

GOVERNORS STATE UNIVERSITY LIBRARY

3 1611 00297 6790

HD
8799
.G53
P45

Peil, Margaret
    The Ghanaian factory
worker: industrial man
in Africa. 48590

THE GHANAIAN FACTORY WORKER:
INDUSTRIAL MAN IN AFRICA

AFRICAN STUDIES SERIES

General Editor: DR J. R. GOODY

THE GHANAIAN FACTORY WORKER: INDUSTRIAL MAN IN AFRICA

by MARGARET PEIL

Centre of West African Studies
University of Birmingham

UNIVERSITY LIBRARY
GOVERNORS STATE UNIVERSITY
PARK FOREST SOUTH, ILL.

CAMBRIDGE

AT THE UNIVERSITY PRESS 1972

Published by the Syndics of the Cambridge University Press
Bentley House, 200 Euston Road, London NW1 2DB
American Branch: 32 East 57th Street, New York, N.Y.10022

© Cambridge University Press 1972

Library of Congress Catalogue Card Number: 73–160091

ISBN: 0 521 08296 X

Printed in Great Britain
by Alden & Mowbray Ltd
at the Alden Press, Oxford

HD
8799
.G53
P45

CONTENTS

TABLES

MAPS

ACKNOWLEDGEMENTS

During my early days as a graduate student of sociology, Joseph P. Fitzpatrick convinced me of the important part industrial workers play in national development. The works of J. Clyde Mitchell were a prime example of the possibilities of research in this field in Africa and provided many insights to guide my work.

This study could not have been carried out without the generosity of the factory managers in allowing us to conduct the lengthy interviews, the willing cooperation of the workers, the interest and hard work of the interviewers and the financial assistance of Grant MH 11793-01 from the National Institute of Mental Health in Washington, D.C. Encouragement and advice in the various stages of the project came from, among others, Jack Caldwell, Jack Goody, André Hauser and Peter Lloyd. As the manuscript took shape, Nelson Addo, Gi Baldamus, Esther Goody, Peter Mitchell, Christine Oppong and Douglas Rimmer were kind enough to read various chapters and suggest improvements. They are not to be held responsible for the result, of course, since their advice was not always taken.

The task of analyzing the data was facilitated by John Koster's expert assistance with computer programs and by many conversations with colleagues and students at the University of Ghana during the five years I taught there. These cannot be credited individually, because it is no longer possible to remember the source of various ideas, but I hope they will be pleased to see the use to which their ideas have been put. To all of these and to my colleagues in Birmingham who encouraged me during the long process of translating the survey into a manuscript, I want to express my sincere gratitude.

MARGARET PEIL

Centre of West African Studies
University of Birmingham
October 1971

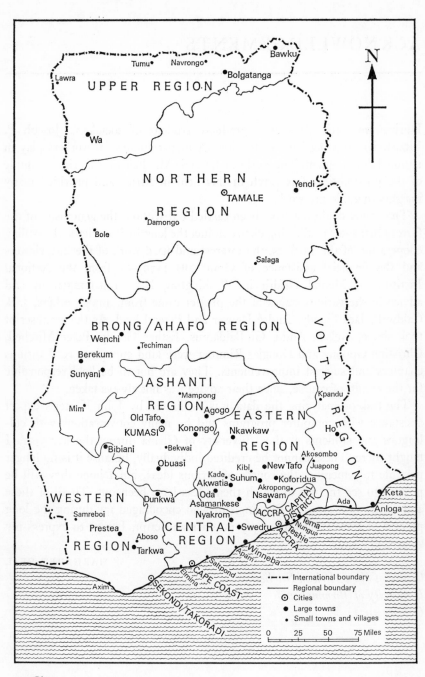

N

UPPER REGION

Lawra
Tumu • Navrongo • Bawku •
Bolgatanga

Wa •

NORTHERN

REGION

Yendi •
⊙ TAMALE

Damongo •

Bole •

Salaga •

BRONG/AHAFO REGION

Wenchi •
Techiman •

Berekum •

Sunyani •

VOLTA REGION

ASHANTI

Mim •
Mampong •

REGION
Agogo •

Old Tafo •
KUMASI ⊙ Konongo •

EASTERN

Kpandu •

Ho •

Bibiani •
Bekwai •

REGION

Obuasi •

Akosombo •

Kade • Kibi • New Tafo • Juapong •
Akwatia • Suhum • Koforidua •
Oda • Akropong •
Dunkwa • Nsawam •

WESTERN

Samreboi •

Asamankese •
Nyakrom •
Swedru ⊙

Keta •
Anloga •
Ada •

ACCRA CAPITAL DISTRICT
Tema •

Prestea •

CENTRAL

ACCRA ⊙
Nungua •
Teshie •

REGION
Aboso •
Tarkwa •

REGION

Winneba •
Apam •

Axim •

Saltpond ⊙
Elmina ⊙ CAPE COAST ⊙

⊙ SEKONDI/TAKORADI

-·-·- International boundary
——— Regional boundary
⊙ Cities
• Large towns
• Small towns and villages

0   25   50   75 Miles

1 Ghana
After a map drawn by the Survey of Ghana

CHAPTER I

INTRODUCTION

In 1957, Ghana became the first sub-Saharan African nation to obtain her independence from colonial rule. She has long been known as the world's foremost producer of cocoa and exports sizeable quantities of gold, timber, manganese and industrial diamonds, but, like most new nations, she aspires to industrialize her economy. Although the country is small by world standards, its eight million people can support moderately sized industries producing relatively inexpensive consumer goods. These provide employment for a gradually increasing number of workers, mostly in urban areas. *Per capita* income was £85 in 1961, which is high for tropical Africa. Ghana is second only to Ivory Coast among the countries in West Africa in the proportion of the population engaged in wage labour (about thirty-five per thousand).

According to the 1960 Population Census, there were over 2.5 million persons aged fifteen or above in the labour force. Of these, 62% were in agriculture, fishing or lumbering, 14% in commerce, and 6% in services. Only 9% of the working population (233,947 people) were engaged in manufacturing. The majority of these are self-employed, small-scale craftsmen (and women) who provide for local needs as carpenters, tailors, fitters etc. Many are part-time farmers, practicing their trade in the dry season or whenever there is a demand for their services. Participation in manufacturing in the conventional sense is limited to less than a quarter of the total.

Factory workers are thus a very small proportion of the total population, but they are important to the future development of the country. In addition, the study of Ghanaian factory workers provides useful information on the adaptation to industrial employment of workers in countries at a similar stage of development. This book is designed to provide a well-rounded view of the lives of Ghanaian workers on and off the job so that their situation and responses can be compared with those of workers elsewhere. This chapter will provide a brief introduction to Ghana for those who are unfamiliar with it, though broader background reading would help the reader to understand those aspects of the industrial situation which are unique to Ghana (see Boateng 1966, Caldwell 1967, Fage 1969, Foster 1965).

LAND AND PEOPLE

Ghana is administratively divided into eight regions and the Accra Capital District (C.D.) (see map 1, p. x). On the basis of geography, culture and level of development, these regions can be conveniently grouped to divide the country into five areas: the north includes Northern and Upper Regions, which were known as the Northern Territories in colonial days; the centre combines Brong/Ahafo Region with Ashanti, from which it was split after independence; the southwest also recombines two recently separated regions, Central and Western; the Accra C.D. is in many ways part of Eastern Region though they are administratively separate; and lastly, the Volta Region, which became British Mandated Territory after the First World War and whose people voted to join Ghana at independence. Parts of the coast have been in contact with Europe since the Portuguese landed at Elmina in the fifteenth century; there were over 200 forts along the coast during the centuries of slave trading which followed. British 'protection' had been extended to the present northern border by 1898. Differences between the north and the rest of the country are greater than differences between central and southern areas; a north–south dichotomy will be used frequently in subsequent discussion.

The north has always been relatively neglected; most of its people are subsistence farmers whose chief source of money income is the remittances of family members working in the south. Many northerners prefer to live in family compounds scattered across the savannah and surrounded by their farms of millet and yams. Southerners prefer to live in villages from which they walk out to their farms in the heavily forested 'bush'. Experience of village life helps southerners adjust to cities, as does their greater participation in the money economy through cash crop farming and widespread trading. Schooling is still rare in the north because of the dispersal of children, poverty, and the opposition of parents who see education as weaning children from traditional ways. Since education is common in the south, most skilled and clerical jobs go to southerners, while northern migrants become labourers on the cocoa farms, mines, harbours etc. Northerners are beginning to demand more development funds and their position in the society will change as education becomes more widespread, but the disparity is marked at present.

Of the southern half of the country, Eastern Region profited from the early introduction of education and cocoa farming. Disease has killed the cocoa in the areas of early cultivation, but farmers have moved west and north, sending back money to provide amenities (especially schools) in their home villages. There are many small and medium-sized towns in Eastern and Central Regions which serve mainly as trading centres; many of the coastal towns were formerly ports. Gold and manganese mining and most of the timber industries are located in Western and Ashanti Regions; diamonds are mined in Eastern Region. Cocoa farming is prominent in the central area; recent expansion has been in Brong/Ahafo. Development of the centre was delayed by the ability of the Asante to keep out European traders and missionaries, but it has largely caught up with the south in recent years; education in Ashanti Region is more widespread than in rural areas of the southwest.

The north is ethnically divided into many groups, of which the main ones are the Dagombas, the Gonjas and the Mamprusis. Several kingdoms flourished in pre-colonial times, often preying on interstitial acephalous societies. Peoples of central and southern Ghana mostly belong to the Akan cluster, of which the Fanti and Asante are the largest groups. The Fanti are fishermen and farmers along the coast in Central and Western Regions. Their contact with European trade and education gave them a head start in development and they hold a notable proportion of clerical and administrative posts. The Asante kingdom was one of the great kingdoms of pre-colonial West Africa; the Asantehene (the paramount chief), who lives in Kumasi, continues to be an important figure in contemporary Ghana. The Ga–Adangme people are concentrated in the Accra C.D. Although many are still fishermen or farmers, large numbers have taken advantage of the opportunities of 'their' town to obtain an education and well-paying jobs in the modern economy.

The Ewe homeland is in the southern and central Volta Region and the contiguous areas of Togo, but outmigration is high (as in the north) because of the poverty of the home area. Ewe fishermen are found along the coast as far as Sierra Leone, up the Volta River and even in Mali, where they dry Niger River fish for shipment to Ghana. Farmland is crowded and not suitable for cocoa in the south, but both cocoa and coffee are grown in central Volta Region. Mineral resources are also lacking in the area, though there is some hope that oil will be found off the coast. Volta Region's chief resource is its people. Early missionaries brought education and training in skills, both of which have been very popular. Manual work is looked on as a good way to get ahead, if one can get training. There is some tribal feeling against the Ewes by the predominant Akan, chiefly based on competition for

3

jobs and development funds, which was exacerbated by the 1969 elections.

Because Ghana is economically advanced compared to her neighbours, immigrants have come from all over West Africa to work there. The foreign-born adult population was over 475,000 in 1960, nearly 10% of the adult population of the country. Differences between Ghanaians from various parts of the country and immigrants will be evident in subsequent discussion. The primary socialization of various peoples has provided them with a wide range of attitudes and behaviour patterns. These result in varying responses to urban, industrial conditions, which provide useful information on the process of social change.

URBANIZATION

Although Ghana is predominantly a rural country, there is also a well-established urban component. Less than a quarter of the population lived in places of 5,000 or more people in 1960, but between a quarter and three-fifths of the population of large towns (over 10,000) in 1960 had been born there. The urban labour force has grown very rapidly in recent years, but it is relatively stable in the sense that most migrants to the urban areas plan a long stay and only return home if they are unable to find work. They go home occasionally to visit, but their major commitment is to the town.

A brief history of the four largest towns will provide some idea of the environment which migrants find there. Accra, Kumasi and Sekondi/Takoradi all date back to at least the seventeenth century, though most of their growth has taken place since the Second World War. They are thus older than most African towns except the Yoruba towns of Western Nigeria. Although they are ethnically heterogeneous, at least a third of the population of each belongs to a single tribe. Their sex ratios are not balanced, but they are relatively low for African towns, indicating that migrants often bring their wives and children with them (see table 1.2, p. 11).

In the sixteenth century, Ga farmers moved down to the coast to take up fishing and trade with Europeans visiting the coast. The first village established, just east of Korle Lagoon, is now part of central Accra. Other villages which are now controlled by the Accra/Tema Municipal Council include Osu, Labadi, Teshie, Nungua and Tema. To establish their presence and improve living conditions for their nationals, the British, Dutch and Swedes built forts within three miles of each other in the mid-seventeenth century. These were originally used for holding slaves awaiting shipment and as trading centres. One is now Government House and the other two, prisons.

The British moved the capital of the colony from Cape Coast to Accra in

TABLE I.I. *Population size of the four towns, 1891–1960*

Year	Accra	Kumasi	Sekondi[a]	Tema
1891	16,267	3,000	1,276	—
1901	14,842	6,280	4,095	—
1911	19,582	18,853	9,122	—
1921	38,049	20,268	9,500	—
1931	60,726	35,809	22,421	898
1948	133,771	71,436	43,898	1,932
1960	337,820	180,642	75,450	30,261[b]
1970	633,880	342,986	161,071	102,838

SOURCES: 1891–1921: Kimble 1963:144. 1931–
60: Census Reports, 1931, 1948, 1960. 1970:
Census Office, May 1970, Provisional results for
City Councils.
[a] 1931–70, Sekondi/Takoradi.
[b] Includes Tema New Town.

1877 and thus stimulated its development as a commerical and transportation centre. Though limited by an open roadstead from which goods had to be landed through the surf in canoes, Accra remained an important port until the Tema harbour was opened in 1962. The railway line from Accra to Kumasi was completed in 1923. It was used mainly for forwarding imported goods, since most of the cocoa and all the minerals and timber were exported through Takoradi.

Manufacturing has developed in Accra because of its centrality in the administrative and communications systems, its convenience to the source of imported raw materials, its pool of skilled and unskilled workers and the concentration of consumers in its large, wage-earning population. Printing, furniture and brewing have been established over a long period; by 1965 a wide variety of goods was being manufactured from imported and local raw materials by about sixty-five large firms (with thirty or more workers) and a multitude of smaller ones. Distribution to other parts of Ghana tends to be limited, especially outside the cities; very few products reach markets in neighbouring countries.

Attempts at municipal government date from the 1890s, but the imposition of rates was strongly resisted by the local populace. Problems of sanitation and overcrowding have been endemic from the early days. A piped water supply was introduced in 1915 and supplemented with water from the Volta River in 1966, but shortages are persistent. Several housing estates were built in the 1940s to rehouse victims of the 1939 earthquake, but these went mostly to middle-income people; the poor found what space they could in

5

the densely settled centre of town and in the fringe settlements such as Nima, where services were almost entirely lacking. Many of these fringe areas have now become part of the city, but they are still grossly neglected and conditions have worsened as their population has grown.

Central Accra has changed relatively little through the years. Fishermen still live there and ply their trade, fiercely resisting government plans for urban renewal. There is as yet no modern, central market and the narrow streets are often badly congested. There is a considerable resident population in the commercial area and manufacturing is carried out throughout the town, though the majority of large firms are found in the industrial estate on the Ring Road (see map 2, p. 158).

Two-fifths of the population are Ga, who regard Accra as their hometown even though some of them grew up in farming or fishing villages elsewhere. The rest of the population is very mixed, since Accra draws migrants from all over Ghana and from most other parts of West Africa. Non-Africans comprised 2% of the population in 1960. They have come from Europe, the Middle East, Asia and America on diplomatic and aid missions and especially to participate in trade and, more recently, in manufacturing. Growth has been very rapid in recent years; the population doubled between 1948 and 1960 and provisional results of the 1970 Census put it at well over half a million (see table 1.1). Since opportunities for employment have grown much less rapidly, unemployment is a serious problem.

Accra has long been an educational centre. Achimota School, opened in 1927, is one of the 'great schools' of West Africa, important in the training of the generation of civil servants and professionals who brought Ghana to independence. The University of Ghana, founded in 1948, shared its buildings for several years before moving from Achimota to Legon. Many other secondary, commercial and technical schools run by the government, the missions and private entrepreneurs are found in and around Accra. Students pour in, often without sufficient means to support themselves and pay school fees. They often become a drain on the resources of urban relatives. Only two-fifths of the adult men in Accra in 1960 had not attended school, which is considerably better than the national average of 70%.

By comparison with an industrialized country, a high proportion of the workers in Accra have remained independent. A quarter of the men and four-fifths of the women who were working were employers or self-employed (see table 1.3, p. 12). Most of the women are petty traders or hawkers, a traditional occupation of Ga women which is also popular with other coastal West African women. A quarter of the men are craft or production workers, often in small roadside workshops or in the compounds of the houses where they live. An eighth of the men are in clerical work, mostly in the civil service; a seventh are unskilled workers. The latter are mostly northern Ghanaians or men from countries to the north of Ghana. (Rouch (1954) describes this group.) The sex ratio for these 'strangers' is much higher than for the rest of the population, since they tend to come for shorter periods and leave their wives behind, whereas the average southern Ghanaian migrant to Accra usually plans a long stay and prefers to have his family with him.

Acquah (1958) provides a detailed study of Accra in the immediate pre-independence period. Although the city has grown considerably, many of her findings are still valid today.

Kumasi, known as the 'Garden City', is 164 miles inland from Accra in the heart of the rain forest and cocoa-growing area. Tradition holds that Kumasi was first built by the fourth king of Ashanti between 1663 and 1697. It became the capital of the Ashanti Confederacy under his successor. The British first visited Kumasi in 1817, when the Ashanti Confederacy claimed a large part of what is now southern Ghana. Later wars between the Asante and the British resulted in the destruction of Kumasi in 1874, the exile of the Asantihene in 1896 and the siege of Kumasi Fort in 1900.

With the coming of the railway line from Sekondi in 1903 and the development of cocoa as an export crop, Kumasi became a great marketing centre. Migrant workers on the gold mines and cocoa farms stop in Kumasi to purchase goods before returning to their homes all over West Africa. A popular saying has it that 'He who has not been to Kumasi will not go to paradise'. The great central market covers about 25 acres and may have up to 9,000 traders at a time (not counting relatives and assistants) (Garlick 1959:6).

The timber industry has also flourished in Kumasi, since the town is surrounded by high forest. Logs are brought on huge timber lorries to the Kumasi sawmills, many of them located on the Asukwa Industrial Estate. Most of the large mills were built after the war, as were other industries. In 1967 there were about thirty-five large manufacturing firms in Kumasi, including producers of bread, beer, minerals, fibre bags, cloth, shoes, furniture and fixtures; but the majority were sawmills.

The population is more homogeneous than in Accra or Takoradi, since Kumasi attracts large numbers of Asante from the surrounding region who bring their wives and children with them. Many cocoa farmers live in Kumasi and go out periodically to supervise their farms outside the city. Many other residents are northerners or non-Ghanaians engaged in trade. Two-thirds of the men and 60% of the women living in Kumasi in 1960 were born elsewhere; a sixth of the men were foreign-born.

B

Introduction

Although a mission was founded in Kumasi in 1839, restricted contact with outsiders allowed the maintenance of traditional practices and slowed the acceptance of Christianity and European education. The Asante have made up for their slow start in the last thirty years, but many migrants to Kumasi come from areas farther north where education is still rare. Thus, half the adult men and three-quarters of the women have never attended school. However, Kumasi is also a centre of advanced education. In 1966 it had eleven secondary schools and the University of Science and Technology, which trains engineers, architects and other applied scientists for the country as a whole.

There were British and Dutch forts at Sekondi (about 140 miles east of Accra) by the late seventeenth century and smaller posts were established at Takoradi (6 miles to the west) at about the same period (Kimble 1963). Sekondi was one of the few ports along the coast suitable for large ships and was chosen as the site for the railway because supplies could be unloaded there. The town's growth is chiefly due to the railway. In 1912, a railway general manager wrote:

Secondee is an upstart town, practically the creation of the railway, and an ever-expanding institution requires constant additions to the staff. Houses are now almost impossible for new men to find, rents are exorbitant and incidentally the cost of living is very high . . . The men live all over the place in wretched conditions. (Quoted by Davison 1956:587.)

The railway location and a railway village were eventually built to provide housing for some of the employees. The railway union has an important place in the development of industrial relations in Ghana. In 1918, before the union was started, railway workers in Sekondi staged the first recorded strike in the Gold Coast (Davison 1956:587).

What Sekondi owes to the railway, Takoradi owes to the port. The deep-water port was opened at Takoradi in 1928 to replace the open roadstead at Sekondi; it was extended in the early 1950s. Though Takoradi has largely been replaced by Tema for imports, it is still very important in exporting timber, manganese and cocoa. Takoradi is prone to the social problems of ports throughout the world. Its delinquency, prostitution, crime etc. are discussed by Busia (1950). This book also gives a vivid picture of the functioning of the municipal government, the educational system, the prevalence of intertribal marriage and the conditions under which people live. Housing has continued to be a problem. In 1952, Takoradi landlords and tenants were complaining that a law forbidding tenants to live in kitchens would result in thousands of people being homeless (*Ashanti Pioneer*, 26 July 1952).

Sekondi and Takoradi are joined in a Municipal Council embracing the

8

two towns and many villages between and near them. The area will hence-forth be referred to as Takoradi, since most of the industry is in Takoradi or between the two towns.

The presence of a port facilitated the development of the timber industry in Takoradi. There is evidence of sawmills and a furniture factory as well as 'motor vehicle construction and repairs' by 1920 (Macmillan 1920). In 1967 there were about fifteen large firms manufacturing cigarettes, cocoa butter, paper products, minerals, furniture, household utensils, cement blocks, metal products and boats in addition to planks and veneers. As in Kumasi, there were also small-scale printing firms and numerous other businesses too small for regular reporting to the Government Statistician.

Nearly three-quarters of the Takoradi population are migrants. Though over half of the people are Ahanta or Fanti from nearby, a fifth of the men and a tenth of the women were born outside Ghana. There are a large number of Nigerians and smaller numbers of Liberians and Voltaics (or were prior to the expulsions of December 1969). The Liberians work on the ships and in the harbour; the Nigerians are prominent in trade. Self-employment is less common in Takoradi than in Accra or Kumasi because Takoradi is a centre of transport rather than of trade. Export goods pass through the town; the money goes elsewhere. The sex ratio is higher than in the other two cities and the labour force participation rate for men is also higher, as befits a migrant town where men come to work and leave when they retire.

An interesting aspect of Takoradi is the varying levels of urbanization available to migrants. The city has a more spacious look than Accra or Kumasi; some of the outlying areas seem rural to the casual observer. Many of the workers do not live in the city centres or the housing estates of Adiembra or Effiakuma (built after the war to house the increasing popula-tion) but in villages between the cities or on the outskirts. Some of these are overcrowded slums, such as Nkontompo (see map 5, p. 162), where services are almost non-existent. Others provide a way of life closer to the migrant's rural experience. Some migrants are able to adjust gradually to urban ways by living in these villages as farmers or fishermen for several years before going in search of an urban job. Others find land to farm in a small way to supplement their income. Thus, many residents of Takoradi remain tied to rural ways.

Tema, about 17 miles east of Accra and joined to it in the Accra/Tema Municipal Council, had housed a Ga fishing village from the early eighteenth century until it was chosen in 1951 as the site of the new port and an in-dustrial town to utilize electricity from the Volta Dam. The fishermen were moved to a newly constructed village in 1959. A town-planning firm was

9

engaged to design a town that would represent the best in modern layout adapted to the climate and social organization of the peoples who would come to Tema. The result is a series of 'communities' divided into 'neighbourhoods' of 3,000 to 5,000 people. Houses are closely spaced, usually with four to six 'houses' in a single building. Many of the buildings are single-storied and provide some 'compound' space for the residents of each 'house'. All houses have electricity, running water and water-borne sanitation, relatively rare amenities in other Ghanaian towns. Houses in Tema proper are all owned by the Tema Development Corporation. Many are under block rental to various firms for their workers, though subletting appears to be common. Unfortunately, building in Tema has never caught up with the demand. This and the relatively high rents have led to considerable overcrowding, with families in the low-income houses usually limited to one of the three or four rooms (Peil 1968c). Sites 1 and 2 of Community 1, built in 1954 for construction workers and supposedly temporary, are still in use.

The large numbers of people who cannot find room in Tema have swelled the population of Ashaiman, about 4 miles from the coast and within the development area. This grew from a village of 2,624 residents in 1960 to about 27,000 in 1968. The houses are privately built; most are of very poor quality and completely lacking in the amenities of which Tema can be justly proud. Large numbers of workers walk from here each day to their jobs in the industrial area or the harbour.

Industrial expansion at Tema has not been as rapid as hoped and unemployment of new arrivals has been augmented by the redundancy of skilled workers in the building trades as major construction projects have been completed and new ones have been delayed (Peil 1969). There were thirteen firms with over thirty workers in 1965, of which only four were privately owned, six were jointly owned by the government and private business and three were state enterprises. Several new firms have opened since then. Tema has tended to attract large firms, with a substantial import component such as car assembly, radio and television assembly, the aluminium smelter and fabricating plants and the oil refinery. Smaller firms and those using local products such as wood and vegetable oil have found it more convenient to locate in Accra where wages are lower.

Because of the recent growth of Tema, demographic data from the 1960 Census has little relevance to the situation in the late 1960s. The central city had over 50,000 people by 1968; the area had over 100,000 people in 1970.

The homogeneity index for the whole country does not tell us much except that Ghana is the home of many subgroups (see table 1.2). Four major ethnic groups account for over four-fifths of the population (Akan, 44%;

TABLE 1.2. *Sex ratio, homogeneity index and percent foreign born, whole country and the three cities, 1960*

	Whole country	Accra	Kumasi	Sekondi/ Takoradi
Sex ratio				
Total population	102	115	113	118
Aged 15+	102	132	133	139
Homogeneity index[a]				
Major tribe	25.1	25.9	52.6	41.9
Subgroup	5.5	19.9	20.7	16.6
Percent foreign-born adult males	16	20	16	19

SOURCE: *1960 Population Census of Ghana*, Special Report E.
[a] This is an indicator devised by census demographers to show the concentration of peoples of one or more ethnic groups. A town where most of the population belongs to one group will have a higher index than a town where no one group predominates. It is computed by the formula

$$\frac{(\text{no. of people in home tribe})^2 + (N \text{ in tribe B})^2 + (N \text{ in tribe C})^2 + \ldots}{(\text{Total population in the administrative district})^2}$$

Mole-Dagbani, 16%; Ewe, 13%; and Ga-Adangme, 9%) but these have many subdivisions. Takoradi is the most heterogeneous of the three cities and has the highest sex ratio, as befits a port and railway town, though it has a higher proportion of Akan than Accra has of Ga-Adangme. Foreigners are more likely to find their way to Accra or Takoradi than to Kumasi. Immigrants who settle in Kumasi are usually from the north, whereas the other two cities draw large numbers of immigrants from coastal countries, especially Togo and Nigeria, as well as northerners.

The distribution of the labour force in the three cities is fairly similar (see table 1.3). The lower rate of employment in Accra is due to the relatively larger numbers of young men who are completing their education there. Professionals, administrators and service workers are over-represented in Accra because they are employed by the central government. Kumasi's markets attract a large number of self-employed sales workers and clerical work is much less important there than in Accra or Takoradi. The proportion of unskilled workers is largest in Takoradi because they are needed on the docks. Kumasi is about half the size of Accra; Takoradi is about half the size of Kumasi. Since these towns are so similar on many other variables, the different reactions of workers living in them may be due, at least in part, to the different scale of the society in which they find themselves. Tema, as a new 'industrial' town, has attracted a more selective group of migrants than the older cities. These differences will be explored further in chapter 6.

TABLE I.3. *Composition of the adult male labour force, whole country and the three cities, 1960 (percentages)*

	Whole country	Accra	Kumasi	Sekondi/ Takoradi
Labour force participation rate, age 15–64[a]	89	86	86	90
Employed[b]	85	74	79	78
Professional, technical	3	5	5	4
Managerial, administrative	1	4	2	2
Clerical	3	12	7	14
Sales	4	9	16	6
Farmers, fishermen	63	6	8	7
Miners, quarrymen	2	—	d	d
Transport, communications	3	9	9	12
Craftsmen and production process workers	13	28	29	25
Labourers and longshoremen	6	16	15	21
Service and sport	2	11	9	9
Employers and self-employed[c]	56	24	40	20
N	1,884,552	135,028	72,081	42,691

SOURCE: *1960 Population Census of Ghana*, vol. IV, and Special Report A.
[a] Employed and unemployed/total population.
[b] Those who did any work for pay or profit during the month preceding the census.
[c] These are all included in the occupational categories above.
[d] Less than 0.5 %.

EDUCATION

A good foundation for industrialization has been laid in the widespread educational system. Because education is an important variable throughout the subsequent discussion, the general plan of the system will be given in some detail here.

Primary school lasts six years and is followed by four years of middle school (known as Middle Forms 1–4). The Common Entrance Examination for entry into secondary school can be taken in Middle Form 2, 3 or 4. About one pupil in ten is successful and enters secondary school. Five years are spent in Secondary Forms 1–5 preparing for the 'Ordinary Level' examinations of the General Certificate of Education (G.C.E.). Those most successful in these examinations are admitted to the two-year sixth forms and sit 'Advanced Level' G.C.E. examinations; university entrants must pass three of these.

Most pupils who complete Middle Form 4 pass the school leaving examination and receive a Middle School Leaving Certificate. The majority then enter the labour force; a few find places in teacher training colleges, private secondary schools, or commercial or technical schools. In 1960, 4%

of the population over the age of fourteen were still in school. Many of these were still in primary or middle school, but nearly 12,000 pupils were attending secondary schools. By 1967 there were 104 secondary schools with 43,889 pupils and 82 training colleges with 16,767 pupils. There is tremendous competition for training-college places. Whereas pupils in secondary schools must pay fees, those in training colleges benefit from government grants and spend four years doing largely secondary-type work. Many continue to study for G.C.E. examinations; a fairly high proportion of university entrants each year have qualified in this way. A few training colleges provide a two-year post-secondary course; this sector is expected to expand in future at the expense of the post-middle-school sector. Commercial and technical schools catering for middle-school leavers have multiplied rapidly in recent years, mostly under private management. Many of these are small and poorly equipped, but they thrive on the felt need for some sort of training to help in the search for employment.

The official age for starting school is six, but many children do not start until they are older. In a country where births and deaths are not usually registered, there may be no record of birthdate and it may not be considered important. Boys leaving middle school average about seventeen years of age, but boys leaving after the age of twenty are not rare. There has been some talk of shortening the primary and middle program to eight years, but having three cohorts leaving school at once would create such extensive unemployment that the suggestion has not been implemented.

The proportion of children in school and wastage vary from one part of the country to another. Early mission schools were established among the Ewe, the Fanti and the Akwapim, and these groups continue to value education more highly than others. Education is still not very popular in the north, because many northern parents see it (quite rightly) as depriving them of their children, who will go to work in town after finishing school. The abolition of fees for primary education in 1952 resulted in a great increase in the numbers attending. By 1960, 44% of the children between the ages of six and fourteen were in school or had attended in the past. Primary and middle school education were made compulsory in 1961. Though this was not strictly enforced, the enrolment in Primary 1 went up from 106,928 in 1960/1 to 231,784 in 1961/2. The numbers continued to increase for several years as the large intake moved up, but total enrolment in primary schools has dropped in every year since 1965/6. Parents are disillusioned when they see large numbers of school leavers without employment, and many have not allowed their children to start school. The reintroduction of school fees in 1967/8 was burdensome for many parents, especially those with several school-age children. Nevertheless, in the 1969/70 school year there were 6,969 primary schools with 975,629 pupils and 3,422 middle schools with 424,430 pupils, representing increases of 121% and 192% respectively in the last nine years (Ministry of Education 1970).

Wastage is low for a developing country and middle schools have not yet shown a decline in registration. About 64% of the 1961 entrants reached Primary 6 and about 81% of these entered middle school in 1967 (Abbey 1970:5). About 4% of those enrolled drop out of middle school each year (Scott 1967:41). Thus, Ghanaian children are more likely to complete ten years of schooling than children in most African countries are to complete a six- or eight-year primary program. This has inevitable implications for the labour force, since middle-school leavers are far more likely to migrate to the towns than young people who have had less education or none at all (Caldwell 1968:370). An estimated 100,000 young people join the labour force each year, of whom over half are middle-school leavers eager for wage employment.

GROWTH OF INDUSTRY

There is not much information on the development of manufacturing in Ghana, since this has been much less important economically than the mining industry or cocoa and timber exports. The first industrial establishment in the Gold Coast may well have been the Presbyterian Press, founded in Accra in 1859 and still in operation. Furniture production, sawmilling, oil crushing and car assembly were established within the next sixty years (Macmillan 1920). The Accra Brewery, the first factory to use large-scale methods, was opened in 1931. During the 1930s there was a brick and tile factory, a squash factory and a printing press at Achimota School near Accra, a bakery at Nsawam and a lime-crushing factory north of Cape Coast. Furniture was being produced at the railway workshops in Sekondi and in Accra and several sawmills were in operation.

Many small enterprises failed during the war due to lack of supplies and trained personnel. After the war, renewed interest in the opportunities available in the colonies led to expansion of existing industries, the installation of more advanced machinery and the introduction of new types of manufacturing. Plywood and veneer factories were established at Takoradi and Samreboi to increase the amount of local processing of raw materials. Extraction of cocoa butter by local millers during the war proved to be uneconomic and lasted only two seasons. In 1949 a mill for commercial extraction was opened in Takoradi. It has proved difficult to compete with

European and American producers; the mill has been closed or operating at only part of its capacity for many years.

TABLE 1.4. *Number of manufacturing firms recorded in 1959 by year operations commenced*

Period	Number of firms
Before 1910	11
1910–19	3
1920–9	19
1930–9	18
1940–9	53
1950–9	130
Total	234

SOURCE: Central Bureau of Statistics, *Statistical reports*, series VII, no. 1, February 1962, table 64.

The highest rate of growth in manufacturing establishments was in the late 1940s and early 1950s, coinciding with the expansion of the market at that time. Cocoa prices were high, many people had money to spend and foreign investors were looking for opportunities. Table 1.4 shows establishments known to the Central Bureau of Statistics which were still in existence in 1959. This is a sample biased toward large firms in Accra, but the general picture of rapid growth is correct. The 1962 Industrial Census found 3,146 enterprises employing more than five persons, of which 1948 were in manufacturing. Though many firms had started since 1959, others had been unknown to the Central Bureau of Statistics or were too small to be included in their records. Growth since 1962 is recorded only for firms with thirty or more workers (see table 1.5). The drop in numbers is due to the change in the number required for reporting (most firms are small), to the omission in 1964 and 1966 of *akpeteshie* (local gin) distillers and motor repair establishments and to the going out of business of many marginal firms.

The great majority of 'manufacturing establishments' in Ghana are very small; only 1% have more than five paid employees and only 16% of the firms operating in 1962 with more than five employees had thirty or more workers and so qualified as large. Fourteen had over 500 employees. Small enterprises tend to be ephemeral, hard to locate and operating with a minimum of capital and a low level of technology; most could be called manufacturers only in an extended sense. Although the large firms employ only a small proportion of those engaged in manufacturing (under 50,000),

TABLE 1.5. *Number of large manufacturing firms and persons engaged, 1958–66*

Year	Number of firms	Number of persons engaged
1958	315	20,650
1960	338	23,491
1962	367	29,708
1964	187	35,849
1966	230	39,482

SOURCES: 1958–62: Central Bureau of Statistics 1967b: tables 50 and 53; Establishments employing 10 or more persons.
1964–6: Central Bureau of Statistics 1967a: tables 2 and 6; Establishments with 30 or more persons engaged.

they serve as an index of future development since they make greater use of modern technology than smaller firms. This study has therefore been limited to workers in large firms, assuming that they will exemplify the most modern non-elite sector of the population. It has also been concentrated in the cities because most of the large firms are found there. Accra, Kumasi, Takoradi and Tema had in 1962 28 % of the manufacturing firms with more than five workers and 51 % of the employees in such firms (Central Bureau of Statistics 1963).

Most of the early factories were owned and run by British or Europeans, though there have been many small enterprises run by local craftsmen (carpenters, printers, tailors) since early in the century. Local entrepreneurs often lacked capital and technical knowledge to make a success of their enterprises or could not arrange for the necessary services, as was the case of the Kumasi proprietor of a laundry whose eight machines had to be filled by carrying water from the standpipe down the road. Ghanaians now run large state enterprises, contribute to the management of foreign-based firms and operate medium-sized firms of their own. Small firms are almost all owned by local businessmen. The 1968 Ghanaian Enterprises Decree limited small business (firms with less than thirty workers and/or capital of less than NC 100,000) to Ghanaians, after a suitable changeover period. This was abruptly shortened by the Ghanaian Business (Promotion) Act of 1970, which required all alien wholesale and retail traders with sales of less than NC 500,000 in the 1967/8 tax year to sell to Ghanaians or otherwise wind up their businesses by 1 August and barred aliens completely from petty trading, commercial transportation, printing, baking and cement block manufacture. Most foreigners owning such firms were Asians (Syro-Lebanese, Pakistanis or Indians), but a few were Nigerians.

It has long been felt that industry cannot be developed solely by private capital. Some industries which are needed for development cannot be profitable for many years and others require such huge sums and/or have such an important effect on the economy that it is thought best to keep them in government hands or at least under partial government control. The Industrial Development Corporation (I.D.C.) was established in 1948. At first it provided loans for prospective entrepreneurs, but later it set up enterprises of its own. Early industries established or aided by the I.D.C. included a soap works, laundry and dry-cleaning plant, a sawmill, casava processing, a brick and tile works, and local potters, hat-makers, weavers and woodworkers. Many of its industries failed due to inadequate planning, poor demand for the products and/or poor management. The remainder were transferred to the Ministry of Industries in 1962.

The number of state-owned industries grew rapidly in the 1960s, partly because of government ideology and partly through the opportunism of foreign businessmen. Plants were established to produce steel (from scrap), paper, jute bags, glass, textiles, sugar and tinned foods, among other things. By 1965 there were thirty-eight manufacturing firms employing 23,378 persons under the State Enterprises Secretariat. The number increased to forty-six in 1966, though several of these were not actually in production (Central Bureau of Statistics 1967a: table 26). These firms were transferred to a new Industrial Holding Corporation after the 1966 *coup*. Some of the least profitable have since been closed or sold to private businessmen.

As the general unprofitability of state enterprises has become apparent, there has been a move toward joint enterprises whereby the state puts up some of the capital and the rest is supplied by private businessmen (usually foreigners) who manage the business and pay the state its share of the profits. There were nine of these joint state–privately owned firms in the Accra Capital District in 1965, twelve state enterprises and about fifty-five privately owned firms with thirty or more workers.

Most of the products recommended by Lewis (1953) as either favourable or marginal for manufacture in Ghana are now being produced. In addition to the products mentioned earlier, plastics, aluminium and rubber products, textiles and clothing, liquor and soft drinks, nails, paint, matches, mattresses and suitcases, batteries, phonograph records, radios and television sets, sweets and a variety of food products, incense and candles, cement, flour and many other products are now produced or assembled locally. Most of these are consumer goods for the local population, but a few products such as plastic sandals are exported to neighbouring countries.

INDUSTRIAL STATISTICS

In attempting to find out more about factory workers, one is inevitably faced with a shortage of information. The availability and accuracy of statistics in a developing country is always a problem. Ghana is fortunate in that a well-run census in 1960 provides basic data of adequate reliability on the population of various towns and villages, with breakdowns by age, sex, education and economic activity. Further information is available on towns of over 10,000 population. An industrial census carried out in 1962 included most of the firms with ten or more workers operating at that time, though a few large firms are known to have been missed and many small firms probably were not located. Many of the firms active in 1962 have since gone out of business and records of new firms are biased toward large firms whose opening receives newspaper publicity. The Factory Ordinance of 1952 required that all factories with ten or more workers register with the Ministry of Labour, but small firms may neglect to do so and the Registrar has no record of factories which have closed. The Central Bureau of Statistics collects data quarterly on firms with thirty or more workers, but this is limited to factories which have come to their attention. They lack the staff to go out and check on the adequacy of the data supplied and are hampered by the lack of interest in statistics of the managers of most firms.

Investigation has shown that in some cases quarterly returns cannot be reconciled to annual returns covering the same period and interviews with managers produce numbers of workers which vary considerably from those reported. This is not necessarily a case of wilful deception. The need to lay off workers temporarily because of lack of raw materials or a drop in demand makes for considerable fluctuation from month to month. Some firms also have considerable turnover of new workers. The manager may report the number of workers he considers normal. A survey of large firms in the Accra Capital District in 1965 found that five of the seventy-four firms were either partly or completely closed.

In addition, most managers have no mathematical training and see no need for accurate records. Others simply do not know exactly how many workers they have. One manager (a graduate engineer) said he had sixty-five workers at a factory thirty-five miles away; only twenty-four were found at the factory. In another case, the personnel manager assured me that he had 350 workers. When the sample had been drawn up, it was pointed out to him that there were only just over 300 names in the wages book. He was quite surprised and spent some time trying unsuccessfully to locate names which might be missing.

Attempts to obtain information on workers in any detail are even more prone to inaccuracy than trying to determine their number. Only a minority of firms keep personnel cards on their workers; many have only the name, job title, labour card number and days worked in the current month. Age may be recorded, since workers have had to give this for participation in the government pension plan. Job classifications vary from one firm to another. Everyone but cleaners and watchmen may be considered semiskilled, or those with some training (such as drivers) may be considered unskilled. Davison (1955) found some men listed as skilled labourers. Thus, it became apparent that the only way to get a comprehensive picture of factory workers in Ghana was to interview a large number of them. The method of obtaining these interviews is reported in the next chapter, and the results in succeeding chapters.

EARLIER STUDIES

Relatively few studies of African factory workers had been published at the time this study was being planned. These were usually carried out by economists rather than sociologists. Elkan (1956) studied the personnel records of two tobacco factories in Uganda and interviewed a small number of workers. His main concern was to analyze the incidence of absenteeism and turnover and suggest ways which management could use to keep these at a minimum. He provides some information on the workers' background and motivation. The workers he studied were mostly short-term migrants without skills who improved their wages by moving from one job to another rather than by moving up within the firm. The situation in Uganda has changed considerably since then, as the expanded school system has turned out large numbers of young people eager for urban employment (Bissman 1969:27; Hutton 1972).

Wells and Warmington (1962) are chiefly concerned with wages, absenteeism and turnover in the Nigerian firms they studied; their approach is management-oriented. Their findings on the differences between large firms and small ones and between southern and northern workers are similar to the Ghanaian findings reported below. Seibel's study (1968) of Nigerian workers is not yet available in English.

Van der Horst (1964) discusses very briefly the social and occupational background of workers in seven South African firms. The responses reported are largely affected by conditions in the country; i.e. long home leaves between jobs were necessary because it was not possible for the workers to have their families with them in town; Africans were not eligible for better paying skilled jobs.

The recent reports on workers in Dakar by Hauser (1968a) and Pfeffermann (1968) are more useful for comparative purposes, the first because it reports on the attitudes and background of workers in several factories, and the latter because he was concerned with the relationships of the workers with their relatives and the position of the workers in the wider society.

Two studies of Indian workers provide a record of the adjustment of factory workers in a developing country which is more industrialized than any in Africa but where problems faced by new workers are often similar. Lambert (1963) carried out a study of five factories in Poona which was similar to the study reported here. Sheth (1968) studied one factory in depth and provided an analysis of the relationships of workers with each other, their supervisors, and their families. This sort of study is best carried out by a native of the country concerned; we can only hope that there will soon be similar work done in African factories.

Slotkin's study (1960) of migrants from southern farms to Chicago and of workers in a sawmill on an Indian reservation is a useful reminder that members of disadvantaged subgroups in an industrial society face many of the same problems as workers in developing countries when taking up industrial employment. However, his 'cultural inadequacy' hypothesis, which limits interest in factory work to those for whom the traditional society is least adequate, does not seem to fit the situation in Ghana. Migration in Ghana is basically an economic action; the culturally satisfied as well as the dissatisfied trek to town to improve their standard of living. This will be discussed further in chapter 5. There was a shortage of urban workers in Ghana earlier in the century, but this shortage was chiefly due to the low wages which were offered. Improvement in the minimum daily wage from 3s. 3d. (16p) in 1950 to 6s. 6d. (33p) in 1960 (Killick 1966:141) brought enough applicants to fill available jobs except where considerable technical training was required. The difficulty in recent years has been the oversupply of prospective workers. The desire of most migrants to return home in their old age indicates that traditional life is still regarded as basically satisfying. Of course, it could also be argued that cultural change has been considerable, at least throughout most of southern Ghana, so that even those who stay at home live a life quite different from that of their fathers.

A recent study of factory workers in Britain (Goldthorpe *et al.* 1968, 1969) provides an interesting framework for comparison of Ghanaian workers with 'advanced' industrial workers. The similarities and differences between the two groups of workers highlight some interesting sociological aspects of the industrial situation.

THE REPORT

The factory worker in a developing country can be looked at from three points of view. In one sense, the study can provide information on the reactions of workers whose cultural background does not include large-scale industrial organizations. Modern methodology can be used to obtain data on attitudes and reactions of workers whose situation is in many ways comparable to that of early industrial workers. Secondly, one can compare these workers with operatives in modern factories in developed countries – the automobile workers of Detroit or the 'affluent' workers of Luton. International competition provides an impetus for modern technology wherever a factory is established. Factory workers in developing countries may seem to have a high income in comparison to other adults in their own societies even though they appear badly off when compared to 'advanced' industrial workers. The third approach is to see them as a unique case, caught between traditional habits and modern demands and responding in a way that is quite different from that of either early or modern industrial workers.

All three approaches will be used here, since each provides a valid interpretation of the data on some aspects of the Ghanaian situation. Industrial workers have common problems of unsatisfactory pay and conditions, of unemployment and poor housing; many have had to migrate to large towns and cities to find work and most maintain contact with relatives outside their nuclear families. Thus, there are aspects of the lives of Ghanaian factory workers which are directly comparable with the experience of workers in other countries and at other times in history. The aspects of their experience which are unique to Ghana or to countries beginning to industrialize in the mid-twentieth century can give us a better understanding of the process of industrialization as it affects workers elsewhere.

The next chapter will report on the methodology used and give a summary description of the workers interviewed and their firms. Reports of surveys made in Africa have often neglected to inform the reader on the techniques used, so that it is difficult to evaluate the representativeness of the sample and/or the reliability of the data. The methods used in studying factory workers were developed in a number of preliminary studies and proved remarkably successful in eliciting cooperation and, insofar as one can tell, reliable answers.

Chapters 3 and 4 are closely connected. The first contains considerable detail on the occupational background of the workers – the career mobility, training and unemployment experience of men in various occupations, some measures of job stability and the wage levels for various jobs in the different cities. Chapter 4 looks at motivation and aspiration as these are shown in the workers' comments on their jobs and their supervisors, in turnover and absenteeism and in their attitudes toward various occupations as desirable for themselves or for their children. It concludes with a study of occupational prestige in Ghana which compares the responses of factory workers with those of middle-school pupils and university students.

Chapter 5 deals with the migratory paths which have led the workers to their present residences and the reasons given for their moves to the city. Chapter 6 shows them as urban residents, with all the advantages and disadvantages of this status. Since factory workers tend to be long-term migrants, their adjustment to the stress and expense of life in town shows us the pattern which seems likely to replace the circulating migration formerly characteristic of African workers. The contacts they make with neighbours and workmates are a measure of their commitment to urban life, though most workers intend to return home eventually and maintain contacts with their relatives at home throughout their stay in town. These contacts are discussed in chapter 7, which also deals with marriage and attitudes toward rearing children.

The final chapter examines the data in relation to recent studies of modernity, indicating the degree to which Ghanaian factory workers are representative of their society and the implications of the findings for the 'Industrial Man' hypothesis. The workers' attitudes and behaviour on the job can only be understood in the context of their origins, yet their ties to tradition and hometown are not unaffected by the fact that they are in modern occupations and many have had a modern education. Throughout the book, place of origin and place of residence, education and occupation are shown to have a constant relevance.

CHAPTER 2

THE FACTORIES

The first half of this chapter will report in detail on the methods used in this study; it can conveniently be omitted by those who are not concerned with the way the data was obtained and not planning studies of their own. The last half of the chapter presents a brief overview of the results, emphasizing the general characteristics of the industrial labour force and differences between factories of various types in terms of management, size, location and type of worker.

METHODOLOGY

In order to obtain more adequate information for the proposed study of factory workers than was available from government statistics, a preliminary survey was carried out during the summer of 1965. Managers were interviewed in seventy-three large manufacturing firms in the Accra C.D. Only five large firms are known to have been omitted. One could not be located and four were not on the Central Bureau of Statistics' lists at that time. Data was collected on the number of workers in various skill categories and, in summary terms, their age, education, training and region or country of origin. Similar data was collected on managers. Information on absenteeism and turnover, work satisfaction and supervisory problems, incentives and training schemes provided a framework for comparing various types of firms. This study will hereafter be referred to as the Management Survey. Its results have been reported elsewhere (Peil 1966).

Plans were then made to interview a large number of workers in the Accra area so that comparisons could be made between those with and without education; of urban and rural background; in skilled, unskilled and clerical jobs; and those working in firms of varying size and type. Since accurate information was available only on the last category, the sample of firms was necessarily based on this. Dr Sen of the Institute of Statistics, University of Ghana, selected firms for the sample using a model with the following specifications:

C

1,000 workers to be interviewed in 10 factories
2 factories in Tema, 4 in central Accra and 4 elsewhere in Accra
2 state enterprises, 1 under joint state–private ownership and 7 privately owned
2 each with under 50 and over 200 workers; 6 with between 50 and 200 workers
Representation of the various industries common in the area: food, metal, wood, textiles, printing and cement

Only firms in operation at least three years were considered, since it was felt that there should be time for the work force to settle down. As it happened, all the firms chosen were at least five years old and all those 'elsewhere in Accra' were in the Ring Road Industrial Estate. All of the selected firms agreed to participate and cooperation was excellent. Table 2.1 shows that

TABLE 2.1. *Comparison of worker sample and factory population, Accra Capital District (percentages)*

Characteristic	Sample	Population[a]
Firms		
State owned	20	16
Jointly owned	10	12
Privately owned	70	72
Total	100	100
Established since 1959	40	45
Management		
Ghanaian	30	25
European	20	18
Lebanese, Indian[b]	30	29
Mixed	20	29
Total	100	100
N	10	74
Workers: Location		
Tema	26	25
Central Accra	27	32
Elsewhere in Accra	48	43
Total	100	100
Workers: Job level		
Unskilled	15	30[c]
Semiskilled and skilled	74	60[c]
Clerical	11	10
Total	100	100
Women employed	12	8
N	994	13,083

[a] Management Survey data.
[b] Some have Ghanaian managers as well.
[c] These may be quite inaccurate, as managers were often guessing.

the sample was representative of factories in the area as to age, ownership, management, location, types of jobs available and the proportion of women workers.

The model suggested numbers of workers to be interviewed among the unskilled, semiskilled, skilled and clerical workers, but the numbers supplied by the firms nine months before were not sufficiently accurate to follow and it was thought better to interview a set proportion of the workers on the books of each firm at the time. It seemed desirable that sampling fractions should be as few as possible and that firms should contribute about equally to the planned 1,000 interviews insofar as their size allowed. In firms with less than 100 workers, all were interviewed. Three-quarters, half or one-quarter of the workers in the larger firms were selected for interviewing by systematic sampling from a random start of all names on the wage list. Since workers are usually listed by location, this provided a representative sample of workers of all grades and departments. Where foremen and charge hands were included in the general wage list and not identified as such, they had an equal chance of being selected. Where it was possible to identify foremen, they were excluded from the general selection and several were chosen randomly for interviewing. Workers who had been on the job for less than two weeks were excluded, since this was too short a time to build up stable attitudes toward the firm and the job. Where a worker selected for interviewing was absent, on leave, on the night shift or had left, the next name on the list was substituted or, in the largest firm, a randomly selected list of substitutes was provided.

Workers were asked about their job and migration history, periods of unemployment and methods of finding work; contacts with fellow workers off the job and with relatives at home; attitudes toward the job, the foreman and the town in which they were living; the age, education, birthplace, year of arrival in Accra or Tema, former residence, tribe, marital status, occupation and place of work of every person living with them; the location of wives, children and siblings not living with them. Half of the workers were also asked to rate thirty-seven occupations as to their prestige in Ghanaian society. Interviews averaged about half an hour without the prestige ranking, which took about twenty minutes. The interview schedule appears in the appendix.

Managers and trade union leaders were asked to announce the forthcoming interviewing to the workers and encourage them to cooperate; the response was excellent. The interviews took place during April 1966, soon after the military *coup*. Workers felt quite free to speak their minds and were anxious to do so. Only two men, a foreman and a clerical worker, refused to be interviewed. In some factories the interviewers had to explain random sampling to the workers to reassure them that those left out were not being discriminated against.

Students in the lower sixth form of secondary school (aged seventeen to twenty) were trained in interviewing in weekly sessions over a period of three months. Most of the interviewers spoke two or more local languages and they were switched from firm to firm so that all workers could be interviewed in their own language if they chose. Forty percent of the interviews were in English or English and a local language. Schedules were in English because it was felt that this made for greater flexibility as well as because it reduced the cost considerably. It was impossible to estimate how many schedules would be needed in various languages and it was thought better for interviewers to have a thorough understanding of what each question meant and to practice translating with each other. They could then interpret the questions to suit the understanding of the interviewees. Some languages were used only a few times. In other cases, two local languages were mixed or the interview was partly in English. This flexibility was possible because the interviewers were operating from one base rather than with a limited number of alternatives.

A room was usually provided for interviewing, but in some factories it was done in shady spots near the buildings or, in one or two cases, on the shop floor. One or more interviewers spent from one to five days at each firm. Because of transport difficulties, some of the interviewers were brought to their factories in the morning and collected in the evening. Others were visited during the day. Each interview schedule was checked within twenty-four hours for omissions and consistency. Defective schedules were returned to the interviewer the next day for correction. In such a structured situation it was more difficult to fabricate answers than if interviewing was done in private households and not subject to close checking. Work improved steadily during the period. Most of the interviewers found the work very interesting; this also improved their performance.

Various checks were built into the schedule to test the accuracy of the data. For example, workers were asked how many people were living with them and then asked to list these and give information on each. In cases where the answer to a 'Why?' question indicated that the original question had not been understood, it could be rephrased. In two factories, statements on wages were checked against wage lists. This indicated that we were getting an accurate statement of take-home pay.

Age at the start of each job could be checked against the number of years on the job, length of unemployment and the year in which the change took place. This increased accuracy by allowing the worker to choose whichever method of reporting was most meaningful to him. There were only three or four workers who were unable to report their job histories in any detail. The most expressive comment of an interviewer concerned an illiterate man in his early fifties who reported fourteen jobs held since about 1927: 'He has wasted a good deal of my time! And confused me with dates.' In most cases, interviewers were able to piece together a coherent work history though details cannot be considered exact. It appears that most workers keep track of time spent on various jobs much more accurately than they do details of home life. Several brought written records from home when they heard we were asking for details. All workers had to establish an 'official age' when the state pension plan was started in 1965, so they were more aware than the general population of the importance of knowing one's birth year.

Preliminary results showed that there were many differences between workers in Accra and those in Tema. It was felt that data from Kumasi and Takoradi would be useful in showing how workers in these smaller towns differed in background and attitudes from the first sample. Luckily, the original grant was sufficient to cover this extension. After checking the list of factories known to the Central Bureau of Statistics, it was decided to interview in four factories, including a sawmill in each town, one factory utilizing largely skilled labour and one having largely semiskilled workers. Three-quarters of the large factories in Kumasi and a third of those in Takoradi are sawmills. One of the firms was to be state owned. Names of firms were written on slips of paper, sorted into appropriate categories and drawn. Alternates were also drawn. Managers of the selected firms were interviewed (using the Management Survey schedule) to obtain further information. Alternates were selected in two cases; one of the first choices was going out of business and the other alternate was chosen to avoid using two state enterprises.

After training a new set of interviewers, workers in Kumasi and Takoradi were interviewed in April 1967. Since only 150 workers were being interviewed in each city, no women or foremen were included in the sample. A systematic sample from a random start was used to provide exactly seventy-five interviewees in each firm. Randomly selected substitutes were provided. Occupational prestige rating was omitted and five questions were added to cover gaps in the data: on attitudes toward overcrowded housing and returning home on retirement, bribes for jobs (which yielded no results), home town and gifts to visiting relatives. Language was less of a problem than in Accra, since almost everyone in these towns speaks some dialect of Akan (either Ahanta, Asante, Fanti or Nzima). Two-thirds of the interviews were conducted in Akan and most of the rest in English and Akan. Cooperation of management and workers was again excellent.

The factories

A third set of interviews was collected in the summer of 1968. There is a great deal of talk about building factories in rural areas so that people will be able to find work at home rather than migrating to the cities. Part of this is based on nostalgia for the 'good old days' and expressed by men who would not themselves be willing to live in a village. Studies of school leavers in Ghana found that about half of them would not leave home if they could get work nearby. However, I have long suspected that workers in rural factories are not local inhabitants but migrants, so that work provided in rural areas allows people to live in a rural environment but not in their hometowns. It was decided to test this hypothesis and obtain some comparative data by interviewing at two rural factories. It was not possible to select randomly, since the factories chosen had to have at least eighty workers and be close enough to Accra to reach before work started (at about 7 a.m.) and to return in the evening. This limited us to a 70-mile radius of Accra. Interviewers working on another project with some of the same questions were given extra training and borrowed for a day in each case. One of the factories selected had been established for several years; the other had been in operation only a few months and parts were still being built. This provided an indication of the attraction of new factories and the degree to which expectations are met. Given the time limitation, we did well to get 138 interviews.

To obtain information on turnover which could be related to statements of job satisfaction, firms in the 1966 sample were contacted fifteen months after interviewing had been completed and the current wage lists were checked against the lists of workers interviewed. Numbers on the schedules were matched with those on the lists of names to show which workers were still employed. This should have been done exactly a year after the interviews, but was delayed because of interviewing in Kumasi and Takoradi and the preliminary processing of these interviews. It was possible to check turnover after fifteen months in only one of the four factories of the 1967 sample. Another was checked after eleven months, just before extensive lay-offs occurred; the third went out of business and repeated requests to the manager of the fourth factory went unanswered.

In reporting the results of this study, the median has been used in preference to the mean because a few extreme deviations could easily result in a false impression. In addition, some measures were more reliable if the ends were left open and if broad categories were used. For example, some men reported extremely low wages, possibly what they had left after paying their creditors rather than their official take-home pay. Most of these were obviously in the lowest wage category, but the exact level of their wages was not available for computation. In reporting work histories, jobs which lasted more than a year were usually reported as two years, three years etc., which was as precise as could be expected from workers with relatively little education. Age is much more reliable in five-year categories than in single years. Categories using numbers have thus been designed to include most of the probable variance.

Although the 0.05 level has been taken as the measure of significant difference, some differences which are too small to be statistically significant are discussed because of their interesting implications and the lines they suggest for future study. This was essentially an exploratory study and the samples were small except in Accra. To avoid constant reference to significance tests, statements in the form 'A is more (or less) X than B' have been used to indicate differences which are statistically significant. Differences stated in other ways may be significant but are not necessarily so.

This research was part of a series of studies made over a five-year period during which the author was lecturing in sociology at the University of Ghana. From time to time the results of other studies will be used to further the analysis. Three national middle-school leaver samples have been used to trace the migration and success in finding work of boys who completed ten years of schooling. Occupational aspirations and expectations and ratings of occupational prestige were obtained from one of these samples. The Tema Network Survey involved interviews at home with residents of Tema and Ashaiman as to their interaction with cotenants, friends, workmates and relatives in town and at home. The factory workers included in that study provided information on their life outside the workplace which supplements that supplied by the Factory Survey. Lastly, a study of unemployment in Tema provided considerable data on skilled workers in the building trades, whose career lines seem to differ somewhat from those of skilled workers in factories.

This book is formally a report on a social survey. Relatively little observation was done in the factories. There is a wide range of information which cannot be obtained by the survey method; a full understanding of worker attitudes and behaviour on the job awaits the work of a participant observer. However, this task should be done by someone with a thorough understanding of most if not all of the languages spoken by the workers and someone who does not stand out as an outsider, before whom one must be on one's guard. The contribution of this study will be to give future researchers a picture of the 'average' factory worker and a framework of hypotheses to guide his observation. We know a good deal about the life of people in traditional villages, but far less about life in town, especially about life at work as opposed to the use of leisure time.

The factories

The advantage of a large survey in an area where little work has been done is that it is possible to establish fairly reliable basic information on which later research can be built. There was very little indication in the literature as to the differences which might be expected between workers in small and large factories, in firms run by expatriates and by local entrepreneurs, in state- and privately managed enterprises; between skilled and unskilled workers, northerners and southerners, new workers and those who had been on the job for several years. A large-scale survey is the only way to get reliable information on all these factors in a single study. Once such data is available, participant observation can be carried out within an established framework and can concentrate on the many aspects of behaviour which are not as reliably studied through interviews – especially the differences between what people say and what they do.

There are difficulties in obtaining accurate data on the past, especially from people who keep no records, but a general knowledge of a person's background is necessary for an understanding of his present attitudes and behaviour and his aspirations and plans for the future. By keeping the questions simple, carefully structured and centred on facts rather than attitudes (which are forgotten or rationalized as time goes on), we have been able to collect a large amount of data on the workers' past lives.

We wanted to find out about industrial workers because they are involved in an environment which cannot be duplicated in traditional society. Workers in large factories were expected to exemplify the townsman of the future, insofar as the nature of one's relationships at work affect one's attitude and behaviour outside the workplace. Small firms are much harder to sample representatively than large ones; they are also less representative of 'modern' society. A craftsman with a few apprentices or family workers in a small roadside business is not required to make changes in his way of life which are asked of the craftsman in a firm employing hundreds of workers and making a standardized product.

Although aspects of their background have both led these men to work in factories and formed their attitudes, so that it is not possible to separate out the influence of the factory from that of education, for instance, the choice of factory workers as a vehicle for the study of social change still seems to be a good one. The direction of social change can be shown through differences between workers of varying occupations and social backgrounds.

In the rest of this chapter we will look at the firms and workers included in this study. In this and later sections of the book, considerable space will be given to a straightforward description of the findings. Description can be limited in a situation where readers are thoroughly familiar with the cultural background of the research. In a situation where most readers are unfamiliar with the cultural assumptions of the people being studied and in an area where little work has so far been published, it is necessary to go into more detail. In addition, it is hoped that the development of comparative studies will be furthered by making the data available in fairly comprehensive form.

THE FIRMS

The sixteen firms are listed in table 2.2. They may be differentiated according to their location, age, ownership, size, turnover rate, or nationality of their managers; or by the skill level, average age, education, or seniority of their workers. The reason for showing all of these characteristics on one table is that comparisons between firms of various types can more easily be made and it is easier to see when expected correlations do in fact occur. For instance, we would expect that older firms would have workers of higher average age than those which have only been open a few years. In this case, however, geographical location appears to be more important than age. The average age of workers in the Kumasi and Takoradi factories is higher than that of workers interviewed in Accra, regardless of the date of opening.

Firms are identified by letter and information on them has been kept fairly general to preserve a measure of confidentiality. In particular, the product of each firm has not been given because in many cases there is only one firm in the country producing this product. It was felt that it would be preferable to maintain freedom to report the reactions of workers in specific firms (having certain management, size and other characteristics) than to identify the firms and have to omit these comments.

Three of the four firms in the provincial towns were older than most of the Accra firms. The Tema firms had been opened comparatively recently, though they were relatively established considering that the town only came into existence in the late 1950s. One of the rural factories was still being built at the time it was studied. None of the workers had been there for more than eighteen months, though some had worked for the parent firm for several years.

Firms on the industrial estate were usually larger than those in central Accra, where space was often limited. Of the central firms, one operated in two sections, one of which was in a small building near the central market. Another had a large workroom on the ground floor and a workroom and office on the first floor of a building housing shops and offices on one of the main streets. A third was part of a complex of two factories involving quite

TABLE 2.2. *Characteristics of the firms*

	A	B	C	D	E	F	G	H	J	K	L	M	N	O	P	Q
Location[a]	T	T	AIE	AIE	AIE	AIE	CA	CA	CA	CA	K	K	TK	TK	R	R
Founded[b]	6	6	5	5	6	5	6	4	5	6	6	5	4	4	5	6
Ownership[c]	S	J	P	P	P	P	P	S	P	P	P	P	P	P	J	J
Management[d]	G/E	E/G	E	G	A/G	A/G	E	G	G	A	A	G	B/G	B/E/G	E	A/E/G
No. of workers	104	312	254	180	91	600	70	252	33	30	117	91	485	274	141	250
No. interviewed	104	155	134	125	81	145	70	117	33	30	75	75	75	75	67	71
Percent[e]																
Unskilled	17	7	45	10	18	6	4	6	3	40	37	15	23	33	15	27
Semiskilled	52	80	11	25	59	26	31	21	60	48	33	9	41	35	57	51
Skilled	17	12	41	61	21	64	65	60	31	8	19	53	27	19	27	11
Clerical	14	1	3	4	2	4	0	13	6	4	11	23	9	13	1	11
Total	100	100	100	100	100	100	100	100	100	100	100	100	100	100	100	100
Women[f]	8	19	1	8	19	22	0	14	33	3	3	—	12	33	15	16
Non-Ghanaians	8	1	37	27	16	24	24	5	0	40	24	9	44	47	57	83
Middle school or more	86	97	30	52	70	64	47	91	82	37	37	57	48	57	73	18
On the job over 5 years	3	10	24	10	68	18	7	45	24	16	25	65	48	57	18	7
Still employed 15 months later[g]	76	65	60	71	74	74	93	96	72	39	—	—	92	89	—	—
Median age	26	25	31	27	28	29	30	29	26	26	32	34	34	31	28	25

[a] T – Tema; AIE – Accra Industrial Estate; CA – Central Accra; K – Kumasi; TK – Takoradi; R – Rural.

[b] 4 – before 1950; 5 – in the 1950s; 6 – since 1959.

[c] S – state; J – joint state-private; P – private.

[d] A – Lebanese, Indian, Pakistani or Chinese; G – Ghanaian; E – European; B – British. The order of letters indicates numerical representation.

[e] Foremen and headmen in firms A–K were omitted when percentaging workers in various categories, since they were not chosen in the same proportion as other workers. In L–Q a few headmen have been included with skilled workers.

[f] Women were interviewed only in Accra and Tema.

[g] These figures relate to all the workers on the lists whether they were interviewed or not (i.e. alternates and men who were absent during the interviewing are included here). Data was obtained only for Accra, Tema and Takoradi firms. The figure for firm O refers to the situation after 11 months, before extensive lay-offs occurred.

different operations with a common management and clerical staff. One of the provincial firms was a branch of an Accra establishment; both rural firms had head offices in Accra. Given the amount of waiting at government offices necessitated by imports of raw materials, payment of taxes etc., lack of an Accra office is a definite disadvantage. This militates against decentralization of industry.

MANAGEMENT

The Management Survey found that over half of the managers of large firms in the Accra C.D. were Ghanaian; only five of the sixteen firms included in this sample had no Ghanaian managers, though they were subordinate to expatriates in seven firms. (In one of these, only the managing director was an expatriate.) Workers were generally more satisfied when under Ghanaian managers than in firms where all the managers were expatriates. Very few of the managers interviewed considered language difficulties important. The advantage of Ghanaian managers is at least partly due to their management style, based on an understanding of local culture.

Lebanese and Indian managers tend to be more paternal than those of other nationalities. Most private firms give their workers a Christmas bonus, but Lebanese firms were more likely than others to do so; some also gave a yearly increment. Indian firms sometimes had parties for the workers, prizes for high productivity and other material incentives. Many Lebanese and Indian firms are small enough for the manager to know the workers individually and to treat them as part of a family. However, this attitude often becomes authoritarian when the manager feels that things are not going well. The casual observer often sees managers shouting at workers. The operation of the extended family system in Indian and Lebanese firms means that Ghanaians have little opportunity for promotion, and this leads to complaints. In firm F, for instance, workers objected to the supervision of Asians who, they felt, held their jobs because they were related to the managing director rather than because of technical or other qualifications.

European-run firms tend to be larger than those run by Asians or Ghanaian private businessmen; the bureaucracy accompanying size is sometimes hard for workers to adjust to. In addition, periodic long holidays in Europe result in relatively frequent changes within top management and a certain lack of continuity. European managers belonging to international companies are less concerned to understand the local culture than the more permanently established Asians.

Large firms do not differ notably from smaller ones in the type of technology employed or in labour intensiveness. There are small firms in Accra which are very similar to large factories in the same industry except for the scale of their operations. The chief difference between large and small factories is in the nature of the relationships between management and workers due to the greater bureaucratization of large factories. This will be discussed in chapter 4.

Detailed personnel records are kept by few firms and the wage book listing is usually by production unit rather than by skill level, so statistics contributed to the government on the use of skilled workers are not likely to be very accurate. An additional problem is that few if any of the managers see the usefulness of statistics, so they feel no pressure to improve their accuracy. Quite a few firms had a lower number of workers by actual count than the number stated by management. In the extreme case, we had been told that there were forty-two workers, but only managed to get thirty interviews (the minimum necessary for inclusion in the sample) by including all the supervisory staff.

THE LABOUR FORCE

The size of the labour force in many firms varies considerably over time. Some firms vary their labour force a great deal from month to month depending on the amount of raw materials they are able to import. Others have shown considerable growth or decline in the past few years because of local or world market conditions. Two firms were operating on three shifts at the time of the study. Since then, the labour force at one of them has been severely reduced and work limited to a single shift because more goods were being produced than could be marketed. Many firms could increase their productivity through more intensive use of capital equipment and/or more efficient use of labour, but the local market in Ghana as in many other African countries is often too limited to make this profitable. Similar problems of overcapacity (in this case, because too many firms are competing for the market) have been noted by Kilby (1965) in his report on the Nigerian bread industry.

Only three of the firms studied do not face local competition and these have considerable competition from imports. In spite of the 'Made in Ghana' exhibition of 1966 and the International Trade Fair of 1967, many Ghanaians remain convinced (with some reason) that 'Made in Here' goods are inferior to those produced abroad. The management of one firm had been taken over by expatriates about a year before the survey. They were systematically cutting the labour force in an attempt to rationalize production and increase the quality of the product. It was about half its former size at the time of the survey and workers felt very insecure since there was no way of knowing who would be laid off next.

The three firms processing raw materials for export were in an insecure position, since the world market was poor. It is often more economic to export raw materials than to process them before exporting. Once capital has been invested and the processing firm established, there may be no choice but to continue uneconomic production, though timber firms with their own sawmills may vary the proportion of sawn timber to logs exported.

The situation at firm Q was just the opposite. It was expected that the number of workers would double in the next six months and would eventually reach 1,500. The workers hired in the first months of production thought their chances of steady work and promotion were good and were willing to endure the poor housing and lack of amenities in the village in view of their prospects.

Although all of the firms included in the sample use relatively simple technology, the skill level of the workforce varies considerably from one firm to another. Lambert (1963:9–13) distinguishes three types of organization of firms which correspond to the skill level of the majority of the workers. They may be characterized as 'gang', 'individual' and 'craft' production. In the first type, which is usually associated with the processing of raw materials, gangs of unskilled workers feed machines under the supervision of a gang leader. They have little control over the machines and little or no training is needed; workers are interchangeable and high turnover does not interfere with production. This type of operation is often found in developing countries because it makes the least demands on the local labour supply.

Firms C, K and L had relatively high proportions of unskilled workers and were characterized by the 'gang' form of organization. Firms N and O, which had somewhat lower proportions of unskilled workers, might also be classified as 'gang', though N is an intermediate case. Its unskilled workers were involved in 'gang' work, only half of its semiskilled workers used machines and a large number of skilled workers were needed to keep the machines functioning continuously throughout the year.

Lambert's second type utilizes largely semiskilled labour. Workers operate different types of machines and have some control over the speed of operation, but the work is repetitive and limited training is needed. Piece rates are probably more successful in this type of firm than in others. Firms which emphasize 'individual' work are A, B, E, J, P and Q. Of these, only firm B pays piece rates, but they appear to be highly successful in increasing production. The plant is noted for the way workers start on time and stick to their work. Firms in this category have the highest proportion of educated workers, because semiskilled work is popular with untrained school leavers. Managers prefer them because they are easier to train than illiterates.

The third type of firm uses largely skilled workers. A worker may take the product through several stages; he must be able to adjust and direct the machine to suit the needs of the moment. 'Craft' production characterizes firms D, F, G, H and M. Most of these workers learned their skills before they joined the firm, though many printers learned on the job. Many of the tailors had spent extended periods in self-employment and many carpenters had worked on their own at some time in the past. This affected their attitude toward their work, as will be shown later.

The proportion of clerical workers in a firm is related to the type of management, the level of development of the firm and administrative arrangements. The Management Survey showed that state enterprises employ, on the average, at least twice as many clerical workers as other firms of the same size and type. The proportions of clerical and unskilled workers at firm Q will be lower when the labour force is fully expanded. The relatively high proportion of clerical workers at firms L and O was due to their timber operations. Workers in the timber section were not included in the total number of workers, but the clerks handled both sides of the business. Since clerical workers at firms G and P were part of the central organization, they were not interviewed.

Ghanaian women have a long tradition of working to support themselves, mainly as traders but also as bakers and seamstresses. Some factories employ no women at all or use them only in clerical positions. In others, there are a considerable number of women doing semiskilled work, usually by hand (assembly, trimming) rather than by machine. There were too few women in the provincial and rural factories selected to gather any significant data, so none were included in the sample.

Factory jobs are not as attractive to women as self-employment because of the regular hours demanded and the lack of day nurseries for children. Women in factories tend (even more than the men) to be young, literate southerners. Two-thirds of the women and 55% of the men interviewed in Accra and Tema were under thirty years of age. Only five of the 124 women interviewed had not completed middle school. There was only one non-Ghanaian. Women were almost twice as likely as the Accra/Tema sample as a whole to have grown up in Accra or the nearby Eastern Region. While two-thirds of the men interviewed in both Accra and Tema were married, 44% of the women interviewed in Accra and 81% of those in Tema were single.

There appears to be no discrimination against non-Ghanaians in factory employment, even in state enterprises, though their general lack of education stands in the way of their obtaining this type of work. Some government services, such as sanitation, are largely dependent on non-Ghanaian labour. Since African immigrants to Ghana are usually illiterate (except for some of the southern Nigerians), they are most likely to be found, with migrants from northern Ghana, in unskilled jobs.

There is relatively little factory employment for labourers and there are likely to be few openings at any given time. A man may be able to join whatever form of commerce is followed by men from his hometown (Rouch 1954) without time-consuming visits to the Labour Office. Varying working hours, which is possible in porterage and other casual labour, is likely to appeal to those unused to working by the clock. Those who prefer wage employment because it provides a regular income are more likely to find it as labourers for local government (especially in the sanitary services), on the docks and railways, or in construction than in factories. According to the 1960 Census, 36% of males from Upper Volta and Mali enumerated in Kumasi were in commerce, and 28% in services (chiefly government labourers and personal services). In Takoradi, 28% of the men from Upper Volta and Mali were employed in transport (docks and railways), 31% in services and 20% in commerce. In Accra, 40% were in services and 23% in commerce. The proportion of northern and non-Ghanaian factory workers in each city was lower than their proportion of the male employed population of that city.

TABLE 2.3. *Labour force participation of the local and foreign-born urban population, selected countries and occupations*[a] *(percentages)*

Country of birth	Craftsmen	Labourers[b]	Clerical	N
Ghana	27	14	9	314,606
Nigeria	22	19	4	26,588
Togo	41	22	3	17,693
Upper Volta, Mali and Niger	7	35	0	32,446

SOURCE: *1960 Population Census of Ghana*, vol. IV and Special Report A.
[a] Urban population: Ghanaians, living in places of 10,000+; for the foreign-born, in places of 5,000+.
[b] Mining and general labourers and longshoremen but not agricultural labourers.

Table 2.3 shows the proportions of men from these countries in various types of work in Ghanaian towns. Early missionaries to the Ewes encouraged their converts to become craftsmen, and Ewes from the Volta Region of

Ghana and from southern Togo are particularly noted as carpenters. Nigerians are often traders; those with skills tend to be tailors. Eighteen percent of Ghana's tailors and 12% of her carpenters were born abroad. Nigerians are more likely than other non-Ghanaians to have the education necessary for a clerical job, but there are also large numbers of Nigerian unskilled workers in the Ghanaian labour force. Migrants from Upper Volta, Mali and Niger, few of whom have either training or education, are mostly employed as labourers.

Half of the 250 men in the survey who grew up outside Ghana were from Togo or Dahomey (mostly the former), 17% were from Nigeria, 16% from Upper Volta, and the rest mostly from Mali or Niger. The proportion of non-Ghanaians in a firm is closely related to the proportion of unskilled workers and, to a lesser extent, to the proportion of skilled workers. Firm C, where 41% of the workers were unskilled, employed 38% of the workers interviewed in Accra who grew up in northern Ghana and 30% of those originating outside Ghana.

TABLE 2.4. *School attendance, median age and birthplace of factory workers and the male population of the cities in which they worked*

Town	% attended school		Median age		% born in locality		N workers
	Total[a]	Workers	Total[a]	Workers	Total[b]	Workers	
Accra[c]	60	69	30	28	42	16	735
Tema[c]	[d]	96	[d]	25	[d]	1	259
Kumasi	49	55	29	33	34	18	150
Takoradi	56	59	31	32	27	23	150
Rural							
Firm P	47	81	32	28	30	19	67
Firm Q[e]	52	86	33	25	36	22	71

SOURCE: *1960 Population Census of Ghana*, vol. II, table 2 and interviews.
[a] Based on male population over age 15.
[b] Based on total male population.   [c] Worker figures include females.
[d] Population increase since 1960 has been too extensive to make comparison meaningful.
Totals are a composite figure for two villages where many workers live.

Factory work tends to draw young, educated men, but this is less true in the provincial towns than in Accra and Tema (see table 2.4). The proportion of factory workers who had attended school was larger in each case than the proportion of the adult male population who were educated. The margin was greatest in Tema and the rural factories, where the median age of workers was lowest and where the factories studied provided semiskilled employment, which school leavers consider a very satisfactory alternative to farming.

The low proportion of workers in Kumasi and Takoradi who attended school is related to their higher average age and to the lower educational level of the area from which the workers come. The educational explosion in Ghana has been so recent that many of these workers missed it. The average age of provincial workers was higher than the median for the general population. Turnover is low, except for firm L, so few young men find jobs there. Industrial growth has been slow in the provincial towns, since most new factories are established in Accra or Tema. The timber industry, which is of primary importance in both these towns, was depressed at the time of the survey and many workers had been laid off. Those remaining tried to hang on to their jobs, since new ones would be hard to find. Unemployment was a greater threat to provincial workers than to those in Accra, because the former were almost twice as likely to be married and many had large families to support.

Ghanaian factory workers tend to be younger than those in Senegal or South Africa. Hauser (1968a:37) reports an average age of thirty-five for workers in four factories in Dakar, Dagoudane Pikine and Rufisque, and van der Horst (1964:42) found that workers in seven Cape Town factories had an average age of thirty-four. Earlier studies of single factories have shown a lower mean age – twenty-nine for a firm in Salisbury, Rhodesia (Bell 1961:54) and twenty-eight for one in Durban (University of Natal 1950:32). Unfortunately, comparable figures for Nigerian workers are not available. It seems likely that workers will be younger in new factories, in those factories experiencing high turnover and in countries where industrial employment is not well established than in countries where workers know what to expect in such work and are committed to it.[1] Although many of the Ghanaian firms studied had been open for more than ten years, in no firm was the average age of the workers over thirty-four and in the majority of firms it was under thirty.

Factory workers tend to be migrants. The proportion of the workers born in the locality was in every case lower than the proportion of the population who were locally born. Except for Tema, the towns and villages included in the sample all had a nucleus of stable population. Birthplace is used here because these data are provided by the Census. A more satisfactory picture of the attachment of workers to the locality is the proportion who grew up

[1] Industrial development in Kenya and Uganda has been roughly parallel to that in Ghana. Only 2% of the 1,300 Kenyan and Ugandan industrial workers interviewed by Bissman (1969:24–5) were under 21, but 60% were between 21 and 30. They were more often educated than the Ghanaians; only 13% had not attended school. Perhaps because of their youth, they were relatively inexperienced; 44% were on their first wage job. Turnover was formerly very high in East Africa, but has dropped recently.

D

locally. Migrant women frequently return to their own or their husband's hometown to give birth. If the child goes back to town with his mother, he will be more influenced by the place where he grows up than by his birthplace. Therefore, future reference to place of origin will be to the place where most of childhood was spent. On this criterion, 19% of the Accra workers and 28% of those in the provincial towns were 'local'.

SUMMARY

Over 1,400 workers in sixteen factories were interviewed. Eight of the firms were in Accra and two each were in Tema, Kumasi, Takoradi and villages in the Accra hinterland. Data was collected fifteen months after interviewing on which workers in Accra and Tema had left their jobs.

An important difference between firms was the style of management, partly due to the size of the firm and partly to the nationality of the managers. European-owned firms tended to be large and impersonal; firms run by Asians tended to be smaller. In some of these, there was an attempt to establish a 'family' feeling, but management was usually autocratic. Workers tended to be most satisfied with Ghanaian managers, though these were not always the most successful from an economic point of view. Several firms faced economic difficulties because of lack of demand for the product, world competition, or problems of importing raw materials.

Firms may also be distinguished as to whether they use 'gang', 'individual', or 'craft' production, involving the predominant use of unskilled, semiskilled, or skilled workers respectively. Since these workers have differing background characteristics, level of turnover and job satisfaction, studying firms of various types provides information on varying constellations of worker behaviour and attitudes. There is a concentration of clerical workers in state enterprises, indicating a higher level of bureaucracy in these firms than in privately owned factories. Some complex firms save on clerical staff by centralizing it in the head office.

Women are not attracted to factory work because of its demand for regular hours and preference for educated workers. Non-Ghanaians are (or were) not discriminated against, but few are in semiskilled or clerical jobs because they lack education. Factory work generally attracts educated young men who are committed to urban employment.

CHAPTER 3

OCCUPATIONS

One of the chief concerns of the study was to learn more about the attitudes and beliefs of workers in various positions in the Ghanaian occupational structure. If factory workers are in the forefront of occupational modernization and if people with different occupations have varying attitudes and do not behave in the same way outside the workplace (because of their differing backgrounds and socialization on the job), as was expected, then comparing workers in various occupations should provide some information on changes to be expected in the society as modernization proceeds.

In a way, different skill levels represent different degrees of incorporation in modern industrial technology. Unskilled workers are often doing jobs which have changed little or not at all over a long period of time. Skilled workers may be using modern machinery and mass production methods, but some of these (especially the carpenters) may be working in much the same way, though under greater pressure for quality and production, as they would if working on their own. The semiskilled workers are more symbolic of a new era; few jobs like these were available in Ghana a generation ago and they are not comparable to non-industrial jobs. Clerical work is largely the same wherever it is done; this work is seldom mechanized in Ghana. Clerical workers are included because of the comparisons which can be made between them and manual workers, especially semiskilled workers. Quite a few of the latter have done clerical work in the past and they tend to have the same social background as clerical workers.

Complete job histories were collected for each worker. Their occupational mobility may be looked at in relation to their own career, their father's major occupation, their aspirations for the future, and their attitudes toward various occupations as expressed in responses to questions on occupational prestige, advice they would give to others, preferred job within the firm and plans for their children. The job histories also provide information on unemployment and migration at various points in a man's career, which may be related to satisfaction with and adjustment to urban labour and to the influence of the family as well as to factors of supply and demand. This chapter will be concerned with details of the workers' occupational experiences. The next chapter will deal with their attitudes toward their own and other jobs.

OCCUPATIONAL CATEGORIES

The bases for classifications were training and pay. Jobs which require no training were considered unskilled, i.e. labourers, storeboys, cleaners and watchmen. A few 'security officers', thus classed as unskilled, made relatively good wages, but most unskilled workers were in the lowest wage category; few earned more than NC20 per month (£10).[1]

Skilled workers were those in jobs for which there is a trade test (carpenters, electricians, masons, printers, tailors, welders) and for which an apprenticeship is required. Their wages average about NC31 per month (£15.50), considerably better than the lower clerical workers. Steel benders were included with skilled workers because almost all of them had had an apprenticeship and their pay level was similar. Very few skilled workers of any type had taken a trade test; the proportion was highest for printers.

Semiskilled workers were subclassified as hand or machine workers. A semiskilled job requires some training, though in many cases this is minimal. Hand workers include those doing assembly, packing, checking and binding (at the printing press). A few of the latter had a level of training and pay to qualify for classification as skilled workers, but most were 'binding assistants' and obviously semiskilled workers. Machine operatives (weavers, casters, riveters, polishers) and drivers form the second category. Drivers have about the same pay and prestige as skilled workers, but their 'apprenticeship' consists of being 'mate' (fare collector, baggage packer, cleaner etc.) to a driver for a period of years during which they pick up the rudiments of driving. Many mates never become drivers and the general skill level is not high. There is a trade test for drivers (in addition to the test for a license), but none of the drivers interviewed had taken it. Wages for machine operatives in Tema were as high as those for skilled workers in Accra; hand workers generally received less.

Semiskilled factory work attracts middle-school leavers who are unable to continue their education or arrange for an apprenticeship. They see it as relatively well-paid work in the modern sector of the economy; it is probably the best job available to them given their lack of qualification. Many factory managers prefer school leavers to the uneducated because those who have

[1] The foreign exchange value of the currency changed twice during the study. Figures given here apply to the middle period, when NC1 = 10s. (50p) or $1.40. After devaluation in 1967, NC1 = 8s. 3d. (41p) or 98 cents.

been to school are likely to plan a longer stay in town than the uneducated (most plan to spend the whole of their working lives there providing work is available), and because literacy and even a limited ability to speak and understand English make communication much easier, especially with expatriate managers. The discipline of schooling, which requires arrival at a set time every day and work on a regular schedule, also makes adjustment to factory life easier than it is for the uneducated, who have formed work habits which vary with the seasons.

All non-manual jobs except watchman/security officer were classed as clerical. These jobs have been divided according to the amount of training required and/or salary received. 'Higher clerical' jobs include trained accounts clerk, secretary, draughtsman, storekeeper and proof reader. Those with little or no training (messengers, clerks, typists, telephonists, receptionists and assistant storekeepers) were relegated to the 'lower clerical' category. Clerical workers are found at every wage level. One-third (32 %) of the lower clerical workers were earning less than NC21 per month; 55 % of the higher clerical workers earned over NC45 per month.

BACKGROUND CHARACTERISTICS

Table 3.1 substantiates comments made in chapter 2 about workers of various types. The median age for skilled workers in each town is over the median age for all workers. Semiskilled workers tend to be younger than average; there were proportionally twice as many semiskilled workers as others under the age of twenty-five. Most of the older unskilled workers were watchmen; the oldest was a Nigerian in his seventies. It is evident that promotion comes fairly early and that education improves one's chances of promotion. An eighth of the foremen were under twenty-five and only a quarter were forty or older. Although five of the foremen had never been to school (they were labourers' headmen), a quarter had gone beyond middle school, compared to only about 5 % of the manual workers.

Three-fifths of the unskilled workers had no schooling; the same was true for almost a third of the skilled workers. The two clerical workers with less than middle schooling were messengers. For some men this is a lifetime occupation or a welcome relief from unskilled labour, while for the majority it is the first step to a clerical career. Although the number and popularity of commercial schools has increased in recent years, the majority of clerical workers in Ghana still learn on the job. The messenger spends his spare time learning to type; the typist may study accounting by correspondence or learn from a friend.

TABLE 3.1. *Background of workers by occupation (percentages)*

	Unskilled	Semi-skilled	Skilled	Clerical	Foremen[a]	Total
Age						
18–24	24	46	16	25	13	29
25–39	57	47	65	62	64	57
40+	19	7	19	13	23	14
Total	100	100	100	100	100	100
Education						
None	61	18	30	1	9	27
Primary, Muslim	14	7	13	1	9	9
Middle	23	70	47	58	57	53
More than middle	2	5	10	40	25	11
Total	100	100	100	100	100	100
Origin						
This region	21	30	26	35	37	26
Other southern Ghana	23	58	56	57	45	53
Other[b]	56	12	18	8	18	21
Total	100	100	100	100	100	100
City[c]	29	22	32	32	43	28
Town[d]	10	24	23	30	27	22
Village	61	54	45	38	30	50
Total	100	100	100	100	100	100
Ethnicity						
Ga	3	14	16	16	27	13
Akan	24	48	42	61	36	43
Ewe	15	23	34	17	23	24
Other	58	15	8	6	14	20
Total	100	100	100	100	100	100
Married	58	57	77	84	89	67
On this job						
1–15 months[e]	44	40	28	21	9	34
16 months–4 years	38	46	41	48	46	43
5+ years	18	14	31	31	45	23
Total	100	100	100	100	100	100
N	252	529	438	157	56	1,432

[a] Accra and Tema only.
[b] Includes those from Northern and Upper Regions and non-Ghanaians.
[c] 40,000+ population; includes all non-Ghanaian urban.
[d] 5,000–39,999 population. [e] 1–18 months for rural workers.

Unskilled work is not limited to the uneducated. Many middle-school leavers are labourers and there are a few with secondary schooling who cannot find better jobs. Although there is a very close connection between education and occupation in Ghana, some people are unable to hold jobs for which their education would seem to fit them. More important, the increasing number of school leavers means that many must be grateful for jobs they might have considered beneath them ten years ago. We hear a great deal about the unwillingness of school leavers to accept manual jobs, which completely ignores the reality that thousands would be grateful for such jobs if they could find them and that other thousands are quite satisfied to hold such jobs. That skilled jobs are preferred to unskilled ones, and higher paying jobs to those which pay less, is hardly surprising.

Occasionally a manager 'tests' a secondary-school applicant by making him work his way up through the factory, but usually those with secondary schooling who are doing non-technical manual work have not completed the secondary course and/or have proved inadequate in earlier jobs. Comments of interviewers on some of the trained men who were doing unskilled work indicate that these may be inadequately trained or motivated. There are others (especially drivers) who are unable to obtain work in their speciality.

Although unskilled workers are often thought of as northerners or non-Ghanaians, there were local people in every town doing unskilled work. There is a 'traditional' element in most of Ghana's towns which does not take advantage of education and continues to live much as in the past. In Accra, these are fishermen; in Kumasi and Takoradi, farmers. (There are also many progressive cocoa farmers living in Kumasi.) Occasionally, some-one from this group may decide after many years in a primary occupation to enter the industrial sector. One Accra man had fished for twenty-three years before quitting and taking up a job in a cement factory. He had been on this job for several months at the time of the interview and was quite satisfied with it.

In a similar way, well-established farmers may decide to apprentice them-selves in some craft, as did one man who became a carpenter when in his forties. These changes tend to come in response to a feeling of lowered vitality, when a man feels he must make some provision for his old age. Some industrial workers, at about the same age, begin to feel that they should look for less strenuous jobs. For example, a labourer in his late thirties said he wanted to become a watchman on his next job (seen as coming in a few years' time) because then he would be 'too old' for other work. The life-span has increased considerably in the last twenty years, but people's expectations have not yet caught up with it.

Unskilled workers are no more likely to be married than semiskilled workers in spite of their higher average age. This is because long-distance migrants, who tend to be unskilled, are less likely to be married than short-distance migrants.

Local workers tend to monopolize the semiskilled, clerical and supervisory jobs. There were quite a few women doing semiskilled hand-work in Accra and Tema. This type of work is largely carried out by local people or migrants from the nearby Eastern Region. In Takoradi, where all such workers were men, they were also mostly local, as were the skilled workers. One-third of the local Asante in Kumasi were in clerical jobs, and another third in semiskilled work. Nearly half of the foremen in Accra and Tema had grown up in Accra; local men were also well represented among the higher clerical workers. Opportunities for higher education and special training, full or part time, are available in the cities; those growing up there can most easily see the advantages of education.

Access to training means that skilled workers are also more likely to come from urban than from rural places. Boys growing up in towns are more likely to see craftsmen at work and to have relatives who are craftsmen than boys growing up in rural places. Rural boys must often migrate to town if they decide to apprentice themselves. Many of them lack either the money for fees or the contacts and thus end up as semiskilled or unskilled workers. Urban boys may also lack money and/or contacts, but they are more likely than rural boys to be aware of the need for further training or education and of ways of bringing this about.

An exception to this is the Ewe, who were encouraged to take up skilled work by early missionaries. The large number of skilled workers originating outside southern Ghana were mostly Ewe carpenters from Togo. Over half of the Ewes interviewed in Accra and 70% of those in Kumasi were skilled workers. It appears that few workers without skills migrate to Kumasi from Western or Volta Regions or from Togo. Over four-fifths of the workers in Kumasi from these areas were doing skilled work. Outside the factories, Ewes in Kumasi are usually on transfer in government clerical posts or in the army or police.

The Akan were over-represented among the clerical workers. Many of these are Fanti from towns along the coast with a long history of mission education or Akwapim from Eastern Region, with an even higher proportion of children in school than the Fanti.

Women workers were usually employed for semiskilled hand-work or as seamstresses. They were more likely than the men to be under twenty-five and to be life-long residents of Accra (where two-thirds of them were interviewed). Tema women were more likely than the men to be recent arrivals and were less often married than the Accra women.

TRAINING

Workers were asked, 'How long did it take you to learn the job you are doing now?' About a quarter of the workers (all of the unskilled and some of the semiskilled) said less than three days' training was needed and another 15% had no more than a month's training. Semiskilled machine workers often took three months or more to learn their jobs. About two-fifths of the workers said they had at least a year of training. This included all the skilled and a few of the clerical workers. About half the lower clerical workers reported less than three days' training, while about half the higher clerical workers had spent at least four months learning their jobs. It is easy to measure training for skilled work, because it is usually set within a formal apprenticeship. Training for semiskilled and clerical work is not so structured and workers' estimates (and their capacities) may vary considerably. It may well have taken some workers much longer than others to learn the proper use of machines. Some weavers, for instance, reported training time of a few weeks while others reported periods of over six months. The management considered that it took at least a year to train a weaver and two or three years' experience would be necessary before any could be appointed charge hands.

Some of the larger firms train skilled workers on the job; others, and most of the smaller firms, prefer to hire workers who are already trained. Half of the firms with over 200 workers included in the Management Survey had an apprenticeship program, while only 13% of the firms with less than fifty workers had one. Some of the programs lasted more than five years. (In one printing firm, completing the apprenticeship and 'trainee' programs took some men eight to ten years.) While these 'on the job' training programs were longer than the average private apprenticeship, other firms had programs lasting only a few months, which could not really be called an apprenticeship though the managers referred to them as such.

A few technicians are sent to home offices in Europe for eighteen months to three years of training, but this is not always as successful as it is hoped. Some of these men change jobs fairly soon after returning and so do not benefit the firm which financed them. Others may not want to pass on what they have learned. One furniture manufacturer complained that men sent to learn to operate machinery refused to teach other workers. The men feel that there are few jobs utilizing such skills and that teaching others might result in the loss of their own jobs.

Another factor which affects the willingness of workers to train others gratuitously is the institutionalized private apprenticeship. Most skilled

workers in Ghana learn their trades by apprenticing themselves to a craftsman for a number of years in return for a payment in money and/or goods
(Peil 1970). In most cases, these masters are self-employed and use the
apprentices as cheap labour in their roadside enterprises. Masters employed
in construction (and sometimes in furniture firms) may bring their apprentices with them, with or without the approval of the management. One of the
firms in the sample had formerly contracted with master carpenters, each
having a certain number of apprentices under him. The arrangement had
been discontinued as too open to abuses. In another firm, one young man
had been hired as a carpenter although he was really the apprentice of another worker, who collected most of the apprentice's wages from him each
payday.

Painters often learn their trade by hiring themselves to a construction
firm and imitating the action of other painters or working with friends for a
short period. Apprenticeships for tailors, carpenters and printers are much
more organized. A tailoring or printing apprenticeship usually lasts three
years; a carpenter may spend four or five years learning his trade and those
who start as young boys often take longer.

About two-fifths of those interviewed (43%) had completed an apprenticeship at some time in the past; a few had had two or three apprenticeships. A
few others had started apprenticeships but not finished them, either because
they lost interest or because their master was too hard on them. Of those who
had completed apprenticeships, three-quarters were working at jobs for
which they were trained; the other quarter had a wide variety of other jobs,
from unskilled to lower clerical. Although most skilled workmen stick to their
trade, some must fall back on other jobs after they qualify. For example, a
twenty-eight-year-old carpenter had finished his apprenticeship at eighteen,
then farmed, sold petrol, worked for three years at his trade, farmed again,
returned to carpentry for a year and then spent eight months as a driver's
mate before starting his present job. The five years of farming had been
spent at home. His apprenticeship was in Kumasi, and his other jobs in two
villages and a town; he had only lived in Accra for a few months when he was
interviewed. His wife of six years was in her hometown, but the children
were living with him and his (mutual consent) wife in Accra. This man
appears to have little or no commitment to his trade.

Most of the craftsmen in large towns are trained in these towns or move
there soon after completing their apprenticeship. Of the Accra workers who
had been apprenticed, 57% (44% of the migrants) were trained in Accra
and another quarter were trained in their hometowns. Two-thirds of the
craftsmen interviewed in the provincial towns were apprenticed there and

another 18% in their hometowns. About half of the apprenticeships were to a private master (who is sometimes a fellow townsman or family friend); the rest were about evenly divided between training on the job and training by relatives, usually a kinsman of the apprentice's father. Very few craftsmen were trained by their fathers or siblings, even in cases where they had the relevant skills. The same principle seems to apply here as in the fostering of children; there is a feeling that better discipline will be maintained and hence better training given if the supervisor is not a member of the immediate family. Among matrilineal groups such as the Akan, the father is responsible for providing his sons with an occupation; it is notable that very few masters for Akan apprentices were chosen from the mother's side of the family.

Only a small number of workers under the age of twenty had completed an apprenticeship, and fewer of those under twenty-five than over had done so. Masters prefer apprentices who have had some schooling, and school leavers are more interested than illiterates in obtaining such training. Since most boys do not leave middle school until they are seventeen, many are nearly twenty before they start an apprenticeship. The average age of apprentices in six trades who were interviewed in Accra was nineteen (Peil 1970). One man began a carpentry apprenticeship at thirty after fourteen years as a steward and another started a masonry apprenticeship at thirty-two after farming since childhood. Both men had long careers as craftsmen after completing their training.

Apprenticeships are very popular with middle-school leavers, who feel that a trade will give them a better income than the low-level clerical work for which they might qualify. The greater utilization of government trade tests as a certification of ability on completing an apprenticeship would simplify hiring procedures and probably increase the quality of this vital sector of the labour force. A system of registering apprentices would also give the government a better idea of how many are being trained, which would improve manpower planning.

OCCUPATIONAL MOBILITY

There is considerable evidence of both generational and career mobility in Ghana. Table 3.2 shows the occupational mobility experienced by the workers in this study. Very few followed in their father's footsteps except for those who initially farmed. Only a minority stuck to the same type of work throughout their careers. The majority of those who had had only one occupation, except for skilled workers, were on their first job when they were interviewed.

TABLE 3.2. *Occupational background of workers by occupation (percentages)*

	Unskilled	Semi-skilled	Skilled	Clerical
Father's occupation				
Farmer	80	67	63	52
Skilled	5	14	17	16
Clerical, professional	3	7	9	15
Trader, businessman	5	5	7	12
Other	7	7	4	5
Total	100	100	100	100
N^a	249	535	431	154
First job				
Farmer	66	34	27	24
Unskilled	15	17	8	5
Skilled	4	9	48	4
Clerical, teacher	5	13	6	38
Other	10	27	11	29
Total	100	100	100	100
Job types[b]				
Manual	71	69	81	0
Non-manual	1[c]	0	0	43
Both	28	31	19	57
Total	100	100	100	100
Career mobility				
One type of job	8	15	40	16
Two types	62	48	42	30
Three or more types	30	37	18	54
Total	100	100	100	100
N	252	529	438	157

[a] A few did not know their father's occupation.
[b] Past and present jobs.   [c] Watchmen.

The strongest relationships between father's occupation and son's first job were among farmers and skilled workers. Nearly nine in ten of those whose first job was farming were sons of farmers. The rest came from a wide variety of backgrounds, including sons of clerks and teachers. Some of these were reared by relatives who were farmers; others went to farm with relatives for a period after they finished their education. Of the sons of skilled workers in Accra and Tema, 44 % started out in skilled work. In the provincial towns, the proportion was much smaller (19 %) and, though a few others were in skilled work at the time of the survey, twice as many were machine operatives as were skilled workers. That the sons of skilled workers were not more likely than others to have an apprenticeship is rather surprising, given the general job satisfaction of skilled workers and the popularity of skilled work in aspirations for children (to be discussed later). Sons of skilled workers were seldom doing unskilled work, but they were as likely to be in semiskilled or clerical occupations as to be working at a trade (not necessarily their father's trade).

In a country where 63 % of the employed population are farmers, it is to be expected that farmers' sons will be predominant in most occupations and that a considerable proportion of intergenerational mobility will be accounted for by the movement out of farming. In Accra, 62 % of the workers interviewed were farmers' sons, thus matching the national population. The sons of farmers were over-represented in the provincial towns. According to the 1960 Census, 55 % of the employed persons in both Western and Ashanti Regions were farmers, but 72 % of the workers interviewed in Kumasi and 65 % of those in Takoradi were sons of farmers. This may be because farmers' sons are moving into these provincial towns for jobs, while urban boys are going off to Accra or Tema in search of work. Workers in Accra and Tema from both Western and Ashanti Regions were disproportionately of urban background.

Clerical workers were less likely than the others to have fathers who were farmers, and clerical workers and skilled workers had farmed as a first job less often than other workers. Not only were clerical workers more likely to have grown up in urban than in rural areas, but some of those who grew up in rural areas were sons, not of farmers, but of village teachers, local council clerks, or traders. These are more oriented toward education than farmers and more likely to live near a school; they usually see to it that their sons are educated.

Many of the fathers of unskilled workers were subsistence farmers in northern Ghana or the countries to the north. Schools in these areas may be far from the homestead and their function is not often understood. (Or, it may be understood only too well; many northern farmers do not want their sons to attend school because this would ensure that they would leave home when their school days are over (Oppong 1966).)

One of the factors militating against the division of African societies on class lines is the occupational heterogeneity of closely knit family groups. A university graduate holding an important government post may have a brother who is a subsistence farmer, another who is an unskilled labourer and a sister who is married to a primary teacher. He will see all of them more or less regularly. Answers of the factory workers to the question on the education and occupations of full siblings showed considerable heterogeneity in their families. In most cases, the worker had at least as much education as others in his family, but a substantial minority of workers had siblings who had gone beyond them in school or who had gone to school when they had not. Several had brothers who were in universities abroad and who would soon return to Ghana as professionals.

TABLE 3.3. *Occupations of brothers by occupation of urban workers*[a]

Worker's occupation	Percent having brothers who are:			N
	Farmers	Skilled	Non-manual	
Unskilled	50	13	8	220
Semiskilled	24	20	22	454
Skilled, foremen	26	34	17	472
Clerical	25	22	22	148
Total	29	24	18	1,294

[a] Percentages do not add up to 100%. 30% of the workers had no brothers and others had brothers in occupations not shown here. Some had brothers in more than one of the occupations shown.

Table 3.3 shows the proportions of workers having brothers in selected occupations. Considering the rural background of the workers, it is interesting that only three in ten had brothers who were farmers, while a quarter had brothers who were skilled workers. This indicates that movement away from farming often includes all or most of the siblings. The proportion of unskilled workers who had brothers farming was double that of other workers; very few unskilled workers had brothers in non-manual occupations. This is a reflection on the more isolated rural background of many unskilled workers and the lack of education in their families. Skilled workers were more likely than others to have brothers in non-manual occupations (including teaching and the professions as well as clerical work). Certain groups (such as the Ewe) are more inclined to skilled work than others and this increases the propensity for members of a family to learn a skill. Sometimes one member trains the others, but often the brothers learn different skills. Non-manual jobs, on the other hand, are almost always learned outside the family, so various families have more equal access to them (given equal education) than they would to skilled work.

Half of those who started as farmers had no education, but many of those who went to school (including 10% of those who went beyond middle school) also farmed at the beginning of their careers (see table 3.4). Rural boys usually help their parents or guardians with the farming while they are

TABLE 3.4. *First work after age 15 by education and age at entering the non-agricultural labour force (percentages)*

	Farmer	Un-skilled	Semi-skilled[a]	Skilled	Clerical, professional	Trade
Education						
None	50	23	6	25	1	5
Primary, Muslim	8	14	12	14	1	10
Middle	39	58	70	51	61	72
More than middle	3	5	12	10	37	13
Total	100	100	100	100	100	100
Age						
Under 16	10	21	6	31	4	18
16–18	24	41	43	36	40	36
19–21	31	26	37	25	40	37
22+	35	12	14	8	16	9
Total	100	100	100	100	100	100
N	511	178	138	290	184	131

[a] Including the army.

in school and continue this after they leave school until they make arrangements to migrate. Nearly a third of those starting in skilled work entered the non-agricultural labour force before they were sixteen. These would have been set to learn a trade when they were very young as a substitute for school. Most other non-farming jobs require that the employee be sixteen or older, though some start trading or find work as labourers before this. (It is not that the employers set an age limit in specific terms, but rather that they aim to hire adults rather than children and this results in few opportunities for those under sixteen.)

Future clerical and semiskilled workers usually complete middle school and so do not enter the labour force until they are in their late teens. Those who enter the urban labour force after twenty-five are almost all illiterates who have been farming or fishing; these form a small proportion of urban workers and are less likely to be committed to a long stay in town than the young school leaver who sees urban work as his best chance to obtain a satisfactory standard of living.

It is difficult to estimate how much occupational mobility represents social mobility. Some might argue that movement from farming to unskilled labour in town involves no change in position or possibly downward mobility. Smelser (1968:162) has pointed out that the peasant or craftsman who becomes a factory worker gives up his economic independence and control over his rate and hours of work. Employees are more attracted to political radicalism and more likely to identify themselves as working class than are the self-employed, though neither of these seems to have occurred to any extent among Ghanaian workers.

Pfeffermann (1968:170, 250) argues that most Dakar workers have about the same standard of living as they would have in a village because demands of relatives serve as an equalizing factor. In Ghana, demands seem to be somewhat lower (this will be discussed in chapter 7) and subsistence farmers who move to town *and find employment* there probably achieve a higher standard of living than they had at home, though in prestige terms their position may be very low. At the other extreme, a wealthy cocoa farmer has considerable prestige in Ghanaian society and his son would have to obtain a fairly good job to equal this. However, since a wealthy farmer can provide a good education for his sons, they may be well equipped in their search for urban employment. Sons of cocoa farmers are much better represented at the University of Ghana than sons of subsistence farmers.

Occupational prestige will be discussed in chapter 4. There is little difference in the ranking of farmer, factory worker and various craftsmen, so status change in a move from one occupation to another may not be noticed by the individual concerned. Movement from manual to non-manual work is generally considered the basic measure of occupational mobility, but in Ghana the movement from messenger to factory worker or craftsman would be a move up; change from rural 'pupil teaching' to a factory job would also be considered upward mobility. It is therefore difficult to give the proportion who have been upwardly or downwardly mobile. Seven percent of the workers were in the same category as their fathers and 41% started work in the same category as their fathers. The difference is mostly due to those who started as farmers. There has been considerable mobility, though much of it has been horizontal or short-distance mobility. This is to be expected, since most of the workers were on jobs about half-way up the status hierarchy.

In estimating career mobility, eleven categories were used: farmer and allied primary occupations, unskilled manual, unskilled non-manual (watchman, messenger), semiskilled, skilled, army and police, trade or business (which represents many levels of economic success but relatively few people in this study), clerical, higher clerical, foreman or supervisor, and professional or semiprofessional (chiefly teachers). The move from clerical to higher clerical parallels the move from semiskilled to skilled among manual workers. There is a considerable range in the prestige rankings accorded various clerical occupations. Foremen and headmen were considered manual workers if the job they supervised was manual, since most of these were labourers' headmen or chief carpenters who continued to work with their men. Where the nature of the supervision was unspecified, it was classed as non-manual work.

Occupational mobility may occur on the job as well as by changing employers. About a fifth of the workers had done more than one type of work for the same employer; some had held three or four different posts. About a third of the changes involved work at the same level: a labourer became a watchman or a semiskilled worker changed from machine to hand-work or vice versa. A quarter of the changes involved moving from manual to clerical work, and 17% from unskilled to semiskilled work. One firm started all untrained workers as labourers and promoted those who showed promise to packers or process workers. Several of the printers and some of the carpenters had done their apprenticeships on the job. One man had moved from apprentice to carpenter to foreman in the same firm. Very few lower clerical workers had moved up to more responsible work; higher clerical workers were usually hired from outside the firm.

Nearly half of the skilled workers started in a trade and two-fifths had never had any other type of work (see table 3.2, p. 50). This was considerably higher career stability than characterized other workers. Clerical workers were also likely to have started in clerical work, though many higher clerical workers had earlier experience in trade (as shopkeepers); others had taught for a time. Many school leavers who start as low-level clerical workers (office boys, levy collectors for local councils) later go into manual work because it pays more and is no more boring. A quarter of the lower clerical workers in Accra and Tema, but only two higher clerical workers, were women. Many of these had been petty traders in the past. Over half of the clerical workers had done manual work at some point in their careers. Those in higher clerical positions had more often done so than those in lower clerical posts, possibly because of a longer career and/or relatively few opportunities available when they started to work.

Many rural craftsmen combine farming with self-employment. They farm most of the year and practice their trade in the off-season and on occasional orders. Craftsmen who are not very successful may abandon their trade, at least temporarily, for farming. An Ewe tailor farmed and worked as a steward before apprenticing himself, then returned to farming after five years of self-employment. He farmed for seven years before seeking employment in the clothing firm where he was interviewed. He was ambivalent as to whether he would continue as a tailor or farm when he left his present job.

The alternation of self-employment with employee status is illustrated by

E

an Ewe carpenter aged thirty-eight. He grew up in Dahomey but did his four-year apprenticeship in Kumasi, where he continued to work. His first two jobs lasted three years each, with six months of self-employment in between. His next two periods of self-employment lasted a year each, with one year on a wage in between. He then found more permanent employment and had been in the job nine years when he was interviewed.

An Awutu mason in a rural factory had spent much less time working for wages than the previous case. He farmed for five years at home before taking up an apprenticeship. Six years later he qualified and spent six months in self-employment until he found a government job. This was terminated eight months later. He moved to the small town where firm P was located and worked there for himself for three years before the manager at firm P asked him to work in the factory. Nine months later he was laid off and returned to self-employment for eight years before being called to work at the factory. Although he liked the steady wages, he was quite capable of maintaining himself without them.

A few further examples of occupational mobility are given to show the possibilities. They tend to be of older men because younger ones have not yet had time for many different jobs. Although they are not typical because they were chosen to demonstrate extensive mobility, the characteristics shown are found to a lesser extent in other workers. For instance, many workers changed jobs frequently early in their careers, then settled down to a longer job.[1] Mobile younger workers are likely to stick with a job later when they have more family responsibilities. Higher educational requirements and unemployment may also limit job mobility in future.

The first two examples are non-Ghanaian watchmen who have settled down in Ghana, though the second has closer ties with his home than the first. The first is a Hausa of sixty-one from Niger. He first came to Ghana at about twenty years of age and worked as a *kayakaya* (porter) for five years, then as a stone cracker for two years, a labourer for three years, a miner for six years and a soldier for seven years before returning home in the late 1940s for two years of farming. Each of his Ghanaian jobs took him to a new place. He returned to Ghana and did contracting for two years, then worked as a watchman for the government for two years before moving back to Accra in 1952 and starting the job on which he was interviewed. In this case there was no commitment to any particular job. He merely took whatever came along and left when he tired of it.

The second man, a Mossi who had grown up in or near Ouagadougou, Upper Volta, had a less varied career. He farmed at home for about ten

---

[1] The same is true of young British workers (Carter 1966:137).

years before moving to Accra, where he found a job as a labourer on the railways. After three years, he moved to Kumasi and worked for nearly two years 'weeding around towns'. In 1936 he moved back home and farmed there for nine years on his own. In 1945 he went into business as a butcher. After about five years of this, he moved back to Ghana – to Takoradi this time. He spent a year as a watchman and then began trading. After $6\frac{1}{2}$ years he moved back to Kumasi and got a job as a labourer at firm M. In his mid-fifties, he transferred to watchman. He thought he would stay at least five years longer before returning home to farm. His wife and children are with him in Kumasi, but he goes home for two weeks every two or three years.

The next three examples are non-manual workers, though the first has spent much of his life farming. He is a Ga supervisor of sixty-eight who grew up in Accra and has only lived elsewhere for three years. He started working at twenty-one as a beach clerk, then moved to Nsawam (20 miles from Accra) as a buyer of foodstuffs on his own account. He returned to Accra in 1921 and worked for six years as a customs clerk, then farmed for five years, spent three years in the army in the early 1930s and returned to farming for about seventeen years. He left this in 1954 to become a customs clerk and later supervisor for his Lebanese employer.

An Adangbe storekeeper aged fifty-two had combined relative job stability with a varied career. He taught for twelve years in a town near Accra, then spent three years in the army just after the Second World War. After a year in a village near Accra as a census clerk for the 1948 National Census, he spent twelve years with the Agriculture Department in another town in Eastern Region. He then got a job at firm A and moved to Tema in 1961.

An Ewe chief storekeeper aged forty-nine also had farming and army experience and had worked his way up within his firm. After nine months' farming at home in Eastern Region, he spent three months on a temporary post as assistant weighing clerk for his uncle in a Western Region village, then spent two years farming in two other villages in Eastern Region. He joined the army in 1946 and was demobilized seven months later. After two years as a labourer in Accra he found another job as store assistant and later moved up to chief storekeeper. He had been on this job for eighteen years when he was transferred to firm Q of which his employers were joint owners.

Two cases of downward mobility were a Fanti semiskilled worker and a Ga riveter, both of whom had trade training. The Fanti, aged thirty-five, taught for two years in a village, then apprenticed himself for two years to learn tailoring. He worked on his own as a tailor for two years in the town where he was apprenticed, then farmed for his father for another two years. This was followed by five years more of self-employment as a tailor in another town, but he could not earn enough on his own and moved to Takoradi, where he found unskilled work in a factory. He was eventually promoted to semiskilled work, which presumably paid more than he had earned on his own.

The Ga was forty-three. He had been apprenticed to a shoemaker in Accra for four years, but had never worked at it. After eight years as a clerk and six months as a timekeeper, he was unemployed for five months before finding a labouring job. This lasted 2½ years. He then moved to Tema and found another labouring job, which lasted only three months. He was employed on his present job soon after the factory opened in 1960, but planned to stay less than a year longer. He said he would like to become a shoemaker, which seems unlikely to provide as high an income as his present job.

The last two are skilled workers. The first learned his skill after a variety of other jobs, while the second has practiced several skills. A Fanti painter aged forty-seven started work as a store assistant in Cape Coast after completing middle school. He left this after three years and worked for four months as a messenger in Accra before joining the army, where he learned to be a telephone linesman. After the war, he worked for six months as a linesman in a gold mine, then spent four years as a salesman and one year each as a steel erector, foreman and skin diver (all in Takoradi). He moved to Tema and learned painting on the job. After 7½ years, he took two years off to farm (while still living in Tema), then started his present job in 1963.

A sixty-year-old mechanic grade 1 grew up in Western Region and attended primary school there. He completed a five-year apprenticeship in tailoring by the age of seventeen and worked at this for six months before beginning a three-year blacksmithing apprenticeship in Accra. He had two blacksmithing jobs, of six years (in Accra) and nine months (elsewhere), before becoming a steward boy. After four months of this, he turned to repairing clocks, typewriters and sewing machines, skills he claimed to have learned as part of his blacksmithing training. This training also apparently covered fitting, because he next worked for three years as a fitter in Accra, for three months in Winneba and for eighteen months as a fitter/blacksmith on a job which involved two further transfers of location. He then moved again to work as a road overseer for the railway for three months before taking up a post as blacksmith at the Prestea gold mine. This lasted for four years. During the 1940s he was in and out of Takoradi, spending one year and seven months on two blacksmithing jobs, four months as a self-employed tinsmith and two years (without further training) as a railway painter. He then transferred to fitting for the railway and stuck to this for about thirteen years. In 1960 he went back to blacksmithing for eight months, then became a village plumber for five years. He had been on his present job for eight months when he was interviewed, and thought he would stay about five years. This long career included residence in ten towns or villages and nine different job titles. He is probably typical (though an extreme example) of many African skilled workers who build on their basic training by learning jobs as they go along.

TIME SPENT ON JOBS

Complete job histories give us some picture of changes in employment over time. One aspect of this is the length of time spent on various jobs. This section refers to urban males only, because patterns of employment for women are often affected by the demands of their families and there were too few rural workers to provide conclusive data. Fifteen percent of the women interviewed were on their first job, so this further cuts down the data available on women workers. Of the women who were not on their first job, two-thirds (compared to 37% of the males in Accra and Tema) had spent an average of less than two years on their previous jobs. Tables 3.5 to 3.7 refer to 3,408 jobs completed prior to the interviews. Omitting the ninety-three men on their first jobs, this comes to an average of 2.8 jobs per man. The number of changes of occupation would be somewhat higher, since some workers did various types of work for the same employer, all of which counted as a single job. (The occupation on which the most time was spent was counted.) Changes of location were not counted if the employer was unchanged; i.e. a period as a self-employed artisan in two or three towns was counted as one job.

TABLE 3.5. *Median length of job (in years) of male workers in various occupations by year ended*

Occupation	1920–49	1950–4	1955–9	1960–4	1965–7	Total	N
Farming	4.1	3.7	2.9	2.1	1.1	2.6	883
Unskilled	1.5	2.2	1.8	1.1	1.0	1.2	641
Semiskilled[a]	5.1[b]	2.3	1.9	1.8	1.9	2.6[c]	355
Skilled	2.1	1.7	1.9	2.3	1.5	1.7	959
Clerical	1.1	1.6	1.8	1.4	1.2	1.4	285
Teaching	0.8	[d]	1.9	2.2	[d]	1.9	83
Trade, business	0.9	2.9	2.6	1.3	1.0	1.7	202
N	367	328	717	1,278	496	3,408	3,408

[a] Includes army and police.   [b] Army and police median 5.5.
[c] Army and police median 5.3; other semiskilled median 2.0.
[d] Less than 10, not calculated.

59

Occupations

Comparison of tables 3.1 and 3.5 shows that factory work is fairly stable compared to other employment. Workers in all occupational categories averaged a longer time on their present jobs than workers in the same category averaged on jobs ending in the 1960s. This is at least in part due to satisfaction with factory work. Increasing unemployment in recent years has also increased job stability insofar as workers can control this.

Farmers had a longer average time per job than anyone except those in the army and police. (The last two involve a relatively small number of jobs, mostly in the 1940s. Men with long periods in the services are considered well qualified to be security officers.) The average time spent farming has decreased steadily through the years. Whereas older men often spent many years farming before migrating to town, the younger ones tend to have farmed for only a few months after leaving school. In addition, trips home for farming are probably shorter now than they were in the past.

Unskilled workers had the shortest average job time, though it was not significantly different from that of clerical workers. Unskilled workers stayed on the job longer prior to 1960 than after. This is partly because those in the service occupations (watchmen and stewards) lose their jobs when expatriates leave the country. There are as many expatriates now as during the colonial period, but most stay only a year or two. It may also be explained by the insecurity of building employment, especially in the late 1960s. Opportunities have severely decreased in recent years; skilled workers often find themselves out of work because their employers have no further contracts or the factory is closed because of lack of raw materials or spare parts. Factory closure affects semiskilled workers even more than skilled ones, because some of the latter are kept on to maintain the machinery. The average length of semiskilled jobs has been fairly stable since the mid 1950s, but it was two-and-a-half times as long before 1950 as at any time after 1955. This is not due to the inclusion of army and police jobs, which averaged five years; other semiskilled jobs prior to 1950 also averaged five years. It may be because of the small number of semiskilled jobs (mostly driving) dating from this period.

Clerical workers have never stayed very long on the job; only 7% of the clerical jobs lasted more than five years, compared to 12% of the skilled jobs and 23% of those in farming. Over two-fifths of the clerical jobs were held by men who spent most of their careers in another field and these, as shown in table 3.6, spent significantly less time on clerical jobs than workers who stayed in this field. Many young men try clerical work when they first come to town, but soon leave it because they are dissatisfied and move into semiskilled or skilled work.

The length of time spent on trading has, like farming, decreased with time. In both cases it should be remembered that there are men who have left these occupations for factory work. Their attitude toward the occupation may be quite different from those who have stuck to it.

TABLE 3.6. *Median length of job (in years) of male workers in various types of work by major urban occupation*

Type of work	Major urban occupation				N
	Unskilled[a]	Semi-skilled	Skilled	Clerical	
Farming	4.0	1.4	2.2	1.2	883
Unskilled	2.1	1.0	1.2	1.0	641
Semiskilled[b]	4.3[c]	2.1	2.3[d]	2.2	355
Skilled	2.2	1.6	1.7	e	959
Clerical	1.4	1.0	1.1	1.9	285
Teaching	e	1.9	1.2	2.3	83
Trade, business	2.8	1.2	1.2	2.3	202
N	813	880	1,328	387	3,408

[a] Two men spent most of their lives trading but were included here.
[b] Includes army and police.   [c] Median without army and police is 1.3.
[d] Median without army and police is 1.1.
[e] Less than 10, not calculated.

Table 3.6 divides the workers according to the urban occupation on which they have spent the most time and shows how much time they have averaged on this and other types of jobs. The hypothesis was that men will spend a longer time on jobs which fall within their career line and a shorter time on other jobs, which may be taken only to fill a period of unemployment. This proved to be true for some occupations but not for others. Unskilled and clerical workers spent longer on jobs in their own fields than did other workers who had unskilled or clerical jobs, but not longer than they spent on jobs in other fields themselves. For example, skilled specialists who had clerical jobs did not work at them for as long, on the average, as did clerical specialists in clerical jobs, but clerical specialists spent as long on semiskilled, teaching and trading jobs as they did on clerical ones.

Semiskilled and skilled specialists, on the other hand, spent longer on jobs in their own fields than they did on jobs in other fields (except for skilled workers who farmed). These jobs are intrinsically more satisfying and better paying than unskilled and lower-level clerical work and this encourages workers to stay on the job longer.

Occupations

Unskilled and clerical specialists who went into trading spent longer at it than semiskilled or skilled specialists who traded. Unskilled careerists who trade for more than a year are usually working for themselves; this is looked on as a better-paying alternative to unskilled work and is very popular with non-Ghanaians (Rouch 1954). Clerical specialists who trade are usually employed as shopkeepers. The successful shopkeeper may save enough to set himself up in business, or may move on to a well-paying higher clerical position.

TABLE 3.7. *Median length of job (in years) by employment status, type of work and proportion self-employed, male workers*

| Type of work | Employment status | | Self-employed (%) | N |
	Employee[a]	Self-employed		
Farming	2.8	2.0	16.1	883
Unskilled	1.2	3.2	4.4	641
Semiskilled[b]	2.6	2.5	7.3	355
Skilled	1.7	2.8	23.8	959
Clerical	1.4	c	1.0	285
Trade, business	1.3	2.7	23.8	202

[a] Includes family workers. [b] Includes army and police.
[c] Too few to calculate.

It was hypothesized that self-employment would usually be for a longer period than wage-employment, because many workers value their freedom and prefer to work at their own pace. The results of comparing the two, as shown in table 3.7, are only a partial confirmation of this. Farmers worked for a shorter period and traders for a longer period when they were self-employed. The difference for farmers is probably due to the fact that the first, long-term farming is usually done on the family farm. Later periods of farming by these basically non-farming urbanites tend to be short. The contrary situation applies to trade; periods spent working for others are usually short time-fillers until enough money is accumulated for a stake, whereas self-employment is more satisfying and tends to last longer. In the only other occupation with enough self-employment for a test, skilled work, the difference was in the expected direction. Many skilled workers prefer self-employment, but it often does not provide a reasonable standard of living and they are forced to seek work for wages. Others use self-employment only as a stopgap for periods when they would otherwise be unemployed; this cuts the average time spent in self-employment. One-fifth of the skilled self-employed jobs compared to a tenth of the skilled wage jobs lasted over five years; this difference is statistically significant.

REASONS FOR LEAVING JOBS

Rural workers were asked why they had left each job. While a certain amount of rationalization comes into the answers to such a question (very few men report that they were sacked), we do get a picture of why men leave one job for another which confirms earlier impressions. The reasons were given for leaving 304 jobs. One-third left because they were laid off (some of these were probably sacked), declared redundant or because the work was 'finished' – the building had been completed, the employer left the country, or the company went out of business. This happened to manual workers more often than to non-manual workers; about half of the unskilled and semiskilled jobs terminated for this reason, compared to two-fifths of the skilled and a third of the clerical jobs. In a study made of unemployed workers in Tema (Peil 1969), skilled workers were more likely to report redundancy than were the unskilled. The difference between the two findings is due to several factors. (1) There were few skilled workers in the rural factories and few of these had been employed in the construction industry, whereas most of the unemployed skilled workers in Tema had been working in construction, where lay-offs are common. (2) Quite a few of the workers at firm P (mostly semiskilled) had been laid off and then taken on again at a later date. Some of the unskilled workers at firm Q had had the same experience.

A fifth of the rural workers had left jobs because they found something better. This was especially true of farming. A fifth of the farming jobs lasted six months or less; one gets the impression that many workers were only putting in time farming to avoid total unemployment. Others left farming 'to find a stable job; this is only seasonal', 'to get money' (because their fathers didn't share the proceeds with them, the farm wasn't paying, or to buy a farm of their own), or in discouragement because of cocoa pests or the death of poultry. One labourer left farming after forty years 'for a regular income job'.

Nearly a fifth left because the job paid poorly. Men left all types of jobs about equally for this reason. Labourers complained that contractors cheated them with late wages and others left teaching in private schools because of irregular pay. All but one of the skilled workers with experience of self-employment found wage-paying jobs because they could not earn enough on their own. A cobbler found he could not get enough money to buy all the necessary equipment. A tailor was out of work when the owner of the sewing machine took it away from him. A carpenter broke from his father because the latter did not share the proceeds of their joint business. It should be emphasized that this sample is biased in that all the men were currently in wage-employment.

Quite a few jobs were terminated because of family influence. In several cases a member of the family became ill and had to be looked after. A fireman went home for three years 'to head the family' and a fitter took eight months off when his father died. A driver spent three years at home farming because he inherited from his uncle and had to look after the farm; he then left because the farm was not as productive as paid employment. Some workers left because relatives said they would find their kinsmen new jobs in another town. One boy's parents decided that his pay in Tema was too small and demanded that he come home. He farmed for a year, then went off to try again. In another case, a man returned to Togo to help his relatives, but his parents advised him after a year to return to Ghana.

Small numbers of jobs were ended for other reasons. Four men resigned to avoid transfer. One had already worked as timekeeper for a contractor in five different places in Togo and Ghana over a period of eleven years and went home rather than move again. Four others left because they could see no prospects of promotion. One of these was an electrician who wanted to be an electrical engineer; the others were clerical workers.

One young man was asked by his father to quit his job so that he could be sent to secondary school. As it happened, he didn't go, but a few did stop work to further their education; a few others stopped to take up an apprenticeship. Only one man reported attending technical school part time while he was working. One man stopped teaching because he could see that he would not get into a training college. Most of those who had taught stopped because they were laid off; none was a trained teacher.

Watchmen are likely to lose their jobs because their employers leave the country, but one left because his mother was convinced he would come to harm if he kept the job and another left suddenly because he saw a strange figure at midnight. (Hardly a useful watchman, but he got another job two days later.)

The proportion of jobs terminated because of redundancy almost doubled in the 1950s and 1960s over earlier years. In the 1960s, men were twice as likely to leave jobs because they found better ones and two-thirds as likely to leave because of poor pay as were men who left before 1960. This seems to contradict the economic facts of life in Ghana in the 1960s; unemployment rose drastically after the *coup* in 1966. However, the cost of living rose steadily and faster than income during this period, making the search for higher pay more important than previously. This matter should be studied with a larger sample.

Length of the job did not make much difference in the reason given for leaving it. Those who left after five years on the job and those who left within the first six months gave reasons which were similar to the group as a whole except that the early leavers were more likely than other workers to quit because they had found a better job.

UNEMPLOYMENT

When collecting job histories, the length of unemployment between jobs was recorded. Most of these periods were short and reporting is less accurate than for the duration of jobs. Nevertheless, since studies of unemployment usually involve interviews with the unemployed about their current period without work rather than investigating various episodes over time, these data are presented as a contribution to a fuller picture of the place of unemployment in a worker's career. Workers were asked twice, at different points in the interview, about periods of unemployment after leaving school, before starting work in the town where they were interviewed and before their current job, so information on these is likely to be more accurate than the data on other periods. Broad categories have been used to summarize the data, as these are likely to increase its reliability.

It is impossible with the present data to separate employment from underemployment or relatively permanent jobs from temporary time-fillers. Working at home as a tailor or carpenter is regular employment for many; for others, it represents a few days' work per month providing a bare subsistence until they can find work on a construction site or in a factory (Peil 1969). Examples have already been given of craftsmen who claimed to have no unemployment but had several periods of self-employment between jobs for others. Unskilled workers may have periods when they engage in casual labour for daily expenses – weeding compounds, unloading ships, acting as mate for friends who drive lorries. Two men in Takoradi reported ten years of casual employment, but the usual period is short.

The Ghana Census counted as employed everyone who had spent at least one day in the previous month working for pay or profit or on their own farms. In this study men were classified as unemployed whenever they considered themselves to be so except for periods spent trading or farming. Boys often look on farming for their fathers as a stopgap until some other work is found, and girls have the same attitude toward trading for their mothers. Workers who spend a few months at home farming between jobs

65

are not, strictly speaking, unemployed, since they are doing work for profit (or at least subsistence) and are not actively looking for work. Even if they are sending off applications to prospective employers, a sufficient part of their time is spent working to merit the classification employed unless they are at home in the north during the dry season. Following some workers' tendency to consider only urban work as employment would result in a false picture of their careers, as the work histories reported above show.

Periods spent outside the labour force have not been counted with unemployment. Some workers had long periods of illness or had to stop work to look after a relative. Others managed to return to school (usually a commercial or technical school rather than an academic secondary school) for two or three years after a period of employment. Women often dropped out of the labour force for several years at marriage. Unfortunately, the number of women included in this study is too small and too selective to give more accurate information on this phenomenon.

The picture is much the same, whether or not these periods are included. A measure of labour force participation which gives the proportion of a worker's time from the beginning of his apprenticeship or his first non-farming job that has been spent in employment, counting self-employment

TABLE 3.8. *Post-school unemployment and first full-time work by location of first job, urban male workers (percentages)*

Length of unemployment	First job						
	Farmer	Un-skilled	Semi-skilled	Skilled[a]	Clerical	Teaching	Other
Non-migrants[b]							
Under 2 months	84	54	52	59	43	58	79
2–6 months	10	24	20	20	30	26	9
Longer	6	22	28	21	27	16	12
Total	100	100	100	100	100	100	100
N	206	50	40	91	53	19	43
Migrants							
Under 2 months	72	50	38	57	30	52	49
2–6 months	14	36	36	19	40	40	33
Longer	14	14	26	24	30	8	18
Total	100	100	100	100	100	100	100
N	43	80	53	97	61	25	51

[a] Unemployment after apprenticeship for skilled workers; those who did not migrate after apprenticeship are classed as non-migrants.
[b] Those who did not move from the place where they grew up in order to obtain their first job.

66

but not farming at home, shows the same basic variance as a measure based on periods of formal unemployment. Workers in Tema and rural factories and those doing unskilled, semiskilled and lower clerical work have had more unemployment than the rest.

Two-thirds of those who had attended school found work within two months of leaving school, including four-fifths of those who farmed and about half of the rest. Non-farmers who found jobs at home were less likely than those who migrated to be unemployed for more than two months, but there was no difference between migrants and non-migrants after six months (see table 3.8). The greater ability of non-migrants to find jobs within two months is due to delays involved in migration and the probability that some of the migrants are going because they have not succeeded in finding work at home.

Young men often do not start looking for work as soon as they leave middle school. Many prefer to 'rest' for a while, using as an excuse the delay of several months in the distribution of Middle School Leaving Certificates. Some are hoping for admittance to secondary school or training college; others are making arrangements for migration. Those who want to work at home but not to farm make the rounds of local government and any other employers. When these possibilities have been exhausted, they also begin to think seriously of migration.

Studies of middle-school leavers in Ghana (Peil 1968b) have shown that those who migrate are less likely to be unemployed six or eighteen months after leaving school than are those who stay at home. Since the young men in these studies left school in the late 1960s, whereas the factory workers had all left school before this, the difference in results may be due to changes in the local situation. With the great increase in school attendance since Independence, it is harder for school leavers to find non-farming jobs at home than it was in the past.

Much of the difference between migrants and non-migrants is due to those whose first job was semiskilled or non-manual. These are more likely than others to migrate to urban areas and take longer to find jobs even when they stay at home.

It was assumed that secondary-school leavers would have a much easier time finding work than middle-school leavers. The former have, until very recently, been relatively rare in Ghana and there are jobs open to them which are not open to middle-school leavers. That there was no difference between them in the proportion who found jobs quickly after leaving school or who took more than six months to find work, either among non-migrants or migrants, may be due to the nature of the sample or the greater willingness of middle-school leavers to go into farming, at least initially. There are few

Occupations

in this sample who attended secondary school and some of them were in jobs which it is unusual for people with their educational background to hold. There may well be personality or other problems which affect their employability. Some of them did not finish the secondary program and so have little more in their favour than men with a Middle School Leaving Certificate. One middle-school leaver in seven migrated initially to a rural area. For many, this was a return home for farming after having lived elsewhere to attend school. Very few secondary-school leavers went into farming and about half became clerks or teachers, jobs which take longer than farming to arrange.

Only provincial and rural workers were asked about unemployment upon first arrival in town. Excluding workers who came on transfer, relatively few of either group found work within a week, but half of the provincial workers and three-fifths of the rural ones were employed within a month of arrival. Skilled workers found jobs more quickly than the unskilled or semiskilled. Migrants from villages found work within a week more often than did those from towns or cities and were less likely to remain unemployed for more than three months. This may be because migrants from rural areas are less committed to staying in town than those from towns and therefore more likely to return home if they remain for several months without work. Aspirations and willingness to take any work that is offered will be discussed in the next chapter.

TABLE 3.9. *Unemployment before current job by place and occupation (percentages)*

| | Length of unemployment | | | | | | |
	Under 1 week	1 week to 1 month	1½–3 months	4–6 months	Over 6 months	Total	N
Place							
Accra	38	25	17	10	10	100	695[b]
Tema	17	28	19	18	18	100	242[c]
Kumasi	37	30	18	9	6	100	150
Takoradi	33	24	16	8	19	100	150
Rural	48	15	14	10	13	100	138
Occupation[a]							
Unskilled	18	36	24	11	11	100	218
Semiskilled	22	25	20	13	20	100	378
Skilled	44	23	14	9	10	100	387
Lower clerical	19	29	18	20	14	100	73
Higher clerical	59	14	15	3	9	100	58
Foremen	52	24	7	5	12	100	56

[a] Urban males only.   [b] 40 unknown.   [c] 17 unknown.

The length of unemployment before the current job varied more between cities, occupations and educational levels than from one time period to another (see table 3.9). Tema workers were only half as likely as those in other towns to have found work within a week; three-fifths of them were unemployed for more than a month before finding their present jobs. Tema and Takoradi workers were out of work for more than six months more often than Accra or Kumasi workers. This difference is partly due to the occupational distribution of the workers interviewed in each city, but the differences remain when occupations are held constant, so the employment opportunities in each town are also relevant.

Foremen, higher clerical workers and skilled workers found their jobs more quickly than did unskilled, semiskilled or lower clerical workers, irrespective of the city in which they were working and the length of time they had been on the job. Nevertheless, skilled workers and foremen in Accra were out of work for a shorter time than those in Tema and skilled workers in Takoradi were more likely to take over six months to find a job than those in Kumasi or Accra. On another measure, skilled and higher clerical workers and foremen had spent a higher proportion of their working lives in employment than had unskilled, semiskilled or lower clerical workers. These are, of course, the least trained sector of the labour force.

Men with no education and those with commercial or technical training found their jobs more quickly than those with middle or secondary education, regardless of how long they had been on the job. The man with no education is willing to take whatever work he can get, whereas school leavers often feel that they should find a 'good job'. The relative success of those with vocational training in finding jobs quickly contradicts the findings of Clignet and Foster (1966:187) and others that these students have more difficulty than those with an academic background in avoiding unemployment. However, this sample is a small one and unrepresentative of secondary-school leavers.

It was expected that workers who had been on the job longer would have found their jobs more quickly than those who had only recently been employed, since it is generally assumed that unemployment has increased in recent years. This proved to be the case, though the difference was not as large as expected. Three-fifths (62%) of the workers who had been on the job five years or longer had been employed within a month of leaving their previous jobs or joining the labour force, compared to 56% of those who had been employed for a shorter period.

The relationships differed from one town to another. In Accra and Tema, employees with only a year of service were least often hired within their first week of unemployment. In Kumasi, only workers hired within the past five years had been unemployed for more than six months, but there was no difference either in Kumasi or in Takoradi between the recently employed and those who had been on the job between sixteen months and four years. In Accra, workers who had been working for their firms over ten years had experienced over six months' unemployment more often than those employed more recently. Thus, it is not possible to trace a clear deterioration in the employment situation from the data available.

There was an inverse relationship between the number of jobs a man had had and the length of time it took him to get his present one. Men on a first and second job most often took over six months to find work and men with several previous jobs were more likely to find the present one in less than a week. This is due to a combination of contacts built up over time, training and experience both on the jobs and in finding jobs and the ability of some men to stay on one job until another has been located.

The unemployment experienced by an individual can be summarized by the number of incidents and their length. Many workers, especially the unskilled, said they had 'wasted no time' between jobs. This is quite possible, since unskilled work was in the past fairly easy to pick up and some workers line up the next job before leaving the current one. However, it seems likely that there is often a period of a week or two between jobs during which the unemployed man rests and investigates the opportunities open to him. Some unskilled workers said they quit because they felt the need for a rest. The category with the lowest unemployment therefore includes all those who had never been unemployed for more than a month: 34% of the urban men, 31% of the women and 33% of the rural workers.

The longest period of unemployment is usually while looking for the first non-agricultural job, since this frequently involves migration and settling down in a new town as well as learning the new role of job-seeker. Two-fifths of the workers reported only one period of unemployment longer than a month, though only 8% of the workers interviewed were on their first job. A third of the workers on their first or second jobs had spent more than three months finding it, compared to a fifth of the workers who had had at least two previous jobs (see table 3.10).

Skilled workers are less affected by unemployment than others, because many can at least support themselves at home, expanding the private work they were doing in the evenings and on weekends while employed. Semiskilled and clerical workers are least likely, or able, to find casual work as a stopgap, yet they face long periods of unemployment more often than do the skilled and unskilled workers.

TABLE 3.10. *Career unemployment by occupation and education (percentages)*

| | Total unemployment | | | | | | |
| | 1 period | | | 2+ periods | | | |
	1 month or less	1–3 months	4+ months	½–6 months	Longer	Total	N
Occupation							
Unskilled	38	28	14	9	11	100	250
Semiskilled	28	20	21	14	17	100	526
Skilled	45	19	16	8	12	100	437
Clerical	26	20	23	11	20	100	159
Foremen	30	20	20	14	16	100	56
Education							
None	51	21	11	9	8	100	386
Primary, Muslim	35	23	17	7	18	100	135
Middle	27	20	20	15	18	100	754
More than middle	34	23	20	7	16	100	153

About one worker in six had experienced at least one period of six months without work. The proportion of workers with two or more periods of unemployment, at least one of which was over six months, is higher for the 25–34 age group than for workers under 25, but does not increase among older workers. It seems likely that most men over thirty-five who are unemployed for a long period decide that the time has come to retire to their hometowns. Younger men are more able to sustain long-term unemployment because they have fewer family responsibilities and because relatives are more willing to support them. An older man finds it harder to turn to relatives for support, even should they be willing to help him.

Just as education increases the propensity to migrate, so even a little education increases the unemployment of those who do migrate. Only half of the workers who had not attended school had been unemployed for more than a month, and only a quarter for more than three months. Workers who had attended only a primary or Koranic school were remarkably similar to those who had gone beyond middle school in their unemployment histories. The workers with a middle-school education had experienced the most unemployment, both in the proportion who had been out of work for more than three months and in the proportion with more than one period of unemployment. They were nearly three times as likely as other workers to have taken more than six months to find their present employment.

F

Occupations

Workers with middle-school education were concentrated in Tema, where the employment process seems to be slower and unemployment is probably higher than elsewhere, and in semiskilled jobs, for which there is less demand than for skilled or unskilled ones. Some school leavers are slow in finding work because their aspirations are too high, but for many it is just a question of too much competition (Peil 1968a). An educated boy may get more willing support from relatives than an illiterate one because there is a hope that he will find well-paying work, but the recent surplus of secondary-school leavers means that this hope is unlikely to be realized. The Mills-Odoi Commission (1967:54) recommended that government clerical jobs should be given only to people who had attended secondary school. The government accepted this recommendation, thus cutting off middle-school leavers from this prime source of employment.

The middle-school leaver thinks he should have something better than an unskilled job, but he lacks training to qualify him for anything else. Semi-skilled work, which suits his capacities, is available only in limited quantity and many school leavers do not find it very satisfying.

Those who spend only a short time on each job are most likely to have long periods of unemployment. This is probably due to lack of adjustment to the work situation and/or lack of motivation. An extreme example is provided by a machine operative who had lived all his life in Teshie, a town between Accra and Tema. At the age of twenty (five years after leaving primary school) he got his first job, as a painter, which lasted eight months. He was then unemployed for seven years before obtaining a post as trainee steel bender, which only lasted four months. It wasn't until two years later that he became an operative in Tema. This job seems to have been more satisfactory than the previous ones. He held it for at least five years. His family had apparently been willing to support him at home over a long period of time, so that he was thirty before he achieved regular employment and thirty-two before he married.

Those who grew up in villages, especially northerners and non-Ghanaians, were more likely to escape long periods of unemployment than were southerners and those of urban origin. This is related to the willingness of the former to do unskilled work and farm, whereas the latter are oriented toward 'school leaver' jobs which take longer to find. Men who entered the non-agricultural labour force before the age of sixteen were more likely than those who started wage employment when they were older to avoid unemployment lasting more than a month. Many of these are skilled workers, who began their apprenticeships in early adolescence. Semiskilled and clerical workers have usually stayed in school until they were seventeen or eighteen.

FINDING A JOB

Workers were asked, 'How did you go about finding this job?' Most employers interviewed in the Management Survey had reported that they obtained workers through the Labour Office. This turned out to be more principle than practice in most firms. In three firms (including the smallest two in the study) only one person or none at all reported getting a job through the Labour Office. Small firms are more likely than larger ones to base their hiring on ascriptive principles; the large ones must be more bureaucratically organized through sheer force of numbers and because they are more liable than smaller firms to government inspection. The law which requires all hiring to be carried out through the Labour Office is backed by a NC200 fine for infractions, but blanket enforcement is impossible because of the lack of Labour Office personnel either to handle the volume of workers seeking employment or to check for offenders. Nevertheless, most firms which do hire at the gate make sure the new worker has registered at the Labour Office and notify the Labour Office that he has been employed.

Many managers prefer to do their own hiring rather than accept men sent by the Labour Office because this gives them more scope for testing an applicant's qualifications and more assurance that he is interested in the job. Labour Offices are not equipped to check the skills which applicants claim to have and selection procedures are not well organized. Limited use of labour exchanges is not confined to tropical Africa. Van der Horst (1964:9) found that firms in South Africa sometimes prefer private recruitment (for which they must get permission). Carter reported (1966:145) that a majority of young British workers prefer to find their own jobs. Only 2% of the Indian factory workers interviewed by Lambert (1963:72–5) had used the employment exchange to find their jobs. In India it was the young, educated, skilled workers who were most likely to have registered at the exchange. In Ghana the majority of men who are unemployed for an extended period probably visit the Labour Office at some time, but those who lack skills and experience are more dependent on it than older and better-trained workers. Those who have gone beyond middle school find their jobs through other means; workers with middle-school education and those with none at all use the Labour Office about equally.

Some unemployed men go to the Labour Office regularly on the theory that officials there know what jobs are available. Others ignore the Labour Office because they feel that there are no jobs to be had or that they could never win the rush to be taken when an opening is announced. Clerical workers and some of the skilled workers prefer writing applications to prospective employers. This method is also often used by schoolboys hoping to line up a job before leaving home, but it does not seem to be as prevalent as in Nigeria, where school leavers are often known as 'applicants'. In five Accra firms over half of those interviewed were employed after application. Unskilled and semiskilled workers are most likely to be employed through the Labour Office; clerical workers (especially higher clerical workers) usually apply; skilled workers and machine operatives are more likely than others to utilize personal relationships in finding work.

In four firms (the two in Tema, one in Takoradi and one rural) the proportion who got their jobs through the Labour Office ranged from 67% to 86%. In only one of the rest was it as high as 25%. Only 11% of the Accra workers found their jobs through the Labour Office. The difference between Accra and Tema is striking, and is symptomatic of the general difference in atmosphere in the two towns. Tema was built as an industrial town. Most of the population have arrived recently and few people have 'connections' to help them find work in the large, bureaucratically run factories. Accra is also growing rapidly, but many industries have been established long enough for their managers and workers to have built up a network of contacts in the city and its hinterland. Firms are often small and workers who are leaving may suggest their successors, or other workers may supply candidates to fill vacant posts.

In Accra, 11% of the workers had the help of relatives, and 21% that of others (townsmen, friends, foremen, gatemen) in finding their jobs.[1] These practices were as often used in Takoradi; they were somewhat less important in Kumasi and seldom used in Tema (for the reasons stated above). Helpful relatives were usually employed at the firm, though a few unemployed men had prestigious relations able to contact employers for them. One man was distantly related to the wife of the assistant director of his firm. In firm E, over a quarter of the workers got their jobs through relatives and more than a third had help from other individuals. This is a small firm with considerable turnover; some of the workers may have been using jobs there as a stopgap until they could find something better.

A European manager of one long-established firm said they often employed sons of workers, because they could have more assurance of good character and loyalty from these than from an unknown new employee. Nearly half (43%) of their workers had help from kinsmen or others in finding their jobs. Two other firms with a fairly high proportion of workers reporting

[1] This is lower than the proportion of British workers whose families help them find work, but the average British industrial worker is less likely than the Ghanaian to have to leave home to find work (Carter 1966: 142, 137).

'contacts' as the source of their jobs were both in the furniture business. Carpenters are often asked to recommend someone when a job falls vacant and they know each other from having worked together on previous jobs.

Northerners and non-Ghanaians often use the 'stranger' network to find jobs. In firm K, a small firm where most of the workers were northerners or non-Ghanaians and where turnover was very high, 40% of the workers had found their jobs through personal relationships. In firm C, which was larger but had a labour force of similar background, a quarter of the workers had done so. In neither of these firms was much use made of relatives, presumably because few workers had any in town.

Rural workers made relatively little use of relatives or other contacts in finding jobs. One of the factories had a Labour Office set up at the gate to process applicants; workers at the other factory had usually applied for their posts, though the manager had contacted some skilled workers in the village and asked them to join the firm. Workers in towns who had done three or more types of manual work were somewhat more likely to use contacts in finding work than those with a less varied career. Rural workers in similar circumstances applied for work, presumably because contacts are harder to develop in the isolated situation of rural factories.

A few workers had transferred to their present jobs from another branch of the firm; this happened to most of the clerical staff at firm Q. Sometimes a worker who does not want to move when his firm leaves town is transferred to another firm with which the manager has connections. Some managers seek out the workers, as did the rural manager mentioned above. One manager in Accra had recruited from the Kumasi Polytechnic and a Kumasi manager had met a worker who suited his needs in Takoradi and urged him to move to Kumasi.

WAGE RATES

The wage structure is treated last because this has an important effect on the workers' job satisfaction, which will be the subject of the following chapter. The problems faced by workers in making their wages cover their necessary expenses are discussed in chapter 6. This section is mainly concerned with reporting wage differentials for workers in various categories and locations.

The minimum wage was established at 6s. 6d. (33p, 65 new pesewas) per day in 1960. This would give a take-home pay of NC16.25 (£8.13) for a month of twenty-five working days. It was raised to 70 new pesewas (35p) per day in 1967 when the cedi was devalued and raised again to 75 new pesewas (37p) in 1968. There is evidence that at least some firms too small to be included in this study pay wages that are considerably below the minimum wage, so the averages for industrial workers are probably somewhat lower than those reported here. Killick (1966:141) has shown that rises in the cost of living have been much greater than rises in the basic wage over a long period, so that the earning power of workers in the mid-sixties was conceivably less than that of workers in the late thirties.

Most workers put in a 5½-day week which averages forty-eight hours with overtime in Accra/Tema and forty-two hours in the provincial cities. National holidays vary from year to year; there were about ten in 1966, but several were dropped after the *coup*. Some firms allow workers one or two weeks' holiday yearly in addition to the four days at Christmas and at Easter.

To check on the accuracy of wage reporting, wage lists were obtained from two factories and the amount reported by each worker was verified. Two of the seventy-five workers in one firm would have been one category lower if the check had not been made. In the other firm, nine of the seventy-five workers reported taking home at least NC 10 less than they should have earned. Most of the misreports were probably caused by the form of the question, 'How much did you earn in the last month – the amount you took home after taxes, pension etc. had been taken out?' A few workers may have reported what they had left after paying the women at the gate for the food obtained on credit since the last payday. The wage lists did not specify deductions and some of the differential could be accounted for by income tax and pension contribution. The practice of taking part of the month's salary at mid-month as an 'advance' may have caused some difficulty, but the interviewers probed about this in the factories where it occurred.

A factor which makes it hard to be precise about 'average' wages is the difficulty some workers have in collecting the money due them. In the second firm where wages were checked, several workers reported not being able to collect their full wages; in another firm, nearly all the workers complained about late pay. This will be treated more fully in the next chapter.

Except for foremen and higher clerical workers, the highest pay is found

TABLE 3.11. *Median monthly wages by occupation* (*new cedis*)

Occupation	Accra	Tema	Kumasi	Takoradi	Rural
Unskilled	19.21	22.09	19.15	18.82	21.32
Semiskilled	20.23	26.98	37.47	25.27	25.00
Skilled	28.94	36.43	38.57	36.43	34.35
Clerical	30.28	38.78	30.91	38.01	55.00

in Tema and the lowest in Accra (see table 3.11). More than half of the un-skilled workers in Tema and the rural factories took home over NC20 per month, while only 75–85% of unskilled workers elsewhere earned NC20 or less. Rural watchmen account for the high average wage of unskilled rural workers. All of the rural labourers but none of the watchmen were in the lowest category. Urban watchmen also tended to be better paid than labourers, but watchmen formed a smaller proportion of the urban than of the rural samples.

Semiskilled work was best paid in Kumasi, where there were some timber drivers earning high wages. (Four earned more than NC45 per month.) Though the median wage for semiskilled workers in Tema and Takoradi was fairly similar, the chance of making more than NC33 per month was much greater in Tema. Only four Takoradi semiskilled workers made more than this, whereas four semiskilled workers in Tema reported earnings of over NC45 per month. Machine work at firm B was on piece rates, making possible a high take-home pay. Semiskilled hand work in Accra pays little better than unskilled labour; machine work is somewhat better, but less well paid than elsewhere.

Skilled workers in Accra are also relatively poorly paid; only 28% earned more than NC33 per month, while 80%, 62%, 59% and 54% of the skilled workers in Kumasi, Tema, Takoradi and the rural factories respectively earned this much. This may be because of the greater availability of skilled workers in Accra, so that employers can easily replace those who leave. Wages for skilled workers in Kumasi appear to be somewhat higher than those for skilled workers elsewhere, but seniority is an important factor here. Two-thirds of the skilled workers in both Kumasi and Takoradi had been with their firms for more than five years. Less than a quarter of the skilled workers in Accra or Tema had equivalent seniority, which emphasizes the relatively high wages in Tema.

Clerical work appears to be best paid in the rural factories, but all of the higher clerical workers at firm Q were interviewed. These men had been brought out from Accra after long service with the parent company; their high pay represented seniority as well as some recompense for the dis-advantages of living in temporary housing on the factory compound. After the factory has grown to its full size, the clerical staff will no doubt be more balanced. The mean wage for Takoradi clerical workers would be farther below the Tema figure than the median. Very few clerical workers in provincial cities earned top salaries and more were in the lowest category than was the case in Tema.

The level of pay appears to have no effect on whether a man walks to work or eats before starting work. Unskilled workers walk to work more often than others, but they tend to live nearer their workplace. They are also most likely to eat before starting work, so evidently the physical demands of the job overweigh their low wage.

SUMMARY

We have seen something of the backgrounds of workers in various occupations, the training and wages they receive, the process of finding a job, the possibilities of occupational mobility in Ghanaian society and the division of time between work and unemployment. Workers from villages usually do unskilled work if they have not been to school or had an apprenticeship, semiskilled work if they are educated. Those from towns and cities have additional opportunities to become skilled or clerical workers and, especially, foremen.

Except for skilled workers, training is usually brief and informal. Workers are expected to pick up the details of their jobs by watching while they assist others. Most jobs are simple enough for this to be practical. Most factories prefer to hire skilled workers who have completed their training, so apprenticeship programs are left to a few large firms and the private system. Many craftsmen working on their own utilize apprentices as cheap labour and provide training which varies greatly in quality from one master to another.

There is little evidence from the workers in this study of the development of exclusive groups on class lines. Although none of the men had a father who could be classed as among the elite, most of Ghana's elite are relatively young and few have sons of the age of these workers. A few workers have siblings who are or may in future be in important positions. The majority reflect the occupational distribution of the Ghanaian population; most of their fathers were farmers and, with the exception of the unskilled workers, who tend to be foreigners or from the less-developed north of Ghana, most have brothers who have also moved into urban occupations. Many have farmed at some time in their careers.

Many of the older men had experienced considerable occupational mobility, including both manual and non-manual jobs. Because there are unskilled, illpaid and non-prestigious jobs among both manual and non-manual occupations, movement across this 'line' in either direction may imply upward mobility or the reverse. The relatively low requirements for most jobs mean that workers can easily move from one occupation to another and there appears to be relatively little resistance to the idea of trying something completely new at any stage of one's career, even if it involves extensive training. This attitude seems ideal for a rapidly changing society, but it does mean that a great deal of training is wasted when the recipient moves on to something completely different.

As a result, many workers in their fifties and sixties have had a very mixed career. It should, of course, be remembered that the older workers still on the job are the remnants of a cohort which has mostly retired to farm and may thus be atypical, but middle-aged workers show the same propensity to change jobs as opportunities arise. Skilled workers more often stick to one occupation, but the difficulties of maintaining a satisfactory standard of living in self-employment have forced many of them to pick up new skills and seek wage employment. However, this sample is biased in that all of those interviewed were working for wages. Artisans who are more successful in self-employment might have abilities which the factory workers lack, but they may just be more attached to their independence and so willing to accept a lower standard of living.

Use of the Labour Office in finding work differs considerably from one place to another. Workers in Tema, where factories are large and bureaucratically run, are more dependent on the Labour Office than are workers elsewhere. Small firms and those which have been established for some time are often more prepared to utilize informal networks to fill vacancies, merely notifying the Labour Office that the job has been filled. Unskilled and semi-skilled workers make more use of the Labour Office than other workers, since there is little they could say in an application to distinguish themselves from other applicants. Clerical workers usually apply, either in person or by post, while skilled workers either apply or use informal networks to locate jobs. In theory, the Labour Office should be able to supply employers with workers having the skills needed, but the lack of testing means that workers may claim more skill than they possess and many employers prefer to make their own choice from available applicants.

The time spent in continuous employment seems to have decreased, and redundancy to have increased, in recent years. This is partly due to the unstable economic situation. Workers are laid off for weeks, months, or permanently because the money for development runs out, import licenses are subject to long delays, import quotas are cut, or increases in the cost of living cut people's ability to buy locally produced consumer goods. The causes of dissatisfaction which lead workers to leave jobs voluntarily have been discussed briefly; they will be treated more fully in the next chapter.

About a third of the workers had never been unemployed for more than a month, and about three-fifths for more than three months, but one in seven had been out of work for more than six months at least once. Semiskilled and lower clerical workers are more likely than others to have a long period of unemployment at some point in their careers. The longest period of unemployment is usually faced when looking for the first non-farming job. About two-thirds of the workers whose first job was not in farming migrated in order to find work; migration inevitably involves delays which prolong initial unemployment. Extended unemployment was most common among Tema workers. This may be related to the continued large flow of migrants into Tema in spite of the slow expansion of its employed labour force in recent years and/or to the necessity of using the Labour Office to find work in Tema.

The young, educated workers in Tema were making wages equal to or exceeding those of older workers elsewhere. Wages in the provincial towns and rural factories were not lower than those in Accra, so the flow of migrants to Accra may be seen as due to the expectation of better opportunities to find work there rather than to better conditions once work is found. Factory openings in Accra are more frequent occurrences than openings in provincial towns and the publicity they receive encourages additional migrants to come even though very few workers are to be hired. Factors affecting motivation and direction of migration will be discussed in chapter 5.

Large numbers of young men are willing to leave home and risk unemployment, or endure its effects for extended periods, because they place a high value on wage employment. Although the sums earned are low by the standards of developed countries and may be not much higher than what is needed to supply the essentials of urban life, they often represent the opportunity of improving one's standard of living considerably beyond the village level. Young men have no standing at home and urban wages represent a chance for independence. This does not mean that wages are not a cause of dissatisfaction; wage differentials are an important reason for valuing one job more than another, as will be shown in the next chapter. But wages are related to experience and opportunities; what is utterly inadequate for one man may be seen as a fortune by another.

CHAPTER 4

JOB SATISFACTION

Early factories brought together men, women and children who had been involved in farming and/or cottage industries. They had to endure low wages, poor conditions and autocratic management because most of them had nowhere else to go. It was a very rare owner who worried about job satisfaction, as workers could easily be replaced. In the past forty years, industrial sociology and business administration have developed as academic specialities. Studies have shown that a man's attitude toward his job and his adjustment to it are important components of his performance on that job. In the same period, there has been a great increase in the complexity of industrial technology in many types of manufacturing, so that the workers' performance has become more difficult to regulate through direct supervision; trained workers who are dissatisfied and leave may be difficult or at least expensive to replace. Job satisfaction has therefore become an important topic of concern for managers as well as for social reformers.

The low point of work satisfaction is often taken to be the large-scale, mass production factory; auto assembly plants are characteristic in that each man does a very small task over and over, with no control over the work process, no sense of participation in the creation of the final product and continual pressure to produce. Considerable nostalgia is expressed for the 'good old days' when independent craftsmen were responsible for a complete production process. However, very few production workers today have ever been independent craftsmen and early factory workers (at least in the cotton industry; see Smelser 1959) usually came from a farming rather than a craft background, so individuals have seldom been able to make this comparison from their own experience. Early recruits found what skills they had being degraded by machines long before the advent of modern mass-production technology.

Blauner (1960:342) found that, for modern workers, job satisfaction is roughly proportional to the prestige of one's occupation in the workplace and in the wider society; to the control a worker has over his physical and social environment, pace of work and decisions affecting his work; and to the relations he has with his workmates on and off the job. He has suggested (Blauner 1964:181–2) that automation will improve job satisfaction by improving the workers' status, giving them more control over their activities and facilitating cooperation of workers with management.

This chapter will examine the Ghanaian workers' image of their occupations and their position in society as this is expressed in positive and negative comments on their jobs, in their attitudes toward supervisors, their willingness to remain on the job and their selection of various occupations as preferable to their own. We will examine the extent to which pay is a focus of discontent and the aspects of their jobs which workers find most satisfying. The reader who is familiar with 'likes and dislikes' studies of modern industrial workers will find both similarities and differences in the Ghanaian situation. For example, the Ghanaian worker resembles the early industrial worker more than the modern one in that his concern with pay is based on subsistence needs rather than a demand for luxuries. (The point can be made even though it would be difficult to categorize all spending as one or the other.) He differs from both in that he can respond to unsatisfactory conditions by returning to the farm. If he has access to farm land in a cash crop area, it may net him an income similar (relative to expenses) to what he would receive in town. This difference is fundamental for an understanding of his motivation and commitment.

Job satisfaction was measured in several ways. Workers were asked what they liked and did not like about their jobs, what job within the firm they would prefer to have and why, how long they thought they would stay on the job and how well their foreman got on with the workers. At the end of the interview, each worker was classified by his interviewer as to how well satisfied he seemed to be. The check of firms in Accra and Tema fifteen months after the survey showed which workers had left, though only some of these had left voluntarily. Attitudes toward various occupations were tested by asking what kind of job the worker would like to have after leaving his present job, what occupational advice he would give to a young man just starting his career and what occupation he desired for his children. The answers to various questions also give us some insight into the workers' expectations in the industrial situation and their attitudes toward various occupations, which is amplified in the study of occupational prestige.

These measures of satisfaction provide fairly similar results. Those who prefer their job to others in the firm are most likely to say that they expect to stay more than five years. The interviewer's estimate of satisfaction was generally based on answers to the occupational preference and intention to stay questions. Those who said they planned to stay longer than five years were about half as likely as those who thought they would leave sooner to have left the firm within fifteen months of the interview. Most men think highly enough of their own jobs to recommend them to others.

LIKES AND DISLIKES

The questions about what the workers liked and disliked about their work appeared early in the interview and proved valuable in increasing rapport. Workers found it easier to say what they did not like than what they liked about their jobs. Some workers had a long line of complaints about the pay, the management, the conditions, the hours and the amenities which the firm ought to supply. Even those who said they liked everything about their work often mentioned some improvement they would appreciate.

TABLE 4.1. *Job likes and dislikes by occupation (percentages)*

	Unskilled	Semi-skilled	Skilled, foremen	Clerical	Total
Likes					
Nothing, don't know	44	47	29	32	38
Job itself, everything	12	29	41	46	33
Having a job, money	36	12	11	8	15
It is my trade	[b]	4	13	3	7
Management	4	5	4	5	4
Other	4	3	2	6	3
Total	100	100	100	100	100
Dislikes[a]					
Nothing, don't know	19	20	29	31	24
Pay	57	50	45	39	48
Management	12	17	19	13	16
Working conditions	8	13	6	8	9
Other	8	11	11	18	12
Total	104	111	110	109	109
N	252	529	496	157	1,432

[a] Some totals are over 100 % because of multiple responses.
[b] Less than 0.5 %.

Many of the workers who said the work was interesting or they just liked it did not elaborate on what they meant by this. It is one of the defects of the survey method that the interview format encourages short answers. Further in-depth interviewing is needed on many aspects of the worker's response to his job. About two-fifths of the workers could not think of anything they liked about their work. Not all of these were thoroughly dissatisfied; some had just not thought about their jobs as something about which one has positive feelings.

Of the rest, half said they liked the job itself; it was easy or interesting or improved their knowledge or training or they could use their experience to make things at home. A quarter were just glad to have any job at all to support themselves and others were glad to be practicing their 'professions', appreciated the amenities and concessions of the management, or enjoyed the congeniality of their workmates or the contacts with outsiders while on business. Only a few workers said the job was easy. Compared to the alternative of labouring, many factory jobs are easy; they are also easier than farming at the height of the season, but farmers have long periods when they can rest and their working hours may be relatively short even during the busy season (Lawson 1967). Factory workers are under considerably more pressure to keep at the job than either farmers or labourers.

Many of the more explicit comments, especially by skilled workers, referred to the occupation rather than to the present job. Workers thought of themselves as tailors or carpenters rather than as workers at X firm.[1] An electrician said he was proud when called on to mend some machine. Tailors and seamstresses said they liked to be able to make their own clothes, and carpenters that they could produce furniture at home. A man is identified in the society by his skill (or lack of skill), not by his employer.

Some workers saw their jobs as episodes in a career; it was the career which was important. A driver of fifty-four said, 'I've done this job all my life; it is part of me', and a tailor commented, 'It is the life profession I have decided on.' Even semiskilled workers sometimes had this view. A machine operative liked his job because 'I am learning a trade.' The urge to improve oneself, to broaden one's qualifications, was also evident in the fitter who thought, 'The company should offer courses in various branches of specialization', and the man who liked proof reading because 'It helps me to improve my English and acquire more vocabulary.'

Some workers commented that they liked the variation in the job and the chance to use their common sense. An upholsterer put it, 'The job requires intelligence and not manpower.' This sort of opportunity is seldom available except to skilled workers and often they resent the constraints of working for someone else when they are used to making their own decisions. A tailor asked that 'concession be made to imagine rather than follow pattern designs'. Tailors have, on the whole, less freedom than carpenters in that they must produce large numbers of the same garment daily on piece rates, whereas

[1] The same is true of British craftsmen (Zweig 1952:29).

carpenters work over a longer period on each piece of furniture and have more variety in the pieces produced. Tailors are part of a mass-production system, whereas carpenters are at least partly involved in craft production. The difference in satisfaction between the two occupations validates the contention that craft production is more satisfying.

Unskilled workers were at least three times as likely as other workers to say they were glad to have a job and/or that they were glad of the money earned. A typical comment such as 'I get my daily bread through it' does not necessarily indicate job satisfaction, but it is enough in many cases to keep the man on the job, especially if the alternative is unemployment. A packer said he was just pleased to be employed after eighteen months without work. A polisher commented, 'In fact, I don't like it, but because I can't get any other I am bound to it.' A watchman said, 'It's the money that keeps me here.' He appreciated being free to farm in the daytime, but farming was not enough to support his family. Two watchmen on the minimum wage were among the few who thought they were earning 'plenty of money', but several other men said they liked the stability of income, a factor often missing in self-employment. The basic concern with money will be discussed below.

The attitude toward machines varied. A carpenter commented that he appreciated having machines to help him in his work; they made it easy. On the other hand, a carpentry machine operator on his first job said he did not like to work on the machine because it was dangerous. There were few complaints about machines, so it can be presumed that most workers become accustomed to them fairly quickly or are moved to other work.

A few workers had favourable things to say about the management. There were appreciative comments on the provision of advances or allowances and on regulations which were helpful to workers. Two-fifths of the employers at firm E, one of the smaller, Lebanese-run firms, gave this type of answer, while only two of the 296 employees of state firms who were interviewed mentioned it. A typist at firm E said, 'When we are in financial straits the management gives help.' This sort of arrangement is much easier to make in a small firm than in a large one. The Management Survey showed that Lebanese and Indian managers make special provisions for their workers such as prizes, parties etc. more often than do other employers. It is part of their paternalistic style of management which, in at least some firms, results in a family feeling which workers respond to positively. Firm E had the lowest proportion of workers who said there was nothing they liked.

Some people said they liked the public relations side of the work or the association with workmates. Drivers enjoyed the chance to travel, except for the inevitable encounters with the police. A foreman said he enjoyed the chance to handle difficult cases and a packer appreciated the chance to chat with friendly workmates on the job. Where they exist, organized work groups are ethnically heterogeneous; managers said this did not cause trouble. Ghanaians generally get on well with each other most of the time, though ethnic rivalry arises occasionally with a suspicion of favouritism in hiring or promotion or in disagreements with foremen or mates.

Aside from the tendency of southern Ghanaians to consider other Africans their social inferiors (a characteristic found among many other peoples the world over), language is the chief differentiating factor. Strangers soon pick up enough of the local language and/or English to get by, but the preference for their own language cuts them off from spending rest periods with members of other ethnic groups and largely determines their choice of companions off the job. This problem is less important for those with a middle- or secondary-school education, since they have a fair knowledge of English and have often picked up other languages from schoolmates.

Workers in Accra were most often satisfied; less than a quarter said they liked nothing and a quarter said they disliked nothing about their jobs. At the other extreme, more than half of the Tema and Kumasi workers could find nothing positive to say about their work and only 7% of the Kumasi workers had no complaints about their jobs. However, this dissatisfaction was not associated with plans to change jobs. Kumasi workers were more likely than those in Accra or Tema to say that they intended to stay on the job for at least five years and the same proportion of Tema workers as of those in firm E (most of whom claimed to be satisfied) were still on the job fifteen months after interviewing.

This leads to the conclusion that there is often little relationship between job satisfaction and stability. Goldthorpe *et al.* (1968:80) have shown that modern workers who feel that they are as well paid as they can expect will stick with a job which they otherwise dislike. In the case of Ghanaian workers and, I expect, of early industrial workers in Europe, there are two factors which impede the effect of dissatisfaction on turnover. Leaving a job voluntarily may have such serious economic consequences in terms of unemployment that the older worker at least does not want to contemplate it and, perhaps more important, workers have not been socialized to the modern concept that one should like work and find it satisfying. One works to live and the unpleasant aspects of work are seen as at least partly unavoidable. This does not prevent a man from leaving one job for another which he knows will pay him more money and/or will be less unpleasant than his present job, but, given a dearth of alternative opportunities, a man may well plan a long stay on a job he finds basically unsatisfying.

A quarter of the workers said there was nothing they disliked about their jobs or were unable to answer the question. Quite a few of these said 'don't know' to both questions and presumably do not think of their jobs in terms of liking and disliking but as the price exacted for living in town. Of the rest, two-thirds complained about the pay, about a sixth objected to the rules and procedures of management or their foremen, and smaller numbers disliked the physical conditions in which they were forced to work (heat, standing, dirt, danger, or the exertion required) or the lack of provision of uniforms, transport, housing, or other amenities to which they felt they had a right.

Pay was mentioned as a source of dissatisfaction by over half of the un-skilled and semiskilled workers, by over half of the workers in Accra and Takoradi and by nearly half of the relatively well-paid Tema workers. Pay was less often mentioned in Kumasi and the rural firms, where it was, on the average, higher than in Takoradi or Accra.

Rural workers were interviewed in June 1968, just after the National Liberation Council had raised the wages of government workers 5%, making the minimum wage 75 new pesewas per day. Most private employers follow the government lead in the minimum wage; only where there is a shortage of qualified workers is it in their interest to pay more (Rimmer 1970). Nevertheless, complaints about pay will no doubt continue. Many workers make only the minimum wage and quite a few employed in small private firms make less than this. Supporting a family on NC 18–20 per month when it costs NC 5 per month to rent a single room is a difficult proposition. A labourer in Accra who said he had had no pay increase since 1953 reported, 'Because the pay is small I don't feel well and I have to come to work on foot [two or three miles] because there is no money for transport.' A watch-man with a wife and two children earning NC 19 per month said, 'A day's pay is less than what I and my family spend in a day.'

Dissatisfaction with pay also involved misunderstandings about deductions and complaints about delayed payment. Several workers said that money was subtracted from their pay without explanation or that they did not receive the right amount. Union dues, contribution to the pension fund and income tax (if any) are deducted at source; it may well be that some workers did not understand why they should not receive the full amount they contracted for.

Several firms pay half the monthly wage as an 'advance' in the middle of the month to those workers who request it (almost everyone). For workers on or below the poverty line, this advance is necessary, since they never save enough to live for a month on the previous month's income. However, Elkan has shown (1956:23) that lower-paid workers in Kampala were less likely to ask for an advance than those who made more. Men paid monthly

G

found it easier to save than those paid bimonthly and the lowest-paid workers were often target workers who subsisted at a very low standard of living so as to save as much as possible. Workers who had settled in town were under more pressure to spend and less pressure to save, so they found the advance useful. Though this hypothesis was not checked with Ghanaian workers, the widespread use of advances may be more related to their commitment to urban employment than to any improvement in their financial situation which results.

One point at which an advance would be particularly useful is when a worker takes up his job. Most new workers have had a period of unemployment during which their resources were used up. In order to support themselves until their first payday they often borrow from a money lender (conveniently stationed at the factory gate) at 25% monthly interest. This indebtedness is likely to remain with them for a long time, since they do not earn enough to pay it off. A small advance when a man starts work which could be deducted from his wages over several months would eliminate this practice and thus mean a considerable increase in real earnings without raising wages. This might be difficult for the management to arrange, especially in firms where many workers stay for only a short time, but the union (to which all workers must belong) might perform a real service by this means.

The workers with the strongest complaint are those in firms where the pay is late. Late pay or failure to pay was given by several workers as the reason for leaving past jobs. In one of the provincial firms included in this study, 83% of the workers complained that the pay was always late. One man said he had had only small 'advances' rather than his regular pay for several months. A public corporation admitted to the press in 1967 that it had no money to pay its workers. Late wages impose considerable hardship on men who are barely able to support their families. The firms concerned were in difficulties because of a depressed market, but the men were also in difficulty; they hesitated to leave because of widespread unemployment.

Withholding of wages was a mark of the authority of the early factory owner over his workers and of their dependence on wages for subsistence. Many industrial workers in developing countries are similarly dependent, which sets them apart from the worker in an industrialized country with advanced and enforceable labour laws and a low level of unemployment. Although minority groups in industrialized societies may seem similarly disadvantaged, welfare provisions are a valuable safeguard and very few employed people are subsisting at the level fairly common in developing countries.

Higher wages may be impossible in firms whose supply of raw materials is irregular, necessitating payment of workers whether or not there is enough work for them to do. (Many firms work at less than half capacity.) For others, an increase might well increase productivity. At present, many workers consciously conserve their energy on their regular jobs so they can work on their farms or at other enterprises in the evenings, since food or earnings from these make an appreciable contribution to their standard of living in the city and/or at least increase their savings for the eventual return home. They could obviously do better if their energies were concentrated on the eight hours in the factory.

Many skilled workmen supplement their incomes by working at home in the evenings or at weekends. Pons (1969) gave an extended description of the life of a Stanleyville carpenter who had a steadily increasing clientele in his private business, so that he needed to work during most of his free time to deliver orders as promised. He had no intention of leaving his factory job and was still on it ten years later. Most carpenters are not as successful as this one, but whatever they earn provides a welcome supplement to their wages.

There was an interesting difference between two firms in the reaction to piece rates. Tailors in an Accra clothing firm complained bitterly that they had to rush and could not do a good job, and maintained that their pay should be stabilized. Semiskilled workers in one of the Tema firms tended to think that piece rates were a good idea and preferred the departments that had them. In one factory they were seen as a penalizing factor; in the other as an opportunity. While self-employed tailors would not be above hurrying if business required it, they are seldom under this necessity. In addition, they can rationalize their dislike of forced production by maintaining their dedication to their trade, which is an important motivation for them. Semiskilled workers have no trade to defend and are denied pride in the product because they only carry out one process; hence, piece rates are an acceptable way of maximizing income. Piece rates have been common in the garment industry in Britain and America, but few of the workers there have experienced self-employment. Half of the workers in the Accra firm had worked for themselves, often for several years. They had problems of adjustment not usual in this business. On the other hand, piece rates were probably essential to prod them to a commercial production level.[1]

It does not appear that workers in either factory were consciously

---

[1] A study of British workers' attitudes to piece work showed that semiskilled workers are sometimes concerned about the disincentive to quality work which results from the emphasis on speed. Although most of the workers had adjusted to piece work, few had no complaints and several would have preferred a flat rate even though it would have meant lower wages, a sentiment shared by a fair number of Ghanaian tailors (Klein 1964:60-1).

restricting output in the way that has often been reported of piece workers in America or Britain. Given their generally low level of subsistence and the families they were committed to supporting, the Accra piece workers were particularly concerned with wage stability because of the security this would give them. The Tema workers were younger and less often married, so some of them could use extra earnings for their own enjoyment; security was less important to them. This is a situation which might give rise to quota restriction, but the layout of the factory (with machines generally well separated from each other) served to inhibit worker solidarity and encourage each man to produce with his own profits in mind.[1]

It is the young, illiterate newcomer to the city doing unskilled or semi-skilled work who is most disappointed with his pay. Reports of urban wages sound very good to the prospective migrant, but it is difficult to anticipate urban expenses. This type of migrant is most likely to return to his village in disillusionment after a relatively short stay in town (Caldwell 1969:62). Old men and those with more education are presumably more able to cope with the urban cost of living and/or to get jobs which pay more. Experienced men are more likely to complain of working conditions and management than younger workers; when older men mentioned pay they often had other complaints as well.

Problems involving the sense of time were mentioned by many workers. These included the management attitude toward lateness as well as the expectation of sustained effort. Comments range from the tailor who said that output per day should be reduced to effect better production, the proof reader who didn't like to be rushed when working, and the clerk who claimed to have too much work for one person, to the many complaints of being pushed by foremen and being penalized for lateness. Workers who arrive late may be sent home and lose a day's pay or have to work overtime without pay at the end of the day. This sort of regulation was common in nineteenth century factories, which had similar problems with promptness.

Management finds it very difficult to get the men to arrive on time and workers, many of whom have never developed the sense of time considered necessary in urban, industrial society, are convinced that justice is on their side. Most people at all levels of the society prefer to operate on 'Ghanaian time', which is much more flexible than 'European time'. One minister created headlines by visiting ministry offices an hour after their supposed opening and finding very few civil servants on duty. While tardiness is not usually as extensive as this, most workers see no reason to worry about fifteen or twenty minutes' delay in starting work. Even with the desire for

[1] Factors inhibiting the 'will to control' among British workers are discussed by Lupton (1963).

punctuality, arriving on time may present severe difficulties. Few workers possess an adequate clock or watch, so they must guess the time from the position of the sun. Buses and lorries do not run on a set schedule and may not run at all if it is raining or (as frequently happens) if they break down.

Problems of timing continue throughout the working day. Again, the greatest problem is psychological. A few workers, with experience only of farming and casual labour, are simply unable to adjust to rigorous time-keeping. Others may take a long time to do so. Education should be of considerable importance in effecting a change to a more time-conscious mentality, since punctuality is required and lessons follow a strict timetable. However, the school leaver who spends some time farming can quickly get out of the habit of time-keeping. Malingering is found among workers everywhere and some of these workers are certainly expending as little energy as possible. But many, having no contact with the Protestant Ethic and belonging to a culture which considers work a necessity for survival, not a duty connected with one's eternal reward, simply do not understand the rationale of continuous labour which the expatriate employer takes for granted. Worker expectations that they should be given frequent 'full resting time' will probably continue. It seems likely that increasing the proportion of time spent actually working will be more dependent on improved supervision than changed attitudes among the workers.

Nineteenth century industrialists faced the same problems with workers who arrived late and seemed incapable of sustained effort. It seems likely that the first generation to take up industrial work in any country will have similar problems of adjustment. This value change is not helped in Africa by the ease with which workers move in and out of industrial employment, since traditional values can be maintained in self-employment. British farmers who found work in the early factories in Manchester were completely separated from their farms and from alternative employment, which speeded their adaptation to industrial requirements.

Shift work introduces something completely new into the workers' lives in its requirement that they work at hours when their friends and families are relaxing or sleeping. Two of the firms ran three shifts covering all twenty-four hours; three others ran two shifts which involved all or part of their workforce. Somewhat more than half of the workers on shiftwork said they liked it or at least did not object to it. Those who did not like it mostly complained that transport was hard to get and more expensive in off-hours. Some had difficulty in getting a hot meal because their wives (most of whom traded) could not make it or keep it hot for them and meals from street sellers were also unavailable in off-hours. One of the three-shift firms provided meals in the company canteen; this was the only canteen which was not subject to complaints. Most workers prefer to buy food from the women at the gate rather than from a factory canteen because it is cheaper and they can get credit.

While the firm with the most complaints about management was Lebanese-owned, a Ghanaian firm was second. Over a third of the workers there said the foremen got on badly with the workers and a third made specific complaints against management – promotions from trainee to regular worker (with associated raise in pay) were too long in coming; equipment, material and personnel were in short supply; orders were accepted which could not realistically be filled on time and then the workers had to rush through the work or put in overtime; the shifts were too long etc. Many of these complaints were made by senior skilled workers who had no intention of leaving, but their dissatisfaction was very real.

Few workers outside of this and one of the Tema firms mentioned promotion. This disinterest may be due, as with British workers (Goldthorpe *et al.* 1968:122, Zweig 1952:22), to a realistic appraisal of the chance of becoming a foreman or an unwillingness to assume what may be an unrewarding responsibility. In the Management Survey, some firms of up to 100 workers said they had no foremen at all; the ratio of workers to foremen was often 1:30 or 40, so the average worker has little chance of promotion. Those who mentioned promotion usually assumed that it should come with seniority. Two headmen complained that 'old hands sit here and see the newly employed earning more' and 'I trained many of the men who have now passed me by.' A new factory which is rapidly building up provides far more opportunities for promotion than most of the factories studied, which had stable or declining labour forces. In the new rural factory, workers who mentioned promotion seemed more optimistic about their chances; the management there was watching them closely with an eye to promoting some of them when their training was completed.

SUPERVISION

The reaction of Ghanaian workers to their foremen seems to be generally positive, but not as favourable as the reaction of British workers to their supervisors. All except the foremen were asked, 'How well does your foreman get on with the workers?' A fifth said that foremen get on badly with the workers and 2% gave an ambiguous answer or said they didn't know, whereas only 14% of the British workers asked a similar question said 'not so well' or 'badly' (Goldthorpe *et al.* 1968:65). The Ghanaian dissatisfaction appears to be due to the different functions which foremen serve in the two countries, to the general lack of training of Ghanaian foremen and to differential expectations and adjustment to industrial labour. With new industrial workers, foremen must provide instruction and discipline, whereas with experienced workers in a technologically advanced firm, their function is more advisory and organizational.[1]

Foremen are often caught between the expectations of management and of the workers, especially if the managers are not African. It is difficult for men who have been socialized only slightly into the values of an industrial society to maintain discipline over people they identify with and to make decisions which conflict with the values instilled in their traditional upbringing. Also, they are often asked to carry out decisions in which they have had no say and of which they may have a very imperfect understanding. They stand between two cultures to a greater extent than the men under them do and need considerable training if they are to cope successfully with the conflicts which arise.

Most Ghanaian foremen are promoted from the ranks and few receive any training in supervision. If better supervision is the key to higher productivity (Kilby 1961:288), then more attention should be paid to careful selection and training of foremen. This training could best be done in centralized adult education courses in the major towns, since most firms are too small to run their own programs and management generally lacks expertise in this field. The Accra Productivity Centre has been working to improve this situation through short courses, but it will probably take a long time to make an impression. Though many foremen in Britain manage well enough without any specific training, they are usually promoted after many years' experience. Ghanaian foremen generally lack this experience; over half of those interviewed had been on the job for less than five years.

The proportion of workers who said they got on well with their foremen (or, at least, that their foremen got on well with the workers) varied with the age, education, sex, occupation and wage of the worker and, especially, with the size of the firm. Southern Ghanaian men who have completed middle school, are in their late twenties and are earning only slightly more than the minimum wage doing semiskilled or skilled work are the most

---

[1] However, an American study of worker–foreman relations in two auto assembly plants (Turner 1955) found only 44 % and 72 % of the workers claiming that foremen got on well with their subordinates. This was related to the frequency of informal contacts, since the assembly line cut down the necessity for formal contacts. Informal contacts are also important in the Ghanaian situation, as was evident in the workers' comments. A study of factory workers at Sapele, Nigeria, found that 28 % said they did not get on well with Nigerian supervisors; 20 % said they did not get on well with European supervisors. In each case, older workers reported poorer relations than younger workers. Clerks were twice as likely as ordinary workers to report that they got on badly with their supervisors, regardless of race (Wober 1967:187).

dissatisfied with supervision. Rather unexpectedly, the proportions of workers who got on well with their foremen were highest among illiterates, non-Ghanaians, older workers, women and those in clerical occupations, a much less homogeneous group than the dissatisfied.

Young southerners come to their jobs with higher expectations than northerners or non-Ghanaians. Since the former are more committed to urban employment, the attitude of their foreman toward them matters. The foreman may have a say when there are lay-offs or when some men are to be promoted to charge hands. In addition, these young men tend to be self-confident because of their education and do not like to be told what to do. They expect to rise quickly to higher wage levels and are disappointed when this does not happen. Experienced older men require less supervision and therefore achieve valued independence; they also tend to have higher wages, which increases their satisfaction. Although women workers are also young and educated, they are less committed to wage employment than the men and have lower expectations for the job. Also, they may well receive more gentle supervision than the men and are often on simple handwork jobs which do not require much direction. Northerners and non-Ghanaians, especially the majority who lack education and training, are less committed to industrial work than the southerners and less likely to expect working conditions or contacts with management to be pleasant. Their goals are more likely to be short-range: to get enough money for the brideprice or to remain in employment until the next planting season or until they save enough to enter trade. Thus, they are more likely than southerners to accept shouting foremen as part of the bargain.

Semiskilled and skilled workers were generally less favourably disposed toward their foremen than clerical and unskilled workers, but this may well be due to the age and educational background of the different types of workers and to characteristics of the firms in which they were working rather than to the nature of their work. The Accra skilled workers were more dissatisfied with their foremen than other Accra workers or than skilled workers in other cities. In this case, the dissatisfied were mainly printers; tailors and carpenters were more satisfied. Among the workers in Tema and the provincial cities, dissatisfaction with foremen tended to be centred in the semiskilled workers, who were young and educated and responded to the situation in the way described above. Clerical workers were most satisfied everywhere, but they got the least supervision. Older clerical workers in good positions were also receiving relatively high wages, but lower clerical workers also thought well of their foremen, probably because their job expectations were more nearly met than was the case for semiskilled workers.

Though age, education and occupation affect the workers' attitude toward their foremen, the size of the firm they work in is even more important. In each category investigated, satisfaction decreases as the size of the firm increases. The most obvious reason for this is that large firms are more bureaucratic than small ones and workers do not like the impersonality which inevitably characterizes large firms.

It is easier to treat workers as individuals in a small firm than it is in a large one. The owner knows all the workers individually and the foreman, if any, performs the role of leader, which workers understand and respond to. Management is closer to the workers in many ways in such firms and is more likely to be understandable to and accepted by the workers. In large firms, on the other hand, senior managers are unknown; they are seldom seen on the shop floor. Workers may look on them only as people who make impossible demands and rules. Inexperienced workers, especially those who are recent migrants to town, have had little or no practice in dealing with impersonal relationships. They feel uncomfortable, not knowing what to expect. This was expressed by a labourer in Takoradi who said of his foreman, 'I don't see him as an individual.'

The state enterprises and one of the joint state–private firms had the lowest proportions of workers thinking highly of their foremen, while firm G, a small Ghanaian firm, had the highest proportion. Important factors here are the excessive bureaucracy of some state enterprises and the influence of politics on managerial appointments.

Comments on the lack of respect shown by foremen to workers under them have the same basis; the workers want to establish a personal relationship with their foreman, and are dissatisfied with a situation in which this is not possible. Foremen, on the other hand, usually have a large number of men under them and are held responsible by the management for training the workers, seeing that they work steadily, and generally maintaining discipline. In firms with a high turnover, it may be difficult for them to get to know the men under them.

The most frequent adverse comment about foremen was that they supervised too closely: 'He comes so often he makes us uneasy while working. He is too enthusiastic.' Two-fifths of the workers said that their foremen told them what to do at least once an hour. The proportion varied little between occupational categories, but was highest for semiskilled workers and lowest for higher clerical workers. Skilled workers in particular object to frequent directions because these deny them the opportunity for individual initiative which they expect. Close supervision may be necessary because of poor training and inadequate work habits, but it is resented. One factor which mediates the situation for skilled workers is that most of their supervisors have titles such as 'head carpenter' rather than 'foreman' and work along with their men. This means that the supervisory role is not so prominent and is shared with the colleague role.

At the other extreme, 30 % of the workers said they were supervised less than twice a day. This included a few higher clerical workers who claimed they had no supervisor, but there were as many unskilled as skilled workers who said they were seldom supervised. Most of the former were watchmen.

Some workers carry over traditional attitudes toward elders into their relationships with their foremen. Supervisors are expected to look after the workers' interests with higher authorities. Those who are seen as always siding with management are strongly criticized. Workers feel they should be able to get help from their foremen when they need it. This includes patient teaching of new workers as well as the ability to handle requests for loans, exceptions to the rules and jobs for relatives and friends without apparent disinterest or favouritism.

Mutual respect is particularly important. Workers and foremen both think they should have respect from the management and from each other. Some of the complaints about being shouted at are due to the lack of respect which such treatment implies. Occasionally an older worker complained that a young foreman did not show him proper respect, but a foreman's age does not appear to be an important factor in his ability to handle the workers.

JOB STABILITY

Absenteeism and turnover are often used as measures of job satisfaction. It is argued that the worker who likes his job attends regularly and does not leave it for another. However, the separation of voluntary from involuntary turnover and absenteeism, which is essential if these are to be used as measures of motivation and which is usual in industrialized nations, is frequently not possible in developing countries where record-keeping is minimal. One must often be content with information on the total number of workers involved. In the present study we have data on the length of time each worker had been on the job, their reports on the number and cause of absences in the previous month and a record of which of the Accra/Tema workers left in the fifteen months following the interviews, but neither the reason for leaving nor the date. Reasons given for terminating past jobs were reported in chapter 3.

In addition, workers were asked how long they intended to stay on the job. This is more useful as a measure of motivation than the turnover or length of service records, because many workers remain in jobs they do not like or leave jobs with which they are generally satisfied. They may see no other opportunities for employment or at least no chance of making more money than they are earning at present and/or improving the conditions, management, or whatever else they object to about their present work. Older workers are less free to quit their jobs than younger men because of their family responsibilities. Even workers who are recorded as having left voluntarily in the sense that they were not dismissed may have been called home by their families or become ill and unable to continue on the job. For all of these reasons, turnover is only moderately related to the worker's attitude toward his job. The connection between absenteeism and attitude toward the job may be even more tenuous, but an examination of its frequency and causes does tell us something about worker behaviour.

Several studies of African industrial workers have utilized management records on turnover and absenteeism (Bell 1963, Elkan 1956, Hauser 1961, van der Horst 1964, Wells and Warmington 1962). Indeed, one of the main reasons for some of these studies was to provide information which would help to increase the stabilization of the labour force. Management has in the past been more concerned with absenteeism than turnover, since most workers lacked skills and could easily be replaced. This is still the case in firms using largely unskilled labour. Increasing complexity of machinery has made it necessary to keep turnover low, but this does not seem to be a serious problem.

Turnover and absenteeism in manufacturing firms in Ghana are not particularly high, though the Management Survey showed considerable variation by industry, ownership and nationality of managers (Peil 1966:34). Turnover was lowest in firms using craft production; annual rates of 5 % and 9 % were reported by furniture and textile firms. The highest rates were reported by firms producing cement blocks; they had an average annual turnover of 72 %.[1] This work is very heavy and workers tend to take a day off from time to time to rest or leave whenever they can find alternative employment, sometimes after only a day or two on the job.

---

[1] These rates are only approximate, since they are based on the number of workers who left during a two-month period and the number of workers employed at the time of interviews. Using the number of workers employed six months before the interviews, the annual turnover rate for private cement firms would be 88 %. However, the majority of those who leave are newcomers. Most firms have a core of long-service workers.

Annual turnover varied from 1 % to 17 % in the four Senegalese factories studied by Hauser (1968a:64). Turnover at the Sapele, Nigeria, sawmill was reported to be 16 % (Wells and Warmington 1962:43), but voluntary resignations accounted for only a 3.5 % rate. Baldamus (1961:22) found that rates over 25 %, though considered excessive, were fairly common in Britain with the full employment of the late 1950s.

Job satisfaction

Turnover was generally lower when some but not all of the managers were Ghanaians. There is a need for further study as to whether the high turnover in private firms owned by Ghanaians is due to management techniques, size, conditions of work, or other factors. Both absenteeism and turnover seem to be higher in Accra and Tema than in the provincial cities. This may be due to more job satisfaction among provincial workers, to their being older and less willing to change jobs, or to the relative lack of other opportunities in these towns. However, the lower rates may be characteristic only of the firms included in the sample, since these towns were not thoroughly surveyed. Firms with high absenteeism were all privately owned, with either Ghanaian or Asian managers. European managers probably put more emphasis on measures to cut down absenteeism.

Several managers said that it was not unusual to have 25% of the workers absent the Monday after payday. However, most firms reported that less than 5% were absent on an average day. When the workers themselves were questioned about their absenteeism, between 8% (firm P) and 43% (firms D and E) said they had been out for at least one day during the previous month. Very few workers admitted to being absent for more than one day. Both workers and managers agree that the chief cause for absenteeism is ill health, so the rate of voluntary absenteeism is very low in comparison to that of industrial workers in Europe or America. The 'affluent worker' can afford a day off now and then to demonstrate his independence of the work situation; the poorly paid workers in a developing country cannot.

Over half of the workers who had been absent in the previous month said they were sick. Given the overcrowded conditions in which many of them are living, the prevalence of diseases such as malaria and typhoid, and the lack of accessible medical advice (it might take two or three days to see a doctor at the local clinic and one only goes if the condition is thought to be serious), it is not surprising that about 13% of the workforce should be ill during the course of a month. The next most important reason for absence is family crises which must be handled immediately. Fathers may be expected to take their children to the hospital; it is sometimes necessary to stay home to care for someone who is ill; visitors from out of town may need someone to help them with their business or in finding a job. It would be hard to classify these cases as voluntary absenteeism, since the worker may have little choice in the matter.

Other workers had less excuse; a few went home for the weekend and did not return in time to work on Monday. Several workers in Accra and Tema missed work because of lateness; a few others rested for a day because they were tired. A small number of Muslims had stayed out on a feast day; this would certainly have involved larger numbers if the survey had been carried out the month after Id el Fetr, which is widely celebrated.

Size of the firm does not appear to be a factor in absenteeism, nor does the proportion of skilled workers in the labour force, though skilled and semi-skilled workers in Accra and Tema reported absence more often than other workers. Unskilled workers were most often absent in the provincial firms; clerical workers had the best attendance record in all firms. Women were absent more often than men in Tema, but there was no difference in Accra, where more of the women were married. Age, marriage and length of time spent in the city appear to have no effect on absenteeism. Firms with high absenteeism do not necessarily have high turnover; in some cases one may compensate for the other.

TABLE 4.2. *Accra/Tema workers still on the job 15 months after interviewing, by occupation, sex and region of origin*

	Accra		Tema	
	%	N	%	N
Occupation				
Unskilled	64	(102)	82	(28)
Semiskilled	74	(180)	71	(160)
Skilled	74	(291)	69	(13)
Clerical	85	(66)	71	(31)
Sex				
Males	74	(600)	71	(212)
Females	83	(75)	68	(38)
Region of origin				
Accra C. D., Eastern	68	(175)	70	(100)
Central, Western	72	(90)	68	(62)
Volta	79	(81)	62	(32)
Ashanti, Brong/Ahafo	66	(44)	78	(41)
Northern, Upper	53	(32)	100	(5)
Outside Ghana	73	(153)	70	(10)
Total	75	(675)	70	(250)

Turnover data in table 4.2 is limited to Accra and Tema because it was possible to get comparable data for only two of the provincial firms and voluntary turnover in these was almost non-existent. In spite of the recent development of the Tema firms and the dissatisfaction of many of their workers, there was no difference between Accra and Tema in the proportion of workers who were still on the job fifteen months after the interviewing.

Though the all-over proportions were similar, there were interesting differences between the two samples in the stability of various categories of workers. Unskilled workers were more stable in Tema, but there were very few of them in the Tema sample. Clerical workers, who also had fewer alternatives in Tema than in Accra, were less stable in Tema. These may have found it easier than unskilled workers to transfer to comparable work in Accra. Women in Tema were more likely to have left their jobs than women in Accra. Since few of the former were married at the time of interviewing, it seems likely that quite a few of them had married in the interval and retired temporarily to start a family.

Workers from Volta Region were more stable in Accra and those from central Ghana more stable in Tema. Tema seems to be more attractive than Accra to migrants from Ashanti, who are mainly young school leavers. They would therefore be more likely to hang on to their jobs than Ewes from Volta Region, who are drawn to Accra by the skilled work available there. The high proportion of non-Ghanaians who stayed on the job is notable. Men from Upper Volta, Mali and Niger seldom go to the cities of Ghana if they plan to stay for only a season. They usually head for the cocoa farms. While half of the northern Ghanaians interviewed in Accra had left their jobs within fifteen months of the interviewing and most had probably left Accra, two-thirds of the Voltaics and Nigerians and 85% of the men from Mali and Niger were still on the job. Their stability was thus at least as good as that of southern Ghanaians, which refutes the management contention that turnover is highest among non-Ghanaians.

In both Accra and Tema, men over thirty-five were less likely to have left their jobs than younger workers. There was a direct relationship between wage level and the proportion who stayed on the job. With each wage increment, more workers stayed. This is a confirmation of the workers' interest in maximizing wages, though long-term workers are likely to be better paid because they have accumulated increments or acquired some training and most turnover is among newcomers. There was a direct relationship between the proportion still on the job and the length of time spent in Accra. Only three-fifths of the workers who had moved to Accra within fifteen months of the survey were still on the job fifteen months later, compared to 83% of those who had been there at least ten years. The new arrivals were no doubt still 'looking around'.

The job seniority of workers represents the turnover patterns of an earlier time and the expansion or contraction of the labour force in the factories in which they work. There is considerable variation in the seniority of workers between firms and between towns, which makes comparison with other studies based on one or two factories rather hazardous. Davison (1955) reported that 32 % of the workers at the Accra Brewery had been there more than five years, which would seem to indicate that job stability in Accra, if not decreasing, is certainly not increasing with time. However, the brewery had been established for a long time and had been expanding its work force, whereas some of the factories we studied in 1966 were relatively new and redundancies were more common than expansion at that time. A study of 1,300 industrial workers in Kenya and Uganda (Bissman 1969:27) found that 21 % of them had been at their jobs for at least ten years. This indicates greater stability than even the provincial workers in Ghana; only 12 % of these had been on the job for ten years or longer. It is strongly suspected that job stability is increasing in Ghana as it has in East Africa because the increased output of school leavers eager for urban work and the very slow growth of the economy have resulted in tremendous competition for the few jobs available. Lack of seniority beyond five years is due to the recency of

TABLE 4.3. *Job seniority by location of worker, occupation, sex, region of origin, migration and wage (percent who have been on the job for a given period)*

	Accra			Tema			Provincial cities		
	1–16 months	5+ years	N	1–16 months	5+ years	N	1–16 months	5+ years	N
Occupation									
Unskilled	50	15	(113)	37	4	(20)	35	31	(81)
Semiskilled	45	11	(202)	32	2	(167)	15	48	(89)
Skilled	32	22	(308)	0	23	(13)	11	68	(88)
Clerical	33	27	(75)	10	13	(30)	5	45	(42)
Wage (NC)									
Under 21	55	7	(243)	54	4	(57)	26	29	(86)
21–33	35	15	(331)	23	4	(120)	16	46	(94)
34–45	22	35	(107)	14	10	(58)	6	69	(86)
46+	7	74	(54)	8	21	(24)	4	83	(24)
Sex									
Males	38	20	(649)	24	8	(221)	18	49	(300)
Females	36	16	(86)	42	0	(38)	—	—	—
Migratory status									
Non-migrant	29	29	(104)	0	0	(7)	5	25	(59)
Migrant	39	18	(631)	27	7	(252)	20	51	(241)
Region of origin									
Accra C.D., Eastern	34	24	(289)	25	5	(103)	20	47	(15)
Central, Western	50	15	(105)	27	6	(66)	17	52	(119)
Volta	39	12	(94)	27	12	(33)	9	63	(11)
Ashanti, Brong/Ahafo	38	21	(48)	29	7	(42)	19	43	(75)
Northern, Upper	41	9	(32)	60	0	(5)	30	55	(20)
Outside Ghana	35	22	(167)	10	20	(10)	17	47	(60)
Total	38	20	(735)	27	7	(259)	18	49	(300)

this situation, to the newness of many factories and to the frequency of redundancies after which workers must start all over again with another firm.

Table 4.3 allows the reader to compare workers in the various samples and note the effects of various occupational and background variables on seniority. Very few provincial workers were new to their jobs; Accra had (rather surprisingly) both more newcomers and more long-term workers than Tema. Those with the greatest seniority tend to be skilled or clerical workers in the higher wage categories. Newcomers tend to be migrants, but migrants are also well represented among the long-term workers. Sex and region of origin do not appear to be very important in seniority except that northern Ghanaians tend to be short-term workers (though this is contradicted by the provincial data).

In every category, the provincial firms kept their workers longer than firms in Accra or Tema. This lower turnover is partly due to the greater stability of older workers, who provided a substantial share of the provincial labour force, but the relative lack of alternative opportunities is certainly important. Workers in Accra and Tema are more able to leave their jobs if they are dissatisfied, even in the present tight labour market, because they have a better chance than provincial workers of finding another job in their area.

The higher proportion of 'new' workers in Accra than in Tema is due to the wider range and larger number of jobs available in Accra (making it easier to find a job there) and to the nature of the labour force in the two towns. Northerners tend to seek work in Accra rather than in Tema because there are far more jobs for the unskilled in Accra, but these low-paid, unskilled labourers are the least stable sector of the labour force.

Wage is directly related to seniority. As mentioned above, workers who stay with the firm are often able to gain increments or move to better-paying work. In addition, a higher wage is an inducement to stay on the job, since it would be difficult to match elsewhere. The better-paid workers are thus usually older than those on the minimum wage and increased family responsibilities make change more hazardous.

Women have only recently begun to work in Tema factories, so few have built up much seniority. However, there seems to be no evidence from Accra that women are less stable on the job than men. Age and marital status are probably more important than sex; older women who are married are more likely to remain on the job than young girls who can readily find other means of support.

The relative commitment of migrants to urban employment is evident in he seniority of migrants. This is less true in Accra, with its relatively high proportion of unskilled workers, than in the other cities. No clear pattern is evident in comparing workers from various areas, but the data demonstrate that non-Ghanaians are as likely to be long-term workers as nationals, providing that discriminatory legislation does not result in their employment being terminated.

TABLE 4.4. *Planned job stability by location (percentages)*

Plans to stay	Accra	Tema	Kumasi	Takoradi	Rural
Under 1 year	13	24	21	1	4
1–3 years	34	38	35	29	19
Longer	36	28	43	69	77
Don't know	17	10	1	1	0
Total	100	100	100	100	100
N	735	259	150	150	138

As mentioned earlier, intention to stay is a subjective factor related to motivation rather than an objective measure of turnover. However, such plans are not entirely unrelated to reality; turnover is higher among the dissatisfied than among the satisfied who plan a long stay.

The length of time workers planned to stay on the job differed more from one place to another than by sex, occupation or place of origin (see table 4.4). Very few Takoradi or rural workers intended to leave their jobs in the foreseeable future, whereas a substantial minority of workers in the other cities thought they would leave within a year. In Accra and Tema, a third of these dissatisfied workers actually left, compared to 18 % of those who said they planned to stay more than five years. (Many of the latter may have left involuntarily.) The enthusiasm of the rural workers was because many were school leavers who were new to the job, glad to have found work when many of their schoolmates were still jobless and enthusiastic about the training they were receiving. There was less commitment in the other rural factory, but opportunities for wage employment in the area were limited and the majority of workers preferred to live there, so they were hanging on desperately in the face of an extensive redundancy program. Although Takoradi workers have more of a choice than rural workers, job mobility is far more limited than in Accra and few workers seem to leave voluntarily.

Attitude toward management is an important factor in this situation. Only one Takoradi worker complained about the management, whereas this was a frequent cause of dissatisfaction in the Kumasi firms. Nearly two-fifths

H

of the provincial workers who complained about the management said they planned to leave within a year, compared to only 3 % of the other workers in these towns. In Tema, where a quarter of the workers thought they would leave fairly soon, those who objected to the pay and those who complained of the management were about equally likely to be thinking of changing jobs, but those who objected to both the pay and management or to the working conditions were even more likely to say they wanted to leave soon. Thus, pay is a more important cause for leaving one's job in Tema than in the provincial towns, but it is not sufficient if other aspects of the job are satisfactory.

Tema workers, being mostly school leavers, have higher expectations of a job than do most provincial workers and so react more strongly to unfavourable working conditions. If the first stage of development allows school leavers to spurn manual labour, the second stage may be indicated by a willingness to work with their hands if the job pays well and is fairly clean, is not too hot and does not involve too much physical exertion. The 'clean' factor may not be too important if the job is fitting, since association with motors is relatively prestigious, or printing, because of the association with literacy, but it is taken into account in estimating the acceptability of other jobs. Some workers are probably attempting to maintain non-manual working conditions in a manual job. This aspect of satisfaction should not be exaggerated; only a small number of workers had anything to say about working conditions and few of these specified that the job should be clean, but it would be an interesting factor to investigate further.

Form (1969, 1970) has carried out a comparative study of automobile workers in the United States, Italy, Argentina and India based on the hypothesis that workers in plants of similar technology will show similar patterns of adaptation, regardless of the level of development of the country in which they are living. This hypothesis seems to have been only partly upheld; the inclusion in the sample of workers in a country such as Ghana, where large-scale industry has appeared more recently and is less widespread, might well have had an important effect on the conclusions. Of interest to the discussion here are his findings on job satisfaction.

It is difficult to compare his results with mine because different questions were asked and because the responses of workers of different skill levels have not been differentiated in the reports. Nevertheless, Form did find fairly general satisfaction with their work among the operatives studied. The proportion of automobile workers who responded favourably to questions on occupational satisfaction, involvement and fulfilment was generally higher than the proportion of Ghanaian workers who indicated general satisfaction when questioned about job likes and dislikes and their attitudes toward factory work in comparison to other occupations. The automobile workers in all four countries were less interested in changing their jobs than were the Ghanaians (except skilled workers); occupational mobility for manual workers may well be more common and easier to achieve in Ghana than in more highly developed countries. The Ghanaians were similar to the others in their relative disinterest in clerical work, which is seen as monotonous and not very satisfying even though it commands considerable respect. Unfortunately, no figures are given on the attitudes of workers in each country toward their pay.

OCCUPATIONAL PREFERENCES

To get some idea of the workers' view of their place within the firm and their plans or hopes for the future, workers were asked which job in the factory they would like if they had complete freedom to choose and what kind of job they would like to have when they left their present one. They were also asked what kind of work they would like their children to do.

TABLE 4.5. *Preferred work in the firm and for next job by present occupation* (*percentages*)

Preferred occupation	Present occupation			
	Unskilled	Semiskilled	Skilled	Clerical
In the firm				
Same as present	29	31	64	35
Unskilled[a]	8	2	1	1
Semiskilled	25	22	9	4
Skilled	25	21	15	16
Clerical	13	24	11	44
Total	100	100	100	100
N	244	518	426	153
Next job				
Unskilled, semiskilled	31	32	9	6
Skilled	20	28	64	13
Clerical	4	18	5	40
Farming	37	15	11	14
Trade, business	8	7	11	27
Total	100	100	100	100
N	224	483	406	140

[a] Mostly watchmen.

Skilled workers were far more satisfied than were other workers, both in preferring the job they were doing to any other available in the firm and in planning to continue the same work on the next job (see table 4.5). Many unskilled and semiskilled workers would prefer skilled work to their own because further training would increase their chances of finding work in future and they could carry on a business on the side. Although most skilled workers prefer to stick to the trade which they already know, one in seven mentioned another skill which he would prefer to his own and others aspired to be drivers.

Watchmen and drivers were almost all satisfied with their occupations. Very few men who had these jobs wanted to change and many men in other jobs would prefer to be watchmen or (especially) drivers. Watchmen see their jobs as easy, allowing free time for other jobs or farming and as a good job for older men. A labourer of thirty-five who wanted to be a watchman said, 'I am quite old and can't do heavy job.' Also, watchmen have very little unemployment. One said, 'The job is well known at the Labour Office so whenever I am sacked I can get another.' The same cannot be said of drivers, of which there seems to be a considerable over-supply. There were quite a few men who had a drivers' license or who claimed to have had training who were working at other jobs because they had been unable to find work as drivers. Men are interested in driving because of the opportunities for travel which it provides, the greater free time (while the lorry is being loaded or unloaded or whenever the car isn't needed) and the relative freedom from direct supervision. It is also seen as lucrative, especially by the unskilled.

Given the opportunity to change jobs within their firms, many men would decline for reasons other than general satisfaction with their present jobs. Age is a factor for some men. A man of thirty-six said he would have to stick to his present job because he was 'too old to learn another'. Many unskilled workers felt that they could not change jobs because they had no qualifications and/or education. Those who did mention another job they would rather have were more likely than other workers to give pay as the reason for wanting to change. Nearly a quarter of the unskilled workers wanted other jobs because they paid more, compared to 5% of skilled workers and 16% of the semiskilled and clerical workers.

The comment 'I have specialized' is used most often by skilled workers and drivers, but some semiskilled machine operatives feel that there is more security in sticking to one job. There is a suspicion that those who are moved about within the firm are more easily laid off. However, resistance to change in this case applies to staying within the semiskilled field rather than to learning a trade. Skilled workers are seen as less dispensable than others: 'When raw materials are short, the tailors are not laid off.'

One of the firms had recently introduced a new machine for making foam rubber. There was considerable competition among the workers as to who would be chosen to run it. One man expressed their attitude, 'This is a new job in the country and I can easily be promoted through it.' This ties in with the workers' general willingness to undertake new training at any stage in their careers if it seems likely to result in new opportunities. Worker attitudes toward innovations that would cut down the number of jobs in the firm would probably be negative only if their own jobs were threatened, because there is a lack of solidarity among workers which would inhibit collective action in such a situation, but this was not investigated in the present study.

Many workers who really want to change jobs (as opposed to those who answered in terms of fantasy) would stay within their own category. This is an indication that placement within a firm is probably a fairly accurate reflection of the workers' abilities or at least that most workers are fairly well satisfied with their placement.

Most of the clerical workers who did not prefer their own jobs wanted to continue in clerical work; often they had a higher-level clerical job in mind. Accounting clerks wanted to be accountants, higher clerical officers wanted to be managers, etc. A third of the men in lower clerical jobs said they would prefer to learn a trade; this would give them a better chance of finding jobs in future and would also pay better than their present jobs. Manual workers who covet clerical work feel differently. A quarter of them said that a clerical post would provide 'heavy pay'. The difference, of course, lies in the wide range of remuneration for clerical work. Those who would like to work in an office visualize themselves in top jobs, which do pay well, but only a small proportion of office workers reach this level.

A few semiskilled workers who had completed middle school also saw office work as the proper fulfilment of their education and as a source of respect unavailable to manual workers. One man commented, 'When well dressed, workers are respected', and another said that clerical work 'broadens the mind'. A labourer said (quite rightly in his case) that 'office clerks have no better qualification'. There were proportionally more clerical workers who would have preferred manual work than vice versa. Ghanaian workers are aware of the possibilities for middle-range occupational success on both sides of the manual/non-manual line and there are probably relatively few manual workers who feel deprived at not having a clerical job.

A few workers said they would like to be foremen or managers. Their comments give us an indication of the workers' picture of these posts. The unskilled wanted these jobs chiefly because of the high salary and because a foreman was seen to work much less hard than a labourer. Other workers thought they knew their jobs well enough to supervise. Over half of the prospective managers were clerical workers or foremen, who had a better chance than other workers to observe management. A carpenter wanted to be made foreman 'so as to improve the company's output' and a sprayer thought he would make a good manager because he was 'interested in ordering people'. A packer said that, as director, he would 'have many friends and better pay'. Another carpenter said, 'Manager, because you should choose the best when you get the chance.'

Several factors influenced answers to the question on the job desired after leaving the present one. Many workers planned to stay where they were until retirement, so they either said 'none', assuming they would be too old to work, or gave farming as their 'retirement job'. This was particularly true for skilled and clerical workers. Secondly, the question asked what job the worker would 'like' to have, leaving him free to state his preference rather than estimate which job was most probable. Most of the semiskilled and unskilled workers who mentioned skilled and clerical work did not expect to get such jobs. The men who said they would like to go into business on their own have a better chance of doing so.

Three-fifths of those who planned self-employment (other than farming), either as a next job or on retirement, had never been on their own before. Foremen and higher clerical workers in Accra and Tema were especially likely to be thinking of setting up a business of their own. Quite a few men have become independent shopkeepers in the past after working as clerks, assistant shopkeepers or artisans (Garlick 1959:10–11; Macmillan 1920), but a major difficulty of those who go into trade after a long career in employment is that they are not as concerned to make a success of it as if they had a longer period of time in which to build up the business. It is looked on as a means of supporting themselves in their declining years rather than as a route to wealth. Skilled workers who had worked on their own in the past were not particularly eager to return to self-employment, probably because of the greater security of wage employment. However, many who did not specify it will probably continue to practice their skill on a small scale in their old age.

Nigerians were often eager to get into trade, which involved a large number of their countrymen in Ghana. Those employed in factories usually lack capital and/or patrons to get started and the low level of their savings means that the goal of independence will be long delayed.

Men over thirty and those who had experienced long periods of unemployment in the past were more likely to be planning to be self-employed than the young and those who had found work easily. We have seen that self-employment is used for support in periods of unemployment; planning for self-employment is a way of avoiding an extended search for work in the future. Men who are beginning to think of their eventual return to the village are more likely to be considering it as a supplement to or substitute for farming than younger men, who are oriented toward a long career in wage employment.

Women were twice as likely as men to plan self-employment in the future, though they had no more experience of it in the past. It is easier for women to combine self-employment with marriage and child-rearing than to keep a job which requires regular hours of attendance. Recently, there has been a movement by both public corporations and private firms to cut down on the liberal maternity-leave provisions which make hiring Ghanaian women very expensive. It has been suggested that a woman only be allowed two maternity leaves with pay regardless of her length of service. Rules at one firm laid down that women who became pregnant during their first year of service should be sacked. Women object to these regulations, but managers feel they cannot finance yearly maternity leaves for a large number of women workers. As a result, women who would prefer wage employment may be forced to become traders.

Clerical workers were less likely than the skilled to plan that their next job would be the same as their present one, but they were more satisfied than semiskilled or unskilled workers, less than a third of whom wanted to find another job in the same field. There are substantial numbers of both unskilled and semiskilled workers who would find a skilled job if they got the chance, and a few who were interested in trade. Nearly a fifth of the semiskilled workers said they would try for a clerical job next time, whereas nearly two-fifths of the unskilled workers planned to return to farming. Men over forty are more likely than younger men to look forward to a return to farming, whereas those under twenty-five are more likely than older men to try for a clerical post. The educational background of the younger men 'qualifies' them for clerical work, whereas farming is much more popular with illiterates. However, even educated men begin to think seriously of farming as they get older.

Skilled work is the most popular choice of workers of every educational level except secondary. Whereas some men say that they could not ever get a clerical job because they lack education, they do not consider lack of training as a permanent bar to skilled work. They are correct in this distinction in that the informal training system can be joined at any age and one can learn on the job. Whereas artisans in Ivory Coast are dependent on paper qualifications to get ahead and hence are eager to attend evening classes, skill training in Ghana is only very loosely articulated with the educational system and thus still open to illiterates. Evening technical classes exist, but they are available only to small numbers of people in the largest cities.

ASPIRATIONS FOR CHILDREN

Many parents are hesitant to say what occupation they would like their children to have. Some have not thought about it; others assume that the child will follow them or will make up his own mind; they say that they have no intention of influencing their children. This situation exists in industrialized countries as well as in developing societies; in both, it is more characteristic of the working class than of parents in professional and administrative occupations. The latter have a better view of occupations at the top of the hierarchy and are able to analyze their children's abilities as fitting them for certain positions. Ordinary people know relatively little about positions further up the hierarchy than their own, do not feel that they can do much to influence events and so are unable to specify an occupation even though many hope that one of their children will some day be a 'big man'. It was thought that parental hopes for mobility might be particularly high in a society such as Ghana where rapid long-distance mobility is possible (as when the son of an illiterate subsistence farmer becomes a judge or Member of Parliament), even if only for a limited number of people. However, the aspirations expressed by the factory workers interviewed were relatively modest.

Because of the difficulty foreseen in getting people to express their aspirations for their children, the question was phrased to get their reaction to factory work as a possibility: 'Would you like your children to work in a factory or would you prefer that they do something else?', and 'Why?' These were only asked of workers who had children. Although the question biased answers to some extent in favour of factory work, those who explained that they were thinking of skilled or clerical work in a factory were classified as preferring skilled or clerical work rather than factory work *per se*. In the few cases where more than one occupation was mentioned, the highest status occupation for a son was counted.

About 30% of the parents said they wanted their children to have a trade and about a quarter each opted for factory work or a profession (including such semiprofessional occupations as teaching and nursing). Only about one in eight mentioned clerical work, including those who said they wanted their children to 'work for the government', which usually implies a clerical job. Very few mentioned farming, trading, or the army or police. Factory work was most popular in Accra, and skilled work in Takoradi. Teaching and trading were twice as popular in Accra and Tema as in the provincial towns; the reverse was true for farming. Those who wanted their sons to be doctors, lawyers or qualified engineers varied from 22 % of the Kumasi parents to 3 % of those in Takoradi.

TABLE 4.6. *Aspirations of urban males for their children by occupation and education (percentages)*

	Wants child[a] to be						
Father's	Factory	Skilled	Clerical	Profes-sional[b]	Other	Total	N
Occupation							
Unskilled	38	26	12	15	9	100	89
Semiskilled	17	38	16	19	10	100	181
Skilled	30	30	13	20	7	100	216
Clerical	23	36	12	24	5	100	83
Foreman	27	24	10	34	5	100	41
Education							
None	36	27	19	9	9	100	179
Primary, Muslim	33	26	12	21	8	100	61
Middle	21	37	11	23	8	100	309
Secondary	16	22	12	50	0	100	32
Technical, commercial	13	42	10	32	3	100	31

[a] If more than one occupation was given, the one chosen for the eldest son was counted.
[b] Includes semiprofessional occupations such as teacher.

The aspirations of workers were generally related to their education and their resulting modernity of orientation and position within the status structure (see table 4.6). Illiterate workers were most likely to favour factory work for their children, especially if they were unskilled. From their comments, many of them had semiskilled work in mind rather than the unskilled work which they were doing, but this still does not involve much expectation of upward mobility. Semiskilled workers, especially those in Tema, were least enthusiastic about factory work; very few favoured clerical work either. Nearly two-fifths said their sons should acquire a skill. This indicates an understanding of the increasing importance of training as a prerequisite for well-paying jobs. Young men who had recently completed middle school, who saw the skilled jobs within their firms as preferable to their own and/or whose fathers were craftsmen were more eager than others that their sons should have a trade. For these men also, minimal mobility was apparently expected or desired, though achievement of technician status would mean a higher position than their own, and an increase in the number of technicians is certainly vital to Ghana's development.

It is in the choice of professional or semiprofessional careers for their children that mobility aspirations are most clearly expressed. Men who were farthest up the hierarchy – foremen and higher clerical workers, those making the best pay – most often thought of their children achieving professional status. The proportions aiming for a profession increased with the level of education from a tenth of the illiterates to half of those who had attended secondary school and from 15 % of the unskilled workers to a third of the foremen. Those who had always lived in towns and those whose fathers had been clerical workers or teachers were more likely to mention a profession than those with a rural, farming background. As in every society, Ghanaian parents in high level occupations can give their children better opportunities to succeed through the school system than rural and lower-income urban parents (Foster 1965). Extra income can be used to provide private schools or extra coaching for examinations. High-level jobs are seen as the logical result of the extensive education they want for their children. While many 'middle level' workers would like their children to go to university, they are often aware that they may not be able to afford secondary-school fees, and this has evidently mediated their occupational aspirations to a realistic level.

The difference between men and women provides an interesting example of the effect of position within the system on aspirations. The women are less likely than the men to have gone beyond middle school, but very few of them have not attended middle school, a much rarer accomplishment for women in Ghana than for men. Whereas men with middle-school education favoured skilled work for their children, the women preferred teaching and professional occupations. So, for a given amount of education, women have higher aspirations than men. There are several possible reasons for this. (1) Some of these women are married to men who have more education and are in higher level occupations than their own, and would tend to have high aspirations for their children and be able to afford the necessary education. (2) Women are less likely than men to be aware of the difficulty of reaching a professional position. (3) Teaching is more attractive to women than to men, partly because flexibility of location (allowing them to follow their husbands when the latter are transferred) is more important than promotion. They are therefore more likely to mention it as a good occupation for their children. It should be mentioned that a much higher proportion of women than of men teachers are trained, so women are probably less likely to think of teachers in terms of the untrained 'pupil teachers' in bush schools who greatly contribute to lowering the status of the profession.

Northerners, who were less concerned about sending their children to school, were most likely to say they wanted their children to be clerical workers. A study of middle-school leavers (Peil 1968a) showed that clerical work will be more often aspired to and will be thought more important in areas where education is not yet widespread than in areas where a substantial proportion of the population attends school and a sufficient number go on to secondary school to make entry into clerical jobs highly competitive. Thus, workers from Eastern and Volta Regions, were education is more advanced than in the north, favour skilled jobs over clerical ones by more than two to one.

Northerners were also more likely than others to say they wanted their children to work in factories. Factory work may well be preferable to construction work (the main alternative for unskilled illiterates) because it is more stable, pays fairly well and provides an opportunity for some to move up to better-paid semiskilled work. Men doing unskilled work who have attended middle school are much less enthusiastic about factory work than those with less education; they want their children to be skilled, as do others with a middle-school education.

It was difficult for many parents to say why they preferred a specific occupation. The reason most frequently given (by 38% of the parents) was that it paid well and/or regularly or provided opportunities for promotion (leading to higher pay). Others said it was a 'good job' or that their children should follow them (16%) or that they should have an occupation which would be useful to the family or the country (11%). A few merely said that they did not want their children to work in a factory.

Northerners, non-Ghanaians and other unskilled workers in the lowest wage category mentioned the pay more often than workers who were better off financially. Older men, who had been in the city for some time, were more concerned with pay than newer migrants and pay was a more frequent basis for choice in the provincial cities than in Accra or Tema. Illiterates were most concerned with security, wanting their children to have an occupation for which there were plenty of openings. Some of those who favoured skilled work said that it paid well, but many wanted their sons to have a trade or 'profession' and/or to be independent – able to maintain themselves independently of the vagaries of employers.

Women placed more emphasis than men on the respect due to those in a 'good' job and in their ability to help the family. Those who favoured clerical work indicated that this would earn respect; some said that such a choice was obvious because the children would be educated. This attitude is not nearly so common as speech-makers across the country would have us believe, but it is probably true that parents are as much responsible as the young men themselves for school leavers vainly seeking clerical jobs.

Chinoy reported (1952: 459) that none of the automobile workers he interviewed wanted their sons to work in a factory except as skilled workers. In the light of the American ideology of unlimited opportunity, these men could not see themselves as successful, but they rationalized their position by putting the responsibility for advancement on their sons.

Ghanaian workers were less likely to reject factory work than the Americans, but they also put considerable emphasis on skilled work. Many parents have a limited knowledge of the occupational structure of their society and make choices from the relatively few occupations with which they have had experience, which are mostly near in status to their own. Nevertheless, they see mobility, at least over a short distance, as characteristic of their society and expect it from their sons. This is not necessarily because they see themselves as failures, since their position in Ghanaian society is relatively prestigious. At the same time, many are aware that long-distance mobility which occurred so often in the years just before and just after Independence is now much less common. There is some understanding that administrative and professional occupations require an expensive education, but it is impossible with the data at hand to say how widespread this understanding is or how many parents adjusted their aspirations as a result of it.

The Ghanaian parents included in this study have an even greater disability than the American parents of whom Chinoy reported (1952: 459), 'with their limited income and lack of knowledge, these fathers can provide little financial assistance or occupational guidance'. Their background, resources and understanding of the process of mobility place severe limitations on their ability to help their children get an advantageous start in life. Lloyd (1967) has shown this clearly by comparing the child-rearing attitudes and behaviour of elite and illiterate parents in Ibadan. Illiterate parents who do not send their children to school yet say they want them to become teachers or doctors are expressing their agreement with the goals of society even though they do not understand the means. It remains to be seen whether this disparity will lead to a serious dissatisfaction with the society.

So far, there is little evidence that a class system is emerging, with the manual workers turning their backs on the clerks and teachers or joining with them to oppose the elites. Although the elites maintain a vastly higher standard of living than ordinary workers and have many opportunities for passing this status on to their children, most of them cannot cut themselves off from their many lower-status relatives. The chance of rising to the elite is smaller than in the past, but it still exists. Parents are aware of the possibility, but do not count on it. The alienation expressed by Duodu (1967) also exists, but it appears to be very rare among ordinary members of the population.

EDUCATION AND OCCUPATION

The fit between the amount of education received and a man's occupational career is closer in developing than in industrialized countries, partly because of the colonial legacy of bureaucracy whereby certification of educational competence is required for jobs at all levels, but also (and more important) because there are relatively few jobs in the 'modern' sector of the economy and most of these require literary rather than technical skills. The amount of education and quality of the resulting certificate are the only officially recognized qualifications separating one candidate from another in a situation of intense competition. It is therefore only natural that certain jobs are seen as available only to those who have achieved a certain level of education, though the amount of education required may be increased over time. Inevitably, other jobs are categorized as suitable only for illiterates, though many men who have been to school may also do them for lack of something better. This situation contributes to the crystallization of a hierarchy of occupations, though other factors are probably of more importance.

In order to get a measure of workers' ideas on the relationship between education and occupation in Ghanaian society as well as measuring in another way their own aspirations, the question was asked, 'If a young man

TABLE 4.7. *Suggested occupations for educated and uneducated young men* (*percentages*)

Occupation	Educated	Uneducated
Profession	12	—
Teaching, police, army	7	a
Clerical, manager	21	—
Skill, factory	56	64
Labour	a	10
Farming	3	23
Trade, business	1	3
Total	100	100
N	1,355	1,355

a Less than 0.5 %.

asked your advice on what is the best work to do, what would you tell him
(1) if he was educated? (2) if he had no education?'

About two-fifths of the workers thought that education did not make any
difference and specified the same occupation for both, or at least occupations
at the same level (see table 4.7). Skilled and factory work were most often
mentioned, both by those who gave the same answer for both and by those
who acknowledged the effect of education on occupational prospects. In the
latter case, the educated young man was usually advised to aim for professional, teaching or clerical work, and the uneducated young man, for
skilled or factory work; or the man with education was to learn a skill, and
the illiterate man to become a farmer or labourer. A few men said that
both should become farmers. A small number mentioned trading or business,
usually for the uneducated and/or thought the educated man should become
a manager. The army or police were recommended occasionally for the
educated man or, rarely, for both. Because of the surplus of school leaver
candidates, these services can now require recruits to have a Middle School
Leaving Certificate.

Two-thirds of the men suggested an occupation at their own level –
skilled workers usually said that a young man should learn a trade, whether
he was educated or not. Clerical workers said the educated man should take
up clerical work, and the uneducated become a farmer. Unskilled workers
frequently recommended unskilled work for the uneducated. The suggested
occupations corresponded even more closely to preferred jobs within the
factory and for the future than to the worker's present occupation.

In all categories except northerners recommending jobs for the educated,
at least half the workers mentioned skilled or factory work, but those who
have little or no education themselves have higher expectations of the rewards
of education and are less likely to think that illiterates should stay at home
and farm than those who have at least attended middle school. Men who had
attended technical or commercial school were similar to illiterates and those
with primary or Muslim education in the larger proportion who suggested
professional work or teaching for the educated and skilled work for the
uneducated, whereas men with middle or secondary-school education more
often thought that the educated should do skilled work and the uneducated
should farm.

There is an interesting difference between illiterates from the north and
those from Togo and Nigeria. The former favoured teaching, whereas the
latter recommended the professions more often than Ghanaians. Teaching
has been the most common occupation of educated northerners. Men from
Ashanti (where cocoa has been most successful) suggested farming more often

than men from other areas. Whereas schoolboys in the cocoa areas are not enthusiastic about farming, men who have moved away think of the income which might be earned from a large farm rather than the living conditions and the work involved. Skilled and factory work was more popular with those who grew up in cities or large towns or who had lived there for at least ten years; recent arrivals more often recommended clerical work, which reflects their more limited view of available occupations.

Recent arrivals mentioned unskilled work more than those who had been in town at least sixteen months, whereas those who had settled down but had not yet spent five years in the city were more likely to suggest farming than either recent arrivals or long-term residents. This was not just a question of age. An equal proportion of men of all ages said that educated men should become skilled or factory workers, but men under twenty-five were less likely than older workers to recommend skilled work for the uneducated; they were equally divided as to whether these should farm or do unskilled work. This is probably due to the high proportion of school leavers among the young men and the great competition for apprenticeships.

OCCUPATIONAL PRESTIGE

People's ideas about the relative position of various occupations within the society have little effect on mobility once a career is started, but probably have some influence on young men in their decision to try for one type of job rather than another and also affect the workers' self-image insofar as they are aware that their jobs are rated high, medium, or low by other people. Of course, their position in the community may be governed more by the importance of non-work roles such as leader of an ethnic association, but generally they profit from the relatively high position of factory work as a 'modern' occupation. The workers' ideas about other occupations were investigated to provide comparative data in this field.

Studies of occupational prestige in developing countries have usually relied on the opinions of secondary school pupils (Mitchell and Epstein 1959, Foster 1965). Xydias (1956) obtained rankings from workers by using pictures of men doing various types of jobs, but this method severely limits the number of occupations investigated (Xydias used twelve). Gamble (1966) used cards with the names of occupations, which were placed on a board divided into five sections. We used the more conventional verbal method with a list of thirty-seven occupations which the workers were asked to rate as 'very high', 'high', 'not high or low', 'low', or 'very low'. They could also say 'don't know' for occupations with which they were not familiar.

The question put to them was, 'This is a list of jobs which men in Ghana have. Some jobs have more standing than others – the men who do this work have more prestige or respect. For each job, put one tick as to how you think this job rates among Ghanaians.' If the worker was illiterate, the interviewer read out each occupation in turn and marked the sheet for him.

TABLE 4.8. *The ranking of occupations*

| | | | | University | |
Occupation	Total	Factory workers[a]	Middle Form 4[b]	First year[c]	Professional certificate[d]
Medical doctor	1	1	3	1	2
Judge	2	2	2	2	1
Member of Parliament	3	8	1	4	4
Diplomat	4	3	12	3	3
Education officer	5	6	4	5	8
Secondary teacher	6	5	7	10	9
Clergyman	7	9	8	8	7
District Commissioner	8	14	5	9	5
Headmaster	9	7	10	7	10
Chief	10	11	16	6	6
Soldier	11	4	6	16	18
Social welfare officer	12	13	9	12	11
Senior clerk	13	16	13	13	13
Businessman	14	12	21	11	12
Journalist	15	17	14	14	14
Policeman	16	15	11	18	19
Farmer	17	10	15	19	21
Football player	18	28	18	15	16
Primary teacher	19	19	20	21	20
Traditional healer	20	27	25	17	15
Factory worker	21	22	17	26	22.5
Storekeeper	22	24	27	20	17
Weaver	23	23	26	23	22.5
Miner	25	18	19	29	29
Lorry driver	25	20	24	25	26
Typist	25	25	23	22	25
Fitter	27	21	22	27	27
Trader	28	30	31	24	24
Carpenter	29	26	28	30	28
Blacksmith	30	29	30	32	30
Shop assistant	31	31	33	28	32
Chopbar keeper	32	32	34	31	31
Building labourer	33	34	29	33	33
Farm labourer	34	33	32	34	35
Steward	35	35	35	35	34

[a] 500 workers in Accra and Tema.
[b] 740 boys and girls in 22 schools throughout the country.
[c] 128 students taking first year sociology.
[d] 56 students studying for advanced certificates in nursing or social administration.

After rating the occupations, the workers were asked to pick one occupation they had marked high or very high and asked to state, 'Why do people respect this job?' They were then to pick an occupation rated low or very low and say, 'Why does this work have low standing?' Only half the workers interviewed in Accra and Tema were asked about prestige (alternate schedules included this page) since it was thought that 500 ratings would be sufficient. In the relatively few cases where workers were unable to cope with this (usually illiterate unskilled workers), the next worker interviewed was substituted.

Ratings of one to five (from very high to very low) were transferred to ranks by a system devised by Yaukey (1955) whereby each prestige category is weighted so that the mean for all ratings over all the occupations will be the same for each group tested. This allows for comparisons between samples even though one group rates consistently lower than another. Table 4.8 shows the rankings given by factory workers and, for comparison, rankings of the same occupations by adolescents in their last year of middle school, students in their first year at the University of Ghana and students studying at the University for certificates in nursing or social administration. The latter all had several years' experience in their fields. Two occupations were rated by factory workers and not by the others; lawyer ranked third, between judge and diplomat, and musician ranked nineteenth, between journalist and miner.

Although urban residents may be expected to have a better picture of the occupational structure of the country than villagers (who may have no personal contact with people in most occupations), and educated people to know more about a range of occupations than illiterates, it can be seen from a casual inspection of the table that the various samples were in agreement on the relative position of most occupations. The Kendall Coefficient of Concordance (W) for the rankings of the thirty-five occupations was significant beyond the .001 level for all four samples and when university students were compared with factory workers who had not been to school. This indicates general agreement in the ranking of occupations among all members of the population. As one would expect, professional occupations come at the top and unskilled manual and service occupations at the bottom. There is, however, considerable mixing of manual and non-manual occupations in the middle, which is more interesting than the predictable extreme placements.

Factory workers were interviewed about two months after the 1966 *coup*, whereas other samples were questioned before the *coup*. This explains the relatively high ranking factory workers gave to soldier and the relatively low ranking given to Member of Parliament and District Commissioner, who shared the odium of the old regime. The army is also popular among school-

I

boys; many more would like to join than the army has room for. It is suspected that soldiers have a higher prestige in most developing societies than they do in America.

Job satisfaction has been defined as 'a function of the disparity between rewards (. . . income and job status) and aspirations and/or expectations' (Wilensky 1960: 459). Although the pay is often considered insufficient, the relatively high-status position of factory work among occupations open to people of limited education (above storekeeper, typist and the skilled trades) should promote satisfaction among factory workers. But factory work appears to be more prestigious among schoolboys than among workers on the job; this is partly accounted for by the prospect being more exciting than the reality. Rural schoolboys ranked it fourteenth and tended to think of it as a 'modern' thing to do, whereas urban pupils, with a better idea of the pay and conditions involved, ranked it nineteenth. Among the factory workers, clerical workers and foremen ranked it higher than ordinary workers, and printers, who are among the best-paid factory workers, ranked it higher than carpenters. The latter ranked their own skill eighteenth, above any other occupation in the manual category. Their view of factory workers obviously did not include themselves; this job was ranked twenty-eighth. Others had a similarly low view of carpentry, which ranked below all skilled and semi-skilled occupations except blacksmithing. Lorry drivers are widely admired and ranked fairly highly in spite of the shortage of employment and in-security resulting from the numerous accidents. It is a job which can be handled by illiterates, which provides the illusion of power and which may pay well.

Farmer (seventeenth) and miner (twenty-fifth) were similar in that those who had little or no education ranked them higher than the university students. The lack of specification (cocoa or subsistence, large- or small-scale farmer) was deliberate, to allow each person to make his own identification. Women, men in Tema and workers who had grown up in cities (especially Accra) or in countries north of Ghana ranked farmer higher than others. In other words, those with the most urban and the most isolated rural background accorded farmers the most prestige, whereas men from the rich cocoa-growing areas thought less highly of farming as an occupation. In either case, farming certainly does not lack prestige, since it is in the upper half for every subgroup of factory workers examined. This is a good example of the difference between occupational prestige and aspirations. Many people think highly of farmers who would not consider being one themselves, whereas others who would recommend farming as a good occupation do not always give it high prestige.

The position of typist (twenty-fifth) shows that most people are relatively sophisticated in discriminating between lower and higher clerical work. Workers from towns outside Ghana and those who had not attended school gave it the highest ranking (nineteenth), whereas male clerical workers and foremen placed it thirty-first. Most other subgroups (including non-Ghanaians of rural origin) placed it between twenty-fourth and twenty-eighth.

The reasons given for rating occupations high or low were centred on the income which the work provided and, to a much lesser extent, the amount of service to the family or community which it involved. Three-quarters of the workers said they based high ratings on the amount of money one could earn and two-thirds said that jobs were rated low because they do not pay well. Foster (1965: 272) has confirmed the importance of income in prestige by having students rate a series of occupations for prestige and then rate them again on the amount of money they think is earned by men doing this work. The two ratings were highly correlated. Southern Ghanaians have been part of a money economy (either with coinage as we know it or with substitutes such as cowries) for centuries. Material goods are considered very important and they are well aware of the function of occupations in providing more goods for some workers than for others. However, non-Ghanaians were more likely to mention money than Ghanaians, and those coming from rural areas mentioned it more often than those who grew up in Accra. In both positive and negative prestige, the length of time spent in town was inversely related to the proportion mentioning money. It may well be that urban experience fosters awareness of the various aspects of prestige or that money is so important to those who have least of it that other aspects of prestige are ignored.

Service was more important as a factor in positive than in negative prestige. One-fifth of the workers said they had rated occupations high because people who had them helped others. Doctors were most frequently mentioned in this connection. In terms of negative prestige, there were some comments that people in certain occupations (especially chopbar keeper) only helped themselves, not the community at large. The same comment was not made about businessmen, so it was not commercial dealings *per se* that were being objected to.

The most prominent factor of negative prestige after money was the physical demands of the job. Occupations were rated low which were hard (or, sometimes, too easy), dirty, tedious, or dangerous. Only one-third as many people used the physical aspects of the job in according prestige as in denying it. Unskilled workers were more likely than others to mention this, presumably because they have more experience of such jobs.

Other aspects of prestige were mentioned by very small numbers of workers. Women were more likely to use education as a criterion than men, and illiterate workers mentioned it more often than those who had been to school. It was, however, more important for university students than for factory workers. Power was sometimes connected with the prestige of judges, and the importance of the work with government officers. Prestige may depend on the character of the people known to be practicing an occupation. Traditional healers were rated low by some who were convinced that they cheat people. Their relative position (twentieth), however, indicates that many people have confidence in them.

SUMMARY

This chapter has been concerned with the reactions of the workers to their jobs, their stability on the job and their attitudes toward their own and other occupations in the factory and in the wider society. The findings are similar to those of Form and Geschwender (1962) and other studies in that older and better-paid workers are the most satisfied. Younger workers are likely to aspire to a greater rise in status than they are able to achieve, especially since many have seen cases of long-distance occupational mobility among their relatives or classmates. However, the average worker is reasonably satisfied with his job, if only because he is glad to be employed when many are out of work.

The workers' primary concern with pay is indicated in their comments on what they like and dislike about their work and in the reasons given for preferring other types of work. The lower the wage, the more people were dissatisfied, but the amount of pay is an imporant source of discontent for workers at every level. This discontent is not necessarily related to turnover because jobs are hard to find and a new one would not in most cases result in increased wages. However, the feeling that the pay is not high enough to justify hard work is fairly widespread.

Ghanaian workers have been compared to nineteenth and to mid-twentieth century factory workers; they have some of the characteristics of each. Like the early industrial workers, their concern with pay is based on a low standard of living and the need to support a large family. These problems continue for a minority of industrial workers in Europe and America today, but the majority have developed consumptionist attitudes based on a relatively high basic wage. The Ghanaian is somewhat better off than the nineteenth century worker (and in this he resembles other modern workers) in that he works much shorter hours and his children are in school rather than working with him in the factory. He is living in a more open society, in which his children may find opportunities for advancement which were not available to him.

Given their limited income, it is just as well that most Ghanaian workers have not yet adopted the consumptionist values so prevalent in industrialized countries. They are too close to their subsistence background in which goods are used again and again to fit well into the 'use once and discard' ethic of modern capitalism. Most would spend extra money on more food, rent for a second room, more frequent visits home and building a house there, responding more generously to requests for aid, or to pay off debts (not necessarily in that order). Though their demand for higher wages is superficially the same as the demand of the modern industrial worker, its base is closer to the need of the early factory operative.

Management's problem is to obtain adequate work for the wages paid. Traditional attitudes toward work and time are sometimes a source of problems, but workers with low productivity are often inadequately supervised. Farm work may be physically exhausting, but it is seasonal and the farmer can stop to rest from time to time during the day. The factory worker is expected to work during set hours $5\frac{1}{2}$ days a week all through the year and to rest only during the noon lunch break. The spread of education should help adjustment to industrial life by teaching 'modern' attitudes toward the use of time. Traditional attitudes which affect supervision may be harder to change.

The average worker is fairly well satisfied with his foreman. Those who are not object most strongly to close supervision and frequent shouting, which is seen as denying the respect which one man owes another. The larger and more bureaucratic the firm, the greater the pressure on the foreman as 'man in the middle', but many foremen lack the training and/or experience to handle the conflicting demands made on them.

Turnover and absenteeism are usually at acceptable levels. They tend to be above average in firms where the work is unskilled and physically exhausting and where management lays off large numbers of workers because of shortages of materials. Sickness is the chief cause of absence, with the needs of the family coming second. The inverse relationship of absenteeism to wages suggests that enabling the workers to pay for better food and housing would increase attendance. Voluntary turnover is closely related to the opportunities for alternative employment available locally, though attitudes toward management, pay and working conditions also have some effect.

The most satisfied Ghanaian workers are the skilled and, to a lesser extent, clerical and semiskilled workers (especially drivers), who feel that they have a career, not just a job. The skilled are in a position to become, to a greater or lesser extent, specialists, in work which can be followed until retirement and in which money earned outside working hours supplements a wage scale which is already higher than that of other workers in the firm. The unskilled worker often quits his job because he feels there is little to lose and he might as well have a rest and/or a change; the skilled and clerical workers stay on the job even though they are dissatisfied because they have more to lose and little to gain from a change.

Pay and opportunities combine to make skilled occupations popular with workers at all levels. Two-thirds of the skilled workers prefer their job to all others and plan to stick with it throughout their working lives. Skilled workers who would consider different work are often interested in another skill. Drivers, watchmen and clerical workers are also generally satisfied, whereas a large number of semiskilled and unskilled workers are not. This is particularly true of middle-school leavers in these occupations, who are disappointed that their education is not worth much in the employment market. They readily compare their position to that of men only slightly older than themselves who got a 'good job' with no more education than they had. Many semiskilled and lower clerical workers would like to move into skilled work and other semiskilled workers would prefer to join the ranks of clerks. Unskilled workers generally feel trapped by their illiteracy and lack of training, which prevent them from improving their situation.

Consideration of the aspirations of parents for their children is useful for the light it sheds on people's ideas of mobility within the society. A man might realize that he had missed the opportunity of a 'good job' because he was unable to get a good education or because he had no training. His estimation of the occupational opportunities open to his children indicates whether he thinks of social status as more or less fixed, open to small-scale mobility, or wide open. From the modest aspirations expressed by most of the parents, we would be safe in assuming that most people expect their children to be only somewhat better placed than themselves. Parents tend to see the future in terms of skills, and they are probably right in that those trained for technical posts will be among the best-paid wage-earners of the next generation.

The high proportion of workers who did not distinguish between those with education and those without in recommending occupations is another indication of the fluidity of the system. Access to training is more important than education and, so far, lack of education is not an insuperable barrier to occupational success. Illiterates have a higher opinion of teachers than those who have been to school and are more ready to think that education should lead to a profession, whereas many of those who have at least completed middle school would prefer it if illiterates would stay at home and farm, leaving urban jobs to the school leavers.

The relative prestige of various occupations in Ghana is similar to that found elsewhere. The mixing of manual and non-manual occupations in the middle of the range indicates that Ghanaians are relatively sophisticated in distinguishing the earning potential of various jobs and are not blind to the 'dead end' nature of some non-manual occupations. Educational prerequisites and the use of mind rather than body are not enough to give an occupation prestige if it does not pay well. This has also been seen in the attitudes of workers toward their own jobs and their aspirations for their own and their children's careers.

CHAPTER 5

MIGRATION

Every year, hundreds of thousands of West Africans leave their homes to live and work, at least temporarily, somewhere else. Migration always requires some adjustment to the new place, but the adaptation required of African migrants to the cities is often considerable. It is least drastic for those who grow up in a town. Less adaptation is required of southern Ghanaians of rural origin than of rural northerners. Southern villages have been under urban influence for generations and many of their residents are able to visit the towns before deciding to move. Northerners, on the other hand, tend to live in dispersed farmsteads rather than in villages and many have never visited even a small town prior to their migration. This chapter is concerned with the geographical aspects of migration and with factors influencing the choice of destination. The problems migrants face in adjusting to life in town will be dealt with in the following chapter.

Studies of African towns often include information about the origins of residents. Censuses can also provide information on the international and interregional flow of migrants, but published data from the 1960 Census in Ghana is limited to birthplace material and even this is not specific for the origins of migrants. Individuals are classed as 'born in the locality of enumeration', 'born in another locality but within the region', 'born outside the region but in Ghana', 'born elsewhere in Africa' or 'born outside Africa'. For the last two categories, there is further information on immigrants from certain countries. For a full description of the migration process, such data are inadequate in that one cannot identify either the direction or the magnitude of migration flows, but only the location of individuals at any one point in time. Some information on the regional origin of migrants has been made available to demographers working on census data, but there is no information on earlier moves of people who had returned home or moved again before the Census was taken.

Caldwell (1969) has attempted to get around this difficulty by obtaining information about past and present residents of urban and rural households, categorizing them as non-migrants, seasonal or long-term migrants, or permanent returnees. This method is useful in measuring attitudes toward migration but, like censuses and most surveys, it assumes that a migrant goes to a town and returns home, whereas many move from one place to another without returning home.

The method used here was designed to provide information about step migration (village–town–city) and other types of movement throughout the migrant's career. Complete migration histories were obtained in connection with the work histories, including stays of at least two months in places where the migrant did not find work. Analysis has been limited to migrant urban men, since there were very few women in the sample and the patterns for women may be different from those of men because their choice of whether and where to migrate is seldom as free as a man's. Workers in the two rural factories have been excluded as well because of the small size of the sample. Although factory workers are a limited segment of the population, their patterns of movement are sufficiently similar to those reported in other studies based on census data (i.e. Caldwell 1967) to indicate that the results may be representative of migrants to Ghana's large towns.

Since many Ghanaian women go to their hometowns to give birth, children often grow up in a town or village different from the one in which they were born. The place where most of childhood was spent has been used instead of birthplace (where these are different) as the 'place of origin' of an individual because his primary socialization has been there. Some families in the cities follow a traditional way of life which differs little from village life. There are farmers in towns of all sizes and many fishermen live in coastal towns and cities. In this case, an urban childhood may differ little from a rural one, but urban origin nevertheless indicates an increased probability of education and acquaintanceship with urban occupations and urban ways. Someone brought to Accra from a small village when very young is likely to be similar in his network of friendships and in his behaviour to someone born in Accra (assuming that both have parents of roughly similar education and occupation). Both are therefore considered to be nonmigrants.

WORKER ORIGINS

Less than one worker in five had grown up in the place in which he was working (see table 5.1). Half of the migrants had made only one move, from home to their place of work. Nearly half of the urban workers had grown up in villages and nearly three-quarters had crossed regional boundaries to find work. More workers had come from large towns than from small towns and more had come from neighbouring countries than from northern or central Ghana (except in Kumasi where people from central Ghana are 'at home').

TABLE 5.1. *Origin of workers (percentages)*

Grew up in	Accra	Tema	Kumasi	Takoradi	Rural	Total
Size place						
This city/village	19	1[d]	27	28	23	18
Other city	7	16	11	9	9	9
Large town[a]	19	23	9	5	12	16
Small town[b]	9	12	6	9	4	9
Village, rural	46	48	47	49	52	48
Total	100	100	100	100	100	100
N	735	259	150	150	138	1,432
Region/country[c]						
Accra C.D.	2	7	2	0	7	3
Eastern	23	31	9	3	55	26
Central, Western	17	26	22	48	13	22
Volta	16	14	7	4	8	15
Ashanti, Brong/Ahafo	8	16	22	8	5	10
Northern, Upper	5	2	13	6	0	4
Outside Ghana	29	4	25	31	12	20
Total	100	100	100	100	100	100
N	588	238	109	108	106	1,149

[a] 10,000–39,999 population.   [b] 5,000–9,999 population.
[c] Migrants only.
[d] 8% of Tema workers were non-migrants. Several men were commuting daily from Accra or its suburbs.

More workers in provincial cities than in Accra grew up locally (either in the city itself or in the region of which it is the capital), since Accra's size and job opportunities ensure it a wider catchment area than the provincial cities. This is especially true of Takoradi, where nearly half of the migrants were from the southwest. Very few Tema workers had grown up there, as it was only a small fishing village when they were growing up. Taking only migrants, Tema most often drew from other towns and cities. The provincial cities were more likely than Accra or Tema to draw workers from villages. About a fifth of those who grew up in Accra and were working there had worked in Tema in the past. There was probably considerable enthusiasm when Tema was being built and many jobs were opening up. The Tema labour force is now expanding relatively slowly, so it is less of an attraction to people in Accra than it was a few years ago. The shortage of housing in Tema has meant that some workers there have had to live in Teshie, Nungua, or even Accra. This is less the case now than in the late 1950s when Tema was being built, but it still happens. If a man is living rent-free in a family house, daily expenses for transport may prove more economical than paying Tema rents.

Migrants from central and southwestern Ghana evidently prefer Tema to Accra, perhaps because they are typically school leavers without training who seek the kind of semiskilled work for which Tema is known. Eastern and Volta Regions are under-represented among provincial workers because it is easier to migrate to Accra or Tema from this area than to Kumasi or Takoradi. There are few northerners in factories in any of the cities and none in the rural factories, because their background makes them more suitable for other types of work. Non-Ghanaians are well represented except in Tema.

About a quarter of the workers in each city had spent all of their working lives there and nearly half (44% in Tema and 47–50% in the other cities) had spent at least three-quarters of their working lives in the survey city.[1] Many of the rest had farmed for several years before going in search of wage employment. Although some men who start as farmers try seasonal migration before they settle down in a town, others go home only for short visits, if at all, once they decide to migrate. An extreme example of this was a Frafra who farmed for thirty-one years before setting out for Accra one dry season in the early 1950s. He had not been home since then.

While there were relatively few workers whose careers showed the circulating pattern of urban and rural work so familiar in early reports on African labour, they were not all illiterate northerners. One man who showed this pattern was an accounts clerk who had been a clerk, a mechanic and a storekeeper in the 1940s and had since spent three periods at home farming (of six, nine and eighteen months) for his father between clerical jobs. These periods were used to cover unemployment and are an example of the ability of southerners to use their homes as a base from which to apply for jobs rather than enduring the privations of living in town while unemployed. Another chief clerk had farmed twice for short periods between jobs. A more typical example of circulating migration is that of a Dagarti labourer who farmed for his father between each job. The farming intervals varied from six months to two years and only one of his jobs (the first away from home) lasted longer than two years. A Malian who had alternated between farming at home and working in Takoradi had returned twice to the same firm. He planned to stay a year or two on his present trip. These cases of circulating migration were relatively rare. One gets the impression that (1)

---

[1] This may be because many of the workers are still young. Some will no doubt move to other places before they retire to their hometowns. One worker interviewed in a rural factory had been employed in firm B when we interviewed there two years before.

seasonal migration early in a man's career may be replaced by long-term migration when he decides to move to a town and (2) few short-term migrants find their way into factory employment.[1]

Men who come to town for a few months or a year or two seldom get jobs in factories, either because other jobs are easier to get or because their abilities and preferences lie elsewhere. Most southern Ghanaians are long-term migrants in intention, though failure to find work may send them home after a short time in town.

Although about a quarter of the workers were fairly new to their jobs, few had lived in the survey city for less than fifteen months.[2] Only in the case of Tema was the median time in the city less than five years and, even here, 44% of those interviewed had been away from home for at least five years.

PRIMARY AND LATER MIGRATION

The direction of first migration is shown in table 5.2. One-quarter of the southern Ghanaians outside the Accra C.D. migrated intraregionally on first leaving home, compared to 4% of northern Ghanaians and 12% of those from Togo, Dahomey and Nigeria. Within southern Ghana, intra-

TABLE 5.2. *Direction of first migration of urban male workers (percentages)*

Region of origin	Region migrated to						
	Accra C.D.	Eastern	Central, Western	Volta	Ashanti, Brong/Ahafo	Northern, Upper	Outside Ghana
Accra C.D.	5	10	5	4	4	7	11
Eastern	21	47	7	14	9	21	0
Central, Western	17	10	57	0	15	0	0
Volta	17	8	3	64	8	14	3
Ashanti, Brong/Ahafo	9	12	10	4	28	21	11
Northern, Upper	3	1	6	0	14	29	0
Upper Volta, Mali, Niger	7	2	5	0	14	0	0
Togo	17	8	2	14	6	7	51
Nigeria	4	2	5	0	2	0	24
Total	100	100	100	100	100	100	100
N	430	120	208	22	174	14	37

[1] This is partly confirmed by Deniel (1968: 101), who found that Mossi seasonal migrants went to the plantations of Ivory Coast; migrants to Abidjan tended to stay several years.

[2] Interviews were conducted in early April. Information was collected by the year the move took place, not the month. A date two years back was thus at least sixteen months previous.

regional migration varied from 12% of those originating in Volta Region (which is mostly rural and has very little industry) to 44% in Western Region (which has several mining towns as well as Takoradi).

Distance and opportunities both affect the direction of interregional migration. Most movement is into contiguous regions.[1] Those moving into Accra are most often from Eastern, Volta or Central Regions. Migrants from Central Region also go west or into Ashanti Region to the north, whereas very few men from Eastern or Volta Regions move to Western or Ashanti Regions for urban employment.[2] Northerners are more likely to go to Ashanti or Brong/Ahafo, the nearest regions with large-scale wage-earning opportunities, than to Accra or Takoradi, which would involve further and more expensive travel.

Volta Region and northern Ghana are areas of extensive out-migration; the few who move there usually plan to farm or have family connections or government appointments. There were very few men who had moved within these regions and later migrated to the towns surveyed. Migrants from these regions in the coastal towns tend to go there directly, or at least without spending time elsewhere in their own regions. It may be that local migrants to the towns and villages in these regions never go any farther (e.g. migrants to Tamale are quite satisfied there and have no wish to travel farther south), but the nature of this sample does not allow us to be sure.

In 1960 there were nearly 170,000 people living in Volta Region who had been born in Togo. It appears that very few of the Togolese who move across the border into Volta Region later migrate to Ghanaian towns. Movement into Volta Region is mostly for farming and most of the southern Togolese in Accra are craftsmen. Of the 9,922 Togolese men in Accra in 1960, 22% were carpenters, 19% were artisans of other types and 23% were labourers. There were far fewer Togolese in Kumasi and Takoradi than in Accra, but the occupational distribution was similar. Migrants in the sample from central and northern Togo were likely to be unskilled workers, but they too had bypassed Volta Region.

Second and later moves are considered together (see table 5.3). Such migration has a somewhat different pattern from primary migration, though the basic flows remain the same. The aggregate of these moves by the more mobile individuals shows less intraregional migration than on the first move, though it was high in moves starting in the Accra Capital District (9% of primary moves and 45% of second and later moves) because of movement from Accra to Tema and vice versa. Only a fifth (22%) of the moves starting

---

[1] Caldwell (1967:123) shows the pattern as reported in the 1960 Census.
[2] They do go to central Ghana for cocoa farming.

TABLE 5.3. *Direction of second and later moves of urban male workers*[a] *(percentages)*

Regional origin of move	Region migrated to							
	Accra C.D.	Eastern	Central	Western	Volta	Ashanti, Brong/Ahafo	North Ghana	Togo
Accra C.D.	13	15	6	10	14	9	7	3
Eastern	25	28	18	2	14	9	3	10
Central	14	13	23	7	0	7	0	0
Western	9	6	7	40	4	16	3	0
Volta	6	2	0	1	41	1	0	3
Ashanti, Brong/Ahafo	16	7	9	17	0	33	13	0
Northern, Upper	5	1	1	3	0	7	7	0
Upper Volta, Mali, Niger	2	1	1	5	0	1	0	0
Togo	6	1	3	0	9	6	0	12
Nigeria	1	1	1	2	0	2	0	0
Returns home[b]	3	25	31	13	18	9	67	72
Total	100	100	100	100	100	100	100	100
No. of moves	424	107	69	126	22	150	30	32

[a] This table applies to the 599 men who migrated more than once.
[b] Counted only if the migrant worked at home and then went to a different place on the next trip.

in southern Ghana and only 5% of those originating in northern Ghana were intraregional.

From the point of view of intake, as shown in the table, intraregional migration is most frequent in Western and Volta Regions. Although the Western Region has several towns offering employment opportunities, the evidence of the Takoradi workers indicates that their attraction is mainly to people who are already living in Western Region. Those living elsewhere are drawn by the greater opportunities of Accra, if they are willing to leave their local area. A study of mine workers in Western Region would show them to be largely outsiders, but this type of work is only available in a few towns and attracts a specific type of migrant. In the case of Volta Region, the high proportion of intraregional moves is because outsiders seldom go to this region.

People moving intraregionally have not necessarily done so on their first move. For example, a carpenter first moved from his home in Volta Region to Koforidua in Eastern Region. Later, he worked in several other towns in Eastern Region before moving to Accra. Primary teachers often work in several towns or villages in the same area, then leave teaching and migrate to the city.

Moves involving a return home have been listed separately, ignoring their starting point. A return home from a first trip was counted as migration only if the migrant stayed at home and worked there for several months *and* went to a different place on a subsequent migration. For example, if a northerner went to Kumasi to work, then returned home for a period of farming before migrating to Takoradi, the second move would be counted as a return home and the third as a migration from the north to the Western Region. Had he returned to Kumasi, his time at home would have been counted as a visit and only the original trip would be counted. If a man merely visited his home for a week or two between towns, he would be considered to have moved from one town to the other. Eastern and Central Regions attracted a higher proportion of returnees than other areas of southern Ghana, but this may be because of the nature of the sample. Men moved to Western and Ashanti Regions for the jobs at which they were interviewed. Returns home account for all but two of the moves to Upper Volta and Mali and most of those to northern Ghana and Togo. A few moves to and from the Ivory Coast (all by Takoradi workers) and two moves to Bamako have been omitted from the table.

None of the Nigerians worked at home once they had moved to Ghana, though a few Ghanaians had spent some time working in Nigeria. Some southern Togolese had considerable international experience. For example, an Ewe foreman of sixty-nine had gardened at home in Lomé for six months before taking up an apprenticeship in Accra. After completing this, he moved to Cotonou, where he spent six years as a fitter and ten as a driver. In 1941 he joined the Ghanaian army and spent the next six years in Accra and Free-

TABLE 5.4. *Rural–urban and interregional migration of urban male workers* (*percentages*)

Moved to	First move from[a]		Later moves from[b]	
	Urban	Rural	Urban	Rural
Same region				
Urban	9	16	14	9
Rural	12	10	9	13
Different region				
Urban	68	65	68	72
Rural	11	9	9	6
Total	100	100	100	100
N	245	530	304	295

[a] Excluding moves originating outside the country.
[b] Excluding returns to hometowns.

town. After leaving the army he was a self-employed fitter for five years in each of two villages in Western Region before moving to Takoradi at the age of fifty.

Table 5.4 divides migrants into urban and rural at both origin and destination, using 10,000 population as the urban threshold. Although the Census classifies all places of 5,000 or more population as urban and at least half of the employed population in most places of this size are in non-farming occupations, it seems better from a sociological point of view to draw the line somewhat higher. Many villages have now grown to more than 5,000 population. Relationships between residents in these small towns (or large villages) are still primary rather than secondary and at least half of the non-farmers are engaged in trade. There is a continuum on most variables, so that division at any point would give much the same results. In this study, small towns have been included with villages as 'rural' unless otherwise specified, and 'urban' or 'town' is used for places the Census classifies as 'large towns' or 'cities' – places of more than 10,000 population.

The large proportion of migrants who went to cities in another region is due to the nature of the sample; 89% of the migrants were interviewed in Accra or Tema, and almost all of these came from outside the Capital District. However, the similarity in destination between those of rural and urban origin and between those in their first and later migrations is independent of the sample.

The first migration is often a return to one's birthplace for a visit to the family and a period of farming, especially for young men who were not brought up by their parents. Thus, a boy who grows up in Accra with an uncle may move back to his village in Eastern Region when he finishes school and farm with his father for a year or two. It is impossible with this sample to find out how many stay at home indefinitely, but most of the factory workers had returned to the city in less than two years. Many stayed at home for less than a year. Other cases of urban–rural migration often involve civil service or teaching posts. Untrained teachers (who are much more likely than trained teachers to later work in a factory) are usually appointed to rural schools.

The only statistically significant differences in table 5.4 involve rural–urban migrants on their first move. Young men from small towns and villages are more likely to go first to a town in their own region than are young men who grow up in towns or rural migrants on later moves. Young men who grow up in towns and decide to leave home tend to think of other towns in their region as offering no more opportunities than their own. They therefore head for the cities, especially Accra. Rural boys, though they are at least partially aware of the limited opportunities of the nearby town, may decide to try their luck there before facing the complexities of the city.

Those who grow up in a large town or city have a first chance at the jobs at home, since they have ample opportunity to look around while living at home. If they do not find satisfactory employment, they tend to head for the capital or for Tema. If the young men who grow up in villages leave home, they are more likely than the urban-reared to think the provincial capital will have the job they need. This hypothesis is confirmed in that migrant workers in Accra and Tema who had come from central or southwestern Ghana were more often from towns than migrants from these areas who were working in Kumasi or Takoradi.

It was thought that uneducated migrants would be more likely than those who had been to school to travel first to places in their own region, since this would maximize the possibility of living near relatives and of speaking their own language. It was also thought that the uneducated would be more likely to move to rural areas of other regions, since they would be more willing than school leavers to take up opportunities in farming. This can be tested for regions as a whole or for subregions with varying levels of educational participation. Volta and Eastern Regions have areas where a relatively high proportion of the population attend school and remain there beyond the age of fifteen and other areas which are near or even below the southern Ghanaian average. Since it was thought that the educated in areas of widespread education might be different in their migration patterns from those in areas where fewer people go to school, migrants from these regions were divided on the basis of the level of education in their Local Authority area rather than on the size of their place of origin.

In table 5.5 'educated' refers to those who have at least attended middle school. There were relatively few men in the survey who only attended primary or Muslim schools and most of these were there for too short a time to be functionally literate and/or lacked literacy in English. They have therefore been included with the uneducated.

The hypothesis of differences between educated and uneducated migrants is confirmed in that uneducated men from rural Central, Western and Ashanti Regions moved first within their own region more often than did the educated men of rural origin or the uneducated men of urban origin. Differences between the uneducated and educated migrants of urban origin were in the expected direction but too small to be significant. Differences between those from high- and low-education areas of Eastern and Volta Regions were also small. The uneducated from high-education areas were somewhat more likely than the educated to go first to a place in their own

K

TABLE 5.5. *First move of migrant urban male workers by place of origin and education (percentages)*

Education and region/country of origin	Same region		Different region			Total	N
	Rural	Urban	Rural	Accra	Other urban		
Uneducated[a]							
Accra C.D.	0	35	18	—	47	100	17
Eastern, Volta							
High education	15	16	4	50	15	100	26
Low education	15	7	6	50	22	100	33
Central, Western, Ashanti[b]							
Urban	14	8	8	31	39	100	36
Rural	9	36	6	23	26	100	65
Northern, Upper	2	0	21	22	55	100	53
Upper Volta, Mali, Niger	0	0	12	42	46	100	68
Togo, Dahomey	3	4	12	61	20	100	94
Nigeria	4	11	12	35	38	100	26
Educated[c]							
Accra C.D.	3	34	16	—	47	100	38
Eastern, Volta							
High education	15	8	9	51	17	100	105
Low education	12	11	6	57	14	100	138
Central, Western, Ashanti[b]							
Urban	13	6	12	39	30	100	94
Rural	9	21	8	30	32	100	166
Togo, Dahomey	11	7	4	60	18	100	27
Nigeria	0	19	0	50	31	100	16

[a] Had not attended middle school.　　[b] Includes a few from Brong/Ahafo.
[c] Northern Ghana and countries to the north have been omitted because there were only 3 educated men from this area.

region, whereas middle-school leavers from low-education areas were somewhat more likely than the uneducated to go straight to Accra, the primary focus of migration from these regions. The uneducated in high-education areas are probably more aware of the disability of lack of schooling than are those in low-education areas. On the other hand, the educated in low-education areas probably have less understanding than those in high-education areas of the devaluation of the Middle School Leaving Certificate due to the oversupply of middle-school leavers in Accra.

Uneducated men from northern Ghana, countries to the north and Togo had seldom spent any time away from home but within their own regions. Opportunities for wage-earning there are rare and those who want jobs must look elsewhere. Those who want to farm stay at home. But while many northern Ghanaians went first to work on Ashanti cocoa farms, migrants from countries to the north of Ghana and from Togo headed for the towns. There are, of course, many thousands of Voltaics working on Ghanaian cocoa farms, but these are mostly short-term migrants and few of them ever move into the towns. The evidence here (and for career migration, below) suggests that most of those working in the towns went there directly and not after a period of seasonal labour in a rural area.

Migrants from rural places in central and southwestern Ghana were, if anything, less likely than those from towns to move to a village on first leaving home. This applies to both the educated and the uneducated and to moves within and outside the home region. Presumably, someone living in a village can farm at home and therefore few migrate to another rural place.

TABLE 5.6. *Type of first move by year of first migration, urban males originating in Ghana (percentages)*

Moved to	1920– 1949	1950– 1954	1955– 1959	1960– 1966/7	Total
Same region					
Rural–rural	8	12	9	4	7
Rural–urban	14	13	13	8	11
Urban–urban	3	4	3	3	3
Urban–rural	7	5	5	2	4
Other region					
Rural–rural	6	9	7	4	6
Rural–urban	33	35	39	54	44
Urban–urban	26	15	20	23	22
Urban–rural	3	7	4	2	3
Total	100	100	100	100	100
N	117	104	203	351	775

In every time period, the majority of first moves were to urban places, usually in another region (see table 5.6). This indicates that migrants who come to the cities have seldom 'tried their wings' by living for a time in a village or small town near their homes. They are a self-selected group who are drawn to urban life from the beginning.

There has been remarkable continuity over time in the type of first move which was made. Although this sample is not representative of moves made before 1950, the pattern for these earlier moves appears to be very similar to moves in the 1950s. In the 1960s there has been a decrease in the proportion of migrants who moved from rural places to towns and villages within their own region and an increase in the proportion who moved from villages to towns in other regions. This is a necessary result of the sample being largely based in Accra and Tema. Some of those who first moved within their own region in the past six years will decide at some future date to move on to Accra.

However, there may well have been an increase in interregional movement to the cities in the 1960s. With the expansion of the educational system, a relatively high proportion of intending migrants have completed middle school. These are more likely than the illiterates to head for the cities. The stable or declining economic situation in the country in the 1960s has probably affected opportunities in Accra and Tema less than elsewhere, and this has no doubt increased the pace of migration to the Capital District. Most of Tema's growth also has taken place during this period, and this has proved an additional attraction.

MIGRATION CAREERS

The main difficulties in using these data in describing migration careers are that they represent workers at different points in their careers (we do not know what the future movements of the young men will be) and that they represent workers who were living in the city at a given time (we do not know about the migration careers of workers who had not yet arrived in the city or who had already left). These limitations mean that we must be careful in drawing conclusions from the data. Nevertheless, they have been presented in spite of these biases because they point to certain aspects of migration which seem worthy of future study.

Migration patterns have been characterized as of six types. Direct migration implies movement from home to the town in which the worker was interviewed without residence in any other place. Some of these have gone home for a period since first moving to the town, but they have not gone elsewhere. 'Side direct' involves movement to another place in the same size category as one's hometown before moving to the survey town, e.g. moving from Akropong to Aburi (both under 5,000 population) and then to Accra. A few Nigerians did the 'side' moving at the top; they moved from their hometowns to Lagos and then to Accra. 'Step' migration implies gradual movement up the hierarchy of size; a man moves from Mampong, Ashanti (a small town) to Kumasi and then to Accra or from Elmina to Tarkwa (a mining town) and then to Takoradi. 'Side step' migration involves an additional move to a place of the same size at some point. Some men who taught moved from one village to another, then to a town before moving to Accra.

Those who showed a 'reverse' pattern moved down the size hierarchy of places at some point. Most of these moved from Accra or Kumasi to Tema or from Accra to Kumasi, but there were others who worked in a town, then were transferred or found a job in a village (not their hometown) before moving to the survey city.[1] An example can be given of a man who had made several reverse moves. He was a Ga carpenter of thirty-four who completed an apprenticeship in Accra by the age of seventeen. He then moved to a village in Central Region to work for a contractor for a year. He continued to work for the same employer for nine months in Winneba (a town in Central Region), for a total of $3\frac{1}{2}$ years in three villages in different regions, for six months in Abidjan, six months in Bamako, nine months in a village in Eastern Region and a year in Lomé. He then returned to Accra, having lived in ten places including three foreign countries by the time he was twenty-six.

Lastly, there is 'in and out' migration. This characterized men who moved to Accra (or the other cities) and then went off and worked elsewhere, later returning to the city where they were interviewed. Men in these last two types may also have been direct, step or side migrants, but it was thought best to put them in a separate category because of the increased complexity of their migration patterns. In allotting individuals to migration types, returns home were ignored. This included both birthplace and the place where they grew up if these were different.

As shown in table 5.7, nearly half of the migrants had come directly to the survey city and not moved again, though the proportion was higher for Accra and Tema migrants (49%) than for those in the provincial cities (42%). This is contrary to what one would expect, since some men work for a time in provincial cities before moving on to Accra or Tema, but it indicates that a large number of migrants to the Capital District are drawn by its greater job opportunities and do not 'waste time' trying other centres. An additional factor is the nearness of Eastern and Volta Regions, which contributed almost two-fifths of Accra/Tema migrants. Men from these regions were more likely to migrate directly than men from southwestern or central Ghana, even when the latter were going to the nearest city.

An illustration of the relationship between propinquity and direct migration is the higher proportion of direct migrants from rural Central and Western Regions to Takoradi and from rural Ashanti and northern Ghana to Kumasi than the proportions from these regions who migrated directly to Accra/Tema. Men from Eastern and Volta Regions, on the other hand,

---

[1] It should be pointed out that a move down the size hierarchy is not necessarily a move to a less urbanized place. Tema is smaller than Kumasi but sociologically more 'urban', as will be shown in chapter 6.

TABLE 5.7. *Career migration by origin of worker and location of firm, migrant urban male workers (percentages)*

Worker's origin	Direct	Side direct	Step	Side step	Reverse	In and out	Total	N
Total sample	46	10	11	2	22	9	100	1,005
Accra C.D.	16	4	0	2	69	9	100	55
Eastern, Volta								
High education[a]	44	14	14	1	20	7	100	131
Other	57	12	12	3	14	2	100	171
Central, Western, Ashanti								
Urban	39	8	2	0	48	3	100	130
Rural	38	13	23	5	15	6	100	231
Northern, Upper	42	16	25	2	13	2	100	55
Outside Ghana	58	11	13	1	11	6	100	232
Accra/Tema sample								
Accra C.D.	16	4	0	2	69	9	100	51
Eastern, Volta								
High education[a]	44	14	15	1	18	8	100	122
Other	59	13	11	4	11	2	100	160
Central, Western, Ashanti								
Urban	44	12	0	0	42	2	100	91
Rural	35	11	26	5	18	5	100	146
Northern, Upper	32	21	23	3	18	3	100	34
Outside Ghana	60	10	16	0	7	7	100	174
Provincial sample								
Eastern, Volta, Accra C.D.	30	8	8	0	50	4	100	24
Central, Western, Ashanti								
Urban	26	0	8	0	61	5	100	39
Rural	44	16	15	5	11	9	100	85
Northern, Upper	57	9	29	0	5	0	100	21
Outside Ghana	50	16	3	5	24	2	100	58

[a] Four local councils in Eastern Region and three in Volta Region with the highest proportions of the population in school.

seldom migrated directly to the provincial towns; very few went there at all. Only 7 % of the men in the sample from these regions were in the provincial towns.

Migrants from towns in southwestern and central Ghana were more likely to migrate directly to Accra than to Takoradi or Kumasi. They showed the reverse pattern much more often than other men. There is a relatively high proportion of urban–rural migration on first moves originating in these areas. Reverses were generally more frequent in the provincial sample, which may be related to the higher average age of the provincial workers. The difference in the proportion of reverses between Accra/Tema and provincial workers was greater for migrants from Eastern and Volta Regions than for other southern Ghanaians, who were better represented in the provincial towns, so it may be due to the small size of the provincial sample.

Men originating in a town are more likely than those starting in a village to show the reverse pattern because destinations that would be 'side' or a step up the size hierarchy for a man of rural origin are 'reverse' for a man of urban origin. Two-thirds of the migrants who grew up in the Capital District had the 'reverse' pattern. Since most of these started in Accra, any move within Ghana was to a place of smaller size.

The proportions of migrants showing the 'side direct', 'step' and 'side step' patterns were about the same regardless of the place of origin or of interview, with the exception that southern Ghanaians originating in towns were less likely to show these patterns than those from rural areas. It was thought that the step pattern of migration would be a useful way of accommodating to urban living. It often fulfils this function among migrants to Stanleyville (Pons 1969: 46) and in Sierra Leone,[1] but apparently is seldom used in Ghana. Educated southern Ghanaians (in the sense used in table 5.5

TABLE 5.8. *Career migration by present age and age and year of arrival, migrant urban males (percentages)*

	Direct	Side direct	Step	Side step	Reverse	In and out	Total	N
Present age								
18–24	61	6	12	2	16	3	100	253
25–29	43	12	13	1	25	6	100	285
30–34	42	11	11	1	26	9	100	187
35–39	34	12	7	5	29	13	100	128
40+	29	10	5	2	36	18	100	152
Age at arrival[a]								
15–24[b]	56	7	12	1	19	5	100	618
25–29	29	16	9	4	33	9	100	197
30–34	20	15	7	3	37	18	100	109
35–39	20	13	7	4	31	25	100	45
40+	14	6	6	0	41	33	100	36
Year of arrival[a]								
1920–49	60	5	0	2	25	8	100	60
1950–4	55	10	7	0	22	6	100	90
1955–9	45	10	13	2	21	9	100	186
1960–7	43	10	11	2	25	9	100	669
Total	46	10	11	2	22	9	100	1,005

[a] Age and year of latest arrival for those who have come more than once.
[b] A few arrived before they were 15.

[1] K. Swindell, personal communication.

of those who had attended middle school) showed the step pattern more often than the uneducated, but the difference is made up by the increased use of 'side step' migration by the uneducated. There were no other pattern differences between educated and uneducated migrants.

Most migrants are young. The most usual time for migration is early adulthood, when the need is felt for employment which will produce the money for bridewealth, household goods and status in society. Early reports on African migrants (e.g. Mitchell 1951) indicated that most migrants had returned home by the age of forty-five. Many had made their last trip by the age of thirty-five. However, recent developments in the economy have encouraged many older as well as younger men to migrate. Only half of the workers who were twenty-five or older had moved for the last time before they were twenty-five and two-fifths of the men over forty had moved since they were thirty-five.

Some young men had moved several times within a short period. For example, a grinder had moved from his home in Kumasi to Winneba on the coast at the age of eighteen. After eight months there, he moved to a village in the same region and farmed for five months before moving to Tema. Another operative had moved from a small town in Volta Region to Kumasi at the age of eighteen. After three years there, spent working as a tally clerk, he moved to an Ashanti village where he served as a clinic assistant for a year, then spent three months as a levy collector in another village before moving to Tema at the age of twenty-two.

A quarter of the urban migrants under twenty years of age had already moved twice, though none had moved more than that (see table 5.8). Two-fifths of the migrants between twenty and twenty-four years of age had lived in three or more places. Among older men, the proportion who had made more than one move was fairly stable. It was 53 % for those between twenty-five and thirty-four and 58 % for older men. However, nearly a third of the men over thirty-five had moved more than twice. This is the generation that was in the army; some of them travelled as far as South Africa and Burma. The proportion of migrants between the ages of twenty and thirty-four who had made more than two moves is about half the rate of the older men.

As expected, the proportion of direct migration decreases with age. The decrease is sharpest between the under-twenty-fives and those who are older. The effect of age on migration patterns is more evident in age at arrival than in present age. This is especially notable in the figures for direct and 'in and out' migration. Only a quarter of the men who arrived in the city after the age of twenty-four had come directly from home and a third of the men who arrived after the age of forty had lived there at some time in the past and were returning for a second or third stay.

Some men continue migrating after most of their colleagues have settled down. This is particularly true of watchmen. A Tema watchman of fifty-five had been a shepherd and farmer in Upper Volta until he was about twenty-five. He then left home and spent five years on an Ashanti cocoa farm and ten years at the Akwatia diamond mine. After a year as a labourer in Accra, he moved to Eastern Region and spent three years farming, then returned to Accra for another three years. He farmed for three more years in Central Region before moving to Tema in 1960, when he was in his late forties. These cases are rather unusual. Most of the older men had lived in the city for a long time. Less than a quarter of the men who were over forty at the time of the survey had moved since reaching that age.

It might be argued that multiple migration should decline with time and the spread of knowledge about living in towns, which is allied to the spread of mass communications and improvements in transportation as well as to the increasing proportion of young people who migrate. As potential migrants now often have friends and/or kinsmen in various towns and are able to get there in relative comfort, they have a better command of the decision factors than former migrants had and, having chosen what they consider the best place, they should be able to remain there throughout their working lives. However, the third section of table 5.8 belies this argument. Recent migrants were less likely than earlier migrants to have migrated directly to the place where they were interviewed.

This seems to contradict the age data, which shows that young migrants (who must have come recently) tended to arrive direct from their homes. However, many older migrants were also recent arrivals. Only half of those who arrived in the 1960s were under twenty-five. What seems to have happened is that many men who were working elsewhere in Ghana in the late 1950s and early 1960s found either that local opportunities were drying up or that opportunities in the Capital District were so much better than those available locally that they moved again in order to participate. It may also be that there has been an increased willingness in recent years to try the nearest town before moving to the big city, though table 5.6 does not indicate it. Four-fifths of the step migrants of the 1960s were under twenty-five. Unfortunately, we do not have enough data to be sure.

Although migration often involves occupational mobility, so that moves may be related to past occupational experience rather than to present job, certain migratory patterns are characteristic of workers in certain occupations. Unskilled workers were more often direct migrants and less often non-migrants than other workers. This is related to the high proportion of direct migrants among workers originating outside Ghana. Semiskilled workers, who have often done clerical work in the past, are very similar to lower clerical workers in the amount and type of migration they had experienced. Very few of the higher clerical workers were direct migrants. They were more likely than the others to be non-migrants (all of the higher clerical workers in Kumasi had grown up there), but those who had moved had done so more often than other workers. Two-thirds of the higher clerical workers had moved more than once. This is partly due to their background in teaching and storekeeping, but it is also probably true that moving up the hierarchy in clerical work often involves transfers from one office to another.

REASONS FOR MIGRATION

It has often been reported that most men migrate to find work which is un-available at home or will pay better than work which can be found at home. (See, for example, Gulliver 1957, Skinner 1960, and Caldwell 1969.) Migrants may express this by saying that they needed work or by mentioning the goal – money for consumer goods, a bigger farm, a better house, or bridewealth. Labour migration is well entrenched in the society; most young school leavers and a large number of young men who have not attended school take it for granted that they will leave home sooner or later. Since it could safely be assumed that most men migrate to improve their standard of living, the questions asked of migrant factory workers were: 'Why did you decide to move to — [this city] instead of going someplace else?' and 'Why did you decide to come to — just at that time?'

Three-quarters of the urban workers (84% of Kumasi workers and 89% of the rural workers) said they chose their destination because of its reputation for jobs. Typical comments were: 'Friends informed me of the many factories here', 'I heard Accra had all the jobs' and 'I heard of people being employed here so I rushed as I had worked too long in the mines.' A Tema worker was even more emphatic: 'Almost all the jobs in the country have been piled in Tema.' A Hausa baker said, 'There were no clothes at my place and we came to work and buy some.' A Togolese sander 'wanted to work in a factory or with a whiteman'. Others came for schooling or apprenticeships which would eventually lead to jobs. A tailor reported, 'My father's brother called me to teach me how to sew. He was in Accra.'

Some young people not yet ready for employment are drawn to the cities by the chance of extending their education. Post-middle day schools (second-ary, commercial and technical) are concentrated in the cities, especially in

Accra, and expenses are considerably lower at these than at boarding schools. Many young middle-school leavers come to the cities each year hoping to continue their education while supporting themselves as stewards, car cleaners, or with other casual work. Accra's Muslim schools also draw students to the city. A baker 'was brought to a Muslim school here because it was supposed to be the best around'.[1]

Of the other factors which influence choice of destination, the main one is knowing someone with whom to stay while looking for work. Migrants often have little money beyond the lorry fare, and it may take several weeks (in recent years, several months) to find work. Meanwhile, food costs money and it is preferable to sleep under a roof rather than in the market or lorry park. Therefore, most intending migrants consider only places where they have contacts. Between 30% and 40% of the workers in each city (but only 15% of the rural workers) mentioned this as a factor in their choice and relatively few of the urban migrants knew no one in town when they moved there.

TABLE 5.9. *Prospective migrants' contacts at their destinations (percentages)*

Relationship	Accra	Tema	Kumasi	Takoradi	Rural
Parent, spouse, sibling[a]	39	36	34	51	21
Other kinsmen	35	31	31	27	26
Fellow townsman, tribesman or other friend	24	23	24	18	10
No contacts	8	13	13	8	44
Total[b]	106	103	102	104	101
N	588	235	110	108	105

[a] A few moved to town with the person mentioned.
[b] Totals are over 100% because of multiple responses.

It had been expected that there would be far more migrants to Tema than to the other cities who knew no one, but apparently this is not the case (see table 5.9). Tema is a new town, but housing is in very short supply. It appears that many prospective migrants choose between Tema and Accra by the availability of someone with whom to stay. If a young man has a 'brother' or other relative in Tema or a school friend working there, he may go to Tema to look for work. If not, he will probably choose Accra instead, since he is far more likely to have a contact in Accra. However, the typical Tema migrant (a young school leaver of urban background) may well be

[1] La Fontaine (1970: 105) found that many recent migrants to Kinshasa came to continue their education.

better able to cope with migration to a town in which he knows no one than is the average migrant to the other cities.

Rural migrants, on the other hand, must often be content to go to places where they are unknown. Over two-fifths of the rural migrants did not know anyone at their destination. Living in a small town or village requires less adaptation from the migrant and it is probably easier to get to know one's neighbours and workmates in such a place than in the city.

Size of place of origin apparently does not affect the decision to migrate to a place where one is unknown. Those from villages were as likely as those from towns or cities to migrate to a city in which they had no contacts. However, workers in Accra and Tema who had come from other cities (Kumasi, Takoradi, Lagos) were more likely than those from smaller places to know only a friend when they arrived. This may be because city-dwellers feel freer to migrate where they have no relatives because the extended family has been less important to them than to villagers.

It was thought that those for whom life in town would be the greatest contrast with life at home would be most likely to move to a place where they had relatives and/or friends. This turned out to be the case. Non-Ghanaians and migrants from northern Ghana more often said they chose their city because they knew someone there than did southern Ghanaians. The desire to go where there are kinsmen or townsmen[1] extends beyond the need for a place to stay. A labourer from Niger said he came to Accra 'to be near fellow tribesmen so as to hear home news quickly'. Contacts are also an encouragement to migrate farther than one would otherwise go. Half of the migrants from Eastern and Volta Regions and the Capital District who were working in Kumasi or Takoradi said they went there because they knew someone, compared to 35 % of the migrants from these regions working in Accra and Tema. Very few Asante working in Kumasi went there because they knew someone. Of course, many more people have friends and relatives in town than go there because of these friends and relatives. They may provide an extra benefit rather than a major reason for choice. This would certainly be the case for Asante working in Kumasi.

In some cases, the choice is made by the relative rather than by the migrant. Responses such as 'My father's brother called me' or 'I went to join my husband' indicate that the individual did not freely select his destination and perhaps was not even free to choose whether or not to migrate. Relatives may find a job and then write for the young man to come. This is cheaper than having him living in town while the search for work is made. Experienced migrants sometimes bring their young relatives with them when

[1] 'Townsmen' is used here in the sense common in Ghana, as men from one's hometown.

they return to town from a visit home. If they are self-employed, the boy may be destined to help them in their business, frequently in exchange for training. This may or may not involve a formal apprenticeship.

Caldwell (1969: 80) shows that dependence on relatives often develops into chain migration. As one man settles in town, he is joined by other members of his family. The larger the number of members of a family who are living in town, the greater the chance that others will join them. The same process operates for villages as for families. A northerner said, 'My townsmen come mostly to Accra.' A young man from Volta Region said, 'Many youths from my hometown go to Accra so I also wanted to come and see for myself.' A casual visit to a relative may result in a longer stay. A Togolese baker said, 'I came to visit my brother and when I saw there was a vacancy in this bakery, I stayed.' Thus, the first migrant from the village or the family chooses a place because of available jobs. Later, members go because he is there and, still later, contacts can be taken for granted and most people wanting work head for that town. Community norms support such directed migration, because it is easier for the village to maintain contact with and control over migrants if they are concentrated in one place.

The attraction of city life was mentioned far less often than work or relatives. About 7% said either that they wanted to see and live in the capital or that they had chosen the nearest city (in the case of rural workers, the nearest factory) to their hometowns. The pull of city life, like the desire to travel (which characterizes many Ghanaians) is a factor in the decision to migrate more than in the choice of destination, which was emphasized in the question they were asked. Insofar as 'bright lights' affect destination, presumably the migrant should be pulled to the largest city in the country. There are certainly some young men who are attracted by the bright lights of the city, but they form a relatively small proportion of the total number of migrants.

There is some evidence that this attitude characterizes young men from towns more than those in the villages. Men from Kumasi, Takoradi and Suhum (which has over 10,000 population) said they left because their hometowns were boring, and a man from Koforidua (with a population of over 34,000) said, 'only Accra is alive'. Village schoolboys do sometimes express a desire to experience life in a big city. However, their actual choice of a town and their reaction to the town when they get there is more often based on the work it provides. Their wages may permit them very little contact with urban high life (Duodu 1967). At least as common is the attitude that jobs are found in cities and the nearest city to one's hometown should be chosen so that contacts with home can be easily maintained.

Precipitating factors are mainly centred on the completion of schooling, arrangements of relatives, the collapse of work at home, notification of a job in town and the availability of money for migration. Typical comments were, 'I was of age and had to migrate to prepare my future', 'That was the time my father had money to finance my migration', 'My sister called me then', 'It was the dry season and there was no farming to do' and 'I came alone with some townsmen who were going then.' There were several labourers in Takoradi who had prepared their cocoa farms and then left them to foreign sharecroppers while they went to town to increase their income. The end of the farming season frequently signals the time to migrate. Some young men reported that they got fed up with farming after a year or two. Young men often object to farming with their fathers when the latter maintain tight control of the proceeds. When the harvest is in, they may be able to persuade their fathers to give them a small sum to finance migration.

An awareness of advancing age occasionally sparks the decision to leave home. A man who had fished for twenty-one years said he suddenly realized that he was getting old and still didn't 'have a job'. This type of migration has not been mentioned in the literature, which is chiefly concerned with the selective migration of educated young men. It would be worth further study, to provide a better understanding of this stage of the life cycle.

Family breakup sometimes precipitates migration. One man reported that the 'father supporting me very much died', and another said, 'My mother left father that year and I had to join father for company.' Some women migrated immediately after a divorce; many others moved to town with their husbands or families. A few young men just wanted to leave home. One said he spent too much money at home and wanted to save. The decision to migrate often involves weighing up the advantages of living at home, where room and board are provided, against living in town and having control over one's earnings. Although relatives often make demands on the urban wage earner (as discussed in chapter 7), these are less frequent than if he were working at home. Fortes (1947:164) gives examples of Asante cocoa farmers who could not save unless they farmed away from their relatives.

SUMMARY

The high proportion of migrants among factory workers has provided an opportunity for examining the types of migration characteristic of southern Ghanaian urbanites. Less than half of the workers had grown up in villages of less than 5,000 population. Most of them originated in the region in which they were interviewed or in contiguous regions. There are few northern Ghanaians working in factories and the proportion of non-Ghanaians in this type of work is lower than the proportion they form of the urban population. Tema has a higher proportion of migrants than the other cities because of its recent origin.

Details have been given of the direction and types of primary and later migration. Movement into the cities usually involves crossing regional boundaries. About half of the migrants moved more than once. Migrants tend to go in the same direction in their first and later moves, but secondary migration involves more moves across regional boundaries than primary migration. Uneducated migrants of rural origin are more likely than the educated or those of urban origin to stay within their home region on a first move, but this depends on the opportunities available in a given locality. Almost all of the migrants from northern Ghana and Volta Region left their regions on the first move regardless of their education or the size of place in which they grew up. Considerable intraregional migration occurs in these areas, but it does not appear to lead to subsequent migration to the cities (or at least to the urban factories) of the south.

Of the types of migration career discussed, direct migration was by far the most common, characterizing over half the moves to each of the cities studied if the 'reverse' and 'in and out' moves which were initially direct are included (i.e. if those who moved from home to Accra, worked elsewhere, and subsequently returned to Accra are counted as direct rather than 'in and out' migration). Migrants to Accra were more likely to go directly there than were migrants to Tema, but this is partly because Tema is of recent creation. Movements to places of the same size and step migration culminating in a move to a city were relatively rare. More people moved to places of smaller size than to places of successively larger size. Having arrived in a city, relatively few people leave it for another city or, if they leave to work in another place (not their hometown), very few return to the city for another stay.

While economic factors are of primary importance in the decision to migrate and in the choice of destination, personal and social factors are also influential. Choice of a destination is chiefly based on its reputation for providing jobs, though knowing someone with whom to stay and distance from home are also important. Only about a tenth of urban migrants knew no one at their destinations, though many who have contacts do not give this as the primary reason for their choice of a place to go. Quite a few migrants have their destination chosen for them because they are sent for, or taken by family or relatives who are already established in town, or are transferred by employers. The 'lure of the town' is a factor in the decision of some young men to leave home, but is certainly much less important than the desire for wage employment.

CHAPTER 6

URBAN LIVING

Migrants face many problems after their arrival in town. They may stay with relatives for a time, but sooner or later they must find a room of their own. This may be located near their relatives, but the shortage of low-rent accommodation means that they may have to move to some other part of the city. As time goes on, they will also find new friends, though the breadth of this network will vary with their background and attitude toward city life. Most of them will marry, if they have not done so already, and encounter the difficulties of bringing up children in town. Most will plan for an eventual return to their hometowns. Like or dislike for city living may have little effect on how long a migrant stays, since the economic reason for being in town remains constant. Most migrants have mixed feelings about the city.

REACTIONS TO CITY LIFE

Workers were asked what they liked best about living in the city and what they liked least. These were open questions; workers could name as many reasons as they chose, but most gave only one answer to each question (see table 6.1). Those living in Kumasi were most favourable in the sense that nearly half said they liked everything or mentioned specific things they liked but could not specify anything they disliked about living in Kumasi. Workers in Tema were least favourable; nearly two-fifths said they liked nothing or mentioned specific things they disliked but could not name any aspect of Tema which they liked. Those in Accra most often had both specific likes and dislikes.

As was expected, given the migrants' primary motivation, the reason most often given for liking the place where they were living was the possibility of getting work there (or the money paid for work). Half of the Kumasi workers and nearly two-fifths of those in Accra had never been out of work for more than a month. Two confident men summed up the feelings of many, 'There are plenty of jobs if you know your contacts' and 'There are a lot of jobs for those who are not lazy.' Work was mentioned much more often

TABLE 6.1. *Migrants' positive and negative feelings about the place in which they are living (percentages)*[a]

	Accra	Tema	Kumasi	Takoradi	Rural
Likes					
Work available	46	20	13	25	40
Living in a city	14	9	19	30	—
Supplies, amenities available	8	16	34	2	16[b]
Relatives, friends here	4	2	4	11	9
Other	9	14	5	13	19
Everything, nothing, DK	19	39	25	19	16
Total	100	100	100	100	100
Dislikes					
Cost of living	56	63	8	43	16
Housing	4	13	13	2	5
Thieves, low morals	2	1	13	19	0
Other	14	6	14	14	69[c]
Nothing, DK	24	18	52	30	16
Total	100	101	100	108	106
N	630	252	118	123	106

[a] Some totals are over 100 % because of multiple responses.
[b] These referred to the low cost of living.
[c] 55 % mentioned lack of amenities.

in Accra than in the other towns; this is probably an accurate assessment of the opportunities available. It was mentioned more often at the rural factory that was hiring workers than at the one that was laying them off, but some of the workers at the latter took into account the needs of other local employers. There is certainly a greater variety of jobs available in Accra than elsewhere and new openings in industry or construction are likely to be in Accra or its environs, regardless of recent talk of decentralization.

The most frequent source of complaint in Accra, Tema and Takoradi was the cost of living. It is hard to get used to paying for everything, but the increasing need for cash in the villages of southern Ghana mediates this change for many migrants. Complaints about the cost of living were most frequent among workers from the north and outside Ghana, for whom the change was greatest and who had the lowest wages. It was of more concern to men than to women and to family men than to young unmarried men who needed to support only themselves. In the provincial towns, where the cost of living was less of a problem, the lowest-paid workers were more likely to complain of it than were workers making over NC20 per month. In Accra, on the other hand, three-quarters of the workers making less than NC46 complained of the cost of living, compared to less than half of the workers making more than this. It evidently takes much more money to be satisfied in Accra than elsewhere.

TABLE 6.2 *Consumer price index for selected towns and rural areas, 1965–8*[a]

Place	1965 Nov.	1966 March	1966 Nov.	1967 March	1968 March
Total					
Accra	152.0	151.3	143.6	139.7	142.7
Kumasi	153.1	159.2	143.2	140.9	144.3
Takoradi	162.5	177.6	171.0	137.4	147.3
Rural	158.9	172.1	167.0	158.9	164.1
Local food					
Accra	165.3	165.6	153.0	139.9	129.4
Kumasi	179.0	181.2	158.0	152.3	146.1
Takoradi	180.7	190.4	191.2	141.5	148.2
Rural	181.9	195.8	190.5	175.2	177.3

SOURCES: Central Bureau of Statistics, *Quarterly digest of statistics*, XV (December 1966), XVI (March 1967) and XVII (March 1968).
[a] March 1963 = 100.

When the survey was carried out in Accra and Tema in 1966, prices had risen 50% in the past three years with no increase in the basic wage (see table 6.2). The increase was even higher in the provincial towns and rural areas.[1] Although food and many consumer goods are cheaper in Accra than elsewhere, rents are higher there and wages tend to be lower for the same type of work (see table 3.11 above). In addition, the very availability of goods means that Accra workers are made aware of their relative deprivation – there are so many things they cannot afford to buy. The consumption pattern of the elite, which is largely centred in Accra, probably adds to the dissatisfaction of ordinary workers there. Some Accra workers complained bitterly that they had come only for money and could not save any.

There was a slight decline in prices between mid-1966 and mid-1967, followed by relative stabilization. The fewer complaints about the cost of living in the provincial towns may be due to the recent decline when the workers were interviewed there in April 1967, as well as to their relatively good economic position in comparison to other residents of provincial towns and the surrounding countryside.

Prices had also declined in rural areas, but the rural index was still higher

[1] See Killick (1966:140–1) for a discussion of wage rates and the cost of living over a longer period.

in March 1968 (after the decline) than in Accra in 1965 (at its peak). Most people expect prices to be lower in the villages than in the cities, especially food prices, but transport costs and increases accompanying break-in-bulk mean that anything not produced in the village will be more expensive there (Lawson 1966:40). Southern Ghanaians have had several generations to develop a taste for imported goods and their consumption patterns assume the availability of sugar, flour, milk, corned beef etc. from abroad. Some of these items are now produced locally, but this has not lowered their cost to the villager. Workers in rural areas who cannot do some farming on the side are subject to the same or greater expenses for purchasing food as urban workers. Two-thirds of the rural workers who commented favourably on the cost of living and all of those who commented unfavourably on it were migrants.

Having arrived in the city, many migrants find urban life to their liking. They enjoy being able to attend films, dances or football matches, and the sense of knowing what is going on. As a tailor put it, one is 'able to witness many prominent events taking place in the capital, not hearsay' (no need to depend on rumours). However, participation in organized entertainment is probably limited to a rather small minority. The advantages of living in a city were commented on more often in Takoradi than in Kumasi or Accra, which are much larger and offer more in the way of 'bright lights'.

Other Takoradi workers disliked these same aspects of the urban environment. Nine percent of them said they did not like the dances and/or film shows and several there and in Tema commented that peace was more to their liking: 'Tema is quiet and I prefer a quiet life.' About 13 % of the workers in provincial towns complained about thieves, fighting, excess drinking etc. Very few (only 2 %) of Accra workers mentioned these aspects of urban life and those who did were usually natives of Accra. Most Takoradi workers had come from villages; few had lived in another large town or city. Thus, Takoradi was very large by their standards though it seems like a small town to people accustomed to cities of developed countries. It seems likely that many long-term migrants to Takoradi do not develop the sophistication which is fairly common in Accra and Kumasi, which are not only larger but more central to national life.

Many people value more highly the amenities of the town – water, electricity, schools, hospitals and stores – than they do the entertainment facilities. Though these may seem to be poorly provided in comparison with industrialized countries, they are often entirely lacking in African villages and small towns and are a considerable inducement to migration to and stabilization in the cities. The lack of such amenities was an important cause for complaint among rural workers; it was mentioned by over half of them, non-migrants as well as migrants.

In addition to electricity and medical services, there are more consumer goods on show in the towns than villagers could imagine. Even though these have been in very short supply in recent years, the goods that do arrive go to Accra stores first, so there is a greater likelihood of being able to buy what you want in Accra than up-country. It is thus interesting that Kumasi workers were four times as likely to mention amenities as something they liked about Kumasi than Accra workers were in relation to their city. This may be partly because residents of Accra *expect* to have all amenities available to them, but it is also because of the concentration among Accra responses on the availability of work. Most people gave only one answer, and work was most salient for Accra workers.

Not all the comments on amenities were favourable. There were complaints about water shortages (which are frequent in Accra), the paucity of public latrines, inadequate medical and social facilities, the poor transportation system and the difficulty of getting food. Inadequate food supplies were a particular problem in Tema prior to the *coup*, but there are periodic shortages of food in all towns because of the delay in granting import licenses and the poor condition of the roads during the rainy season.

The majority of the workers spend less than half an hour on the journey to work. Nevertheless, those who are dependent on city buses or mammy lorries often find the service inadequate, especially in wet weather. Municipal bus systems are characterized by frequent breakdowns, limited routes and a demand for service which far exceeds the number of buses available. This has been a persistent problem. (See, for example, comments in the *Ashanti Pioneer* of the early 1950s on the Kumasi bus system.) 'Trotro' passenger lorries run by private entrepreneurs are used more often than municipal bus services because the former run more frequently and cover a wider variety of routes. One-third of the Accra workers walk to work; over half take lorries. In Tema, there are about equal numbers of walkers and those who ride lorries. Most of the provincial and rural workers walk to work. The cost of transport seldom exceeds 5 new pesewas per day in the cities, but most of those at firm Q who rode paid between 10 and 20 new pesewas a day (5–10p) in fares. Many workers walk to avoid the expense. Worker demands that employers should supply transport are an obvious reaction to the situation, but few employers can provide such a service.

The literature on urban life often mentions its anonymity and the problems of adjustment which sometimes result in anomie. Migrants are said to lack the support of family and friends. Even though they have relatives in town, these may live some distance away and be visited only on special occasions (Leslie 1963). Such a situation does not seem to be characteristic of Ghanaian cities, where there is a considerable amount of visiting with friends and relatives in town and (especially if the hometown is within a day's travel) fairly frequent visits to and from home as well (see chapter 7). Where workers commented on this aspect of urban life, it was usually with appreciation rather than the reverse. 'I like Accra because it makes me learn to solve my own problems alone.' 'Everybody here cares for himself.' 'Nobody interferes with his fellow's life.' They do not feel alone: '. . . there are many people around'. Only sixteen workers in Accra and Tema mentioned interpersonal conflicts, including ethnic and family problems, disrespectful children and lack of friends. Five times that many (both migrants and non-migrants) said they liked living in the city because they had relatives and/or friends there. They will probably have fewer close friends than at home and their networks will be loose rather than close-meshed (Mitchell 1969), but this does not necessarily mean that the friendships are less satisfying.

The important point here is that city life allows the migrant to choose his associates to a far greater extent than would be possible in the village. Kinship obligations may be called for by men so distantly related that they would hardly be considered kin at home, but obligations may also be neglected to an extent that would result in a severe reprimand at home. A man can spend all of his free time with kinsmen and townsmen, or he can choose friends from a wider range and see kinsmen only occasionally. He can be selective in which kinsmen or townsmen he sees. Only the elite can afford to cut their ties completely and very few of them do so, but there are many men who appreciate the freedom urban life gives them to avoid people they do not get on with and to be alone when they prefer solitude.

Inter-ethnic relations did not appear to be a salient problem. Only four men mentioned ethnic attitudes. Three were Ewes who said there was 'tribal feeling' and the fourth, a Ga (the local tribe in Accra) said that the local people were hard on foreigners. Another Ewe said that people were very cooperative and a Kotokoli from Togo said he had found very little ethnic discrimination. Northerners are probably more looked down on than Ewes, since they are usually illiterate and in unskilled work and often do not maintain the same standards of cleanliness as southern Ghanaians, but the Ewes are in more direct competition with other southern Ghanaians for jobs and influence than are the northerners. While the usual stereotypes are resorted to in times of conflict of interests, people generally are taken on their merits as individuals and a considerable amount of mixing is taken for granted as part of urban life. Studies of housing in Madina (a suburb of

Accra) and Tema (Peil 1967, 1968c) showed very little clustering of ethnic groups. Few houses with more than two households are ethnically homogeneous and neighbours usually get on well together.

The problem of housing will be discussed below. Noise and congestion, the fast pace of life, lack of parks, dirty streets and 'lunatic' lorry drivers, heat and mosquitoes also came in for occasional adverse comment. Nevertheless, there were those who found the towns not only peaceful but beautiful (both the buildings and the layout); the people clean and nicely dressed; the accommodation good; and the libraries, churches and resting seats all that they could desire. A few coastal people who had worked inland were very glad to get back to the seaside.

Rural workers were asked, 'Have you ever thought of moving to Accra? What would be the advantages and disadvantages of such a move?'

TABLE 6.3. *Rural workers' reactions to the possibility of moving to Accra* (*percentages*)

Negative	
No, satisfied, have work here	28
High cost of living in Accra	25
Don't like city life	8
Don't know anyone there	7
Other negative answers	11
Positive	
Amenities, standard of living there	18
Jobs, better working conditions	14
City life pleasant	13
Other positive answers	4
Total[a]	128
N	138

[a] Total is over 100 % because of multiple responses.

The preponderance of negative comments over positive ones is a measure of the self-selectivity of rural workers. Many had not thought about moving to Accra even though they could give reasons for not going. Those who had already worked there often had mixed feelings about it. Some of those who indicated that they were quite content to stay where they were as long as they remained employed said that they might go to Accra if they needed to look for another job. However, there was an awareness of unemployment in Accra. Some said they would go there if they had a job lined up. Some of those who thought of Accra as a good place to find work considered it so because improved working conditions might be expected. One man mentioned the possibility of being able to change jobs, which he could not do in the community in which he was then living.

The reason given most often for avoiding Accra was the well-known high cost of living, especially of rent. The rent index for Accra in May 1968 was 109.9, lower than Takoradi's and showing considerably less rise than the cost of living generally. Nevertheless, table 6.5 (p. 165) shows that the average monthly rent paid by workers in Accra was 75% higher than the average rent paid by rural workers, whereas wages were about the same in both places. Rural workers were also more likely than those in Accra to get more than one room for their money. In addition, most of those in the 'other negative' category said that accommodation was very hard to find. The cost and poor quality of transport also came in for criticism.[1]

Not only were there fewer men who said they liked city life than who wanted to avoid it, but several of the positive comments were ambivalent. An operative on his first non-farming job said, 'Yes; sometimes I like to go to enjoy city life and to come back', and a young electrician said, 'I just want to visit there and see city life and come back. But if I get the opportunity I would like to stay there and work. I hear life is hard there but I think city life will be interesting.' An operative who had spent 3½ years in Accra on a previous job said, 'Even though I like city life, I may not be able to cope with high rent.' Several of those who preferred city life had only recently been transferred to firm P from Accra and had left their families there. One of these summed up the social aspects of life in a big city: 'One can have access to library, watch films and go to football matches; exchange ideas with friends, but friends encroach upon leisure hours and this retards studies.' Although quite a few young men would like to sample city life, it seems likely that the present shortage of opportunities for wage-earning in towns will keep the majority of them from flooding into the cities; they will be content to sample the city as an occasional visitor and avoid its high cost of living.

RESIDENCE IN TOWN

It has been noted that migrants often cluster in the part of town nearest their home. Early migrants build houses where their road enters the town and later migrants tend to live in the same area (Leslie 1963:33, Pons 1969:34). This pattern does not seem to characterize the Ghanaian cities studied and

---

[1] Deniel's study of the attitudes of Mossi farm labourers toward Abidjan had the same results (1968:143–4). They could see that a higher standard of living was possible in Abidjan, but that life was often very hard for the poor and illiterate.

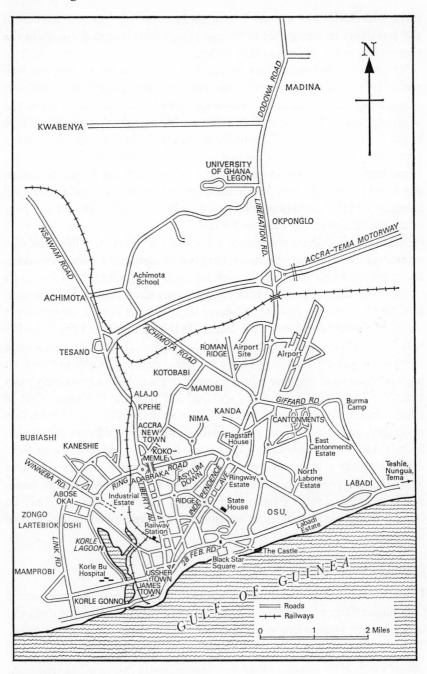

2 Greater Accra
Courtesy of the Geography Department, Cape Coast University College

may be less applicable to West African cities generally than to cities of East and Central Africa. Housing in Tema is all owned by the Tema Development Corporation and applicants must be grateful for any house allotted to them, so clustering there is impossible. There are notable concentrations of ethnic groups in other Ghanaian towns, but these tend to be in areas of early settlement of local people (in the villages from which the towns grew) and of strangers (in the zongos where the first 'strangers' were localized). All parts of town now show considerable ethnic heterogeneity, though the core area (such as James Town/Ussher Town in Accra; see map 2) is less mixed than areas farther from the centre of town. Newcomers are forced to scatter throughout the city because of the difficulty of getting housing. They are free to scatter because of the low level of ethnic prejudice. The concentrations which are evident can be explained by tribe, income and, rather surprisingly, size of place of origin.

Workers from places of the same size tend to live in certain parts of the city; not only are non-Ghanaians and northerners likely to be living in Nima and those who grew up in Accra, in James Town or Ussher Town, but those who grew up in towns (of from 5,000 to 40,000 population) are most likely to be living in Kaneshie (regardless of their tribe) and those from villages, in the Bubiashi/Kotobabi area. The proportion of non-Ghanaians of urban and rural background also varied considerably from one part of town to another. Areal differences are significant when tribe is held constant (though tribe is a more powerful predictor of location than size of place of origin, as would be expected). Patterns similar to those in Accra were found in the provincial cities, but the numbers were too small for statistical tests to be applied.

These differences are partly accounted for by ability and need to pay rent. The majority of Accra workers who own, or whose families own, the houses they are living in grew up in Accra. One-quarter of the workers living in Osu or along the coast from James Town to Mamprobi owned their houses or lived in family houses; rents in these areas are relatively high, considering that much of the housing is old and substandard. If local people rented a room, they paid a relatively high rent for it more often than the migrants did, presumably because they could afford to.

Migrants from villages are found in the lowest wage category more often than those from towns or cities. Almost all northerners are of rural origin (see table 3.1, p. 44). This necessitates living in those parts of town where rents are lowest. Some of them settle in the suburbs, where it may be possible to build a small house or where rents are low because of lower demand and services, though most prefer a central location. It has been noted in

Ibadan that workers prefer enduring severe overcrowding in the centre of town to more room on the outskirts because of the cost and inadequacy of public transport (Mabogunje 1968:214). This appears to be true of Accra as well.

Many low-paid workers go to areas like Nima, where three-fifths of those renting paid NC2.00 a month or less. Rents were somewhat higher in Accra New Town and the Bubiashi/Kotobabi area which forms the next ring outward from Nima and includes the Kanda Estate. Many middle-level factory workers live in this area because it is convenient to the Ring Road Industrial Estate. Rents were higher in the more central Adabraka/Asylum Down area, which was more popular with clerical than with manual workers.

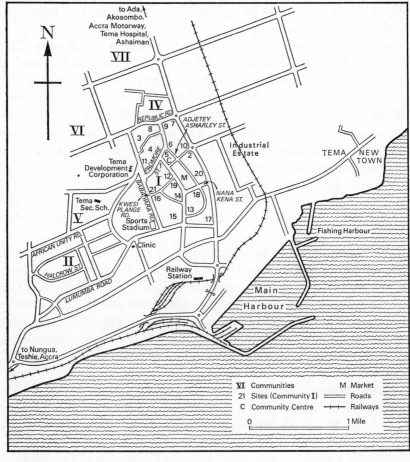

3   Tema
Courtesy of the Geography Department, Cape Coast University College

However, income is not the full answer to a person's residence in town just as tribe is not. Workers originating in cities, towns and villages are still concentrated in separate areas when wages are held constant.

There was usually some concentration of workers near their firms. Between a third and two-fifths of the work force at each firm had less than a twenty minute walk to work each day. Men try to find work near where they are living, but few move if they happen to find employment at a distance.

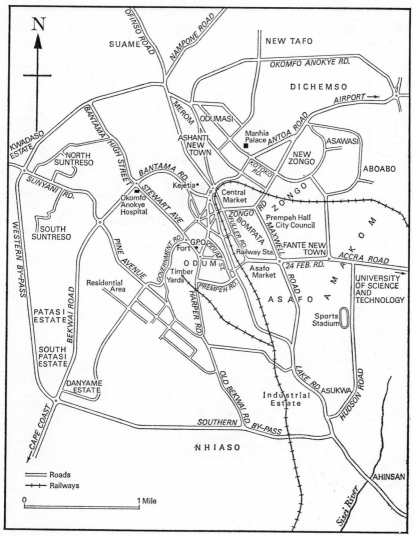

4 Kumasi
Courtesy of the Geography Department, Cape Coast University College

Urban living

Accommodation is hard to find and it is better to stay put than risk a rise in rent by moving.

Workers in Tema have less say about where they live than workers elsewhere. Since there is a severe shortage of housing, some of the firms lease houses for their workers, but about a third of the population of greater Tema (and at least a third of the factory workers) lives in Ashaiman, a very poorly serviced suburban development of private housing on T.D.C. land about two

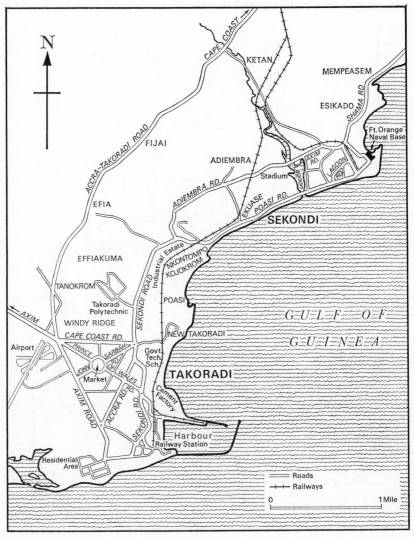

5   Sekondi/Takoradi
Courtesy of the Geography Department, Cape Coast University College

miles north of Community VII (north of the area covered by map 3). The majority of Tema workers are thus too far away from their firms to conveniently walk to work.

The smaller number of workers interviewed in Kumasi and Takoradi makes detailed discussion of their location impossible, but the degree of their concentration around the factories can be noted. A fifth of the Kumasi workers lived in the area around the Industrial Estate and just over half were living in the centre or the southeastern quarter of the city, where the factories are located (see map 4). Quite a few lived in or near the Zongo, a low-rent area three or four miles away on the north side of the city. Only three workers owned their houses, though home ownership is said to be common in Kumasi.

The two factories in Takoradi were several miles apart. The only concentration of workers was in Nkontompo and Kojokrom, villages next to each other and between the two towns where many workers live in very poor conditions (see map 5). Nearly half of the workers paying less than NC4.00 monthly rent lived in this area, which is a convenient walking distance from the Industrial Estate. The rest of the workers were fairly evenly scattered throughout the area, including many in other villages which are within the Municipal Council area. Very few lived on the housing estates at Adiembra or Effiakuma. Only a fifth lived in either central Sekondi or central Takoradi, which are both a considerable distance from the factories studied. Home ownership was more common than in Kumasi and more scattered arealy than in Accra. A number of long-term migrants to the Takoradi area have built houses there and some consider themselves to have settled permanently in town.

HOUSING

The problems of finding and paying for satisfactory accommodation, the overcrowding experienced and interaction with co-tenants and neighbours are important factors in the life of the worker. Most migrants make their first urban contacts in the process of finding a place to spend the night, whether this is with relatives or friends, a tribal chief, or a chance acquaintance who agrees to let the stranger stay with him.

As shown in table 6.4, very few migrants to towns have their own room from the start, even though they may move to town with other members of their families. Nearly two-fifths of the rural migrants had to find accommodation for themselves from the start. A few of those at firm P were in housing supplied by their employer. Space is not always found with the

TABLE 6.4. *Host and time spent sharing accommodation on first arrival in town (percentages)*

	Accra	Tema	Kumasi	Takoradi	Rural
Host[a]					
Sibling[b]	32	28	33	46	17
Other kinsman	31	28	30	22	22
Friend, other[c]	31	35	30	28	23
None, own place	6	9	7	4	38
Total	100	100	100	100	100
N	588	238	109	108	106
How long shared[d]					
Up to 2 months	19	13	38	18	40
2½–12 months[e]	48	49	31	45	56
Longer	33	38	31	37	4
Total	100	100	100	100	100
N	536	213	99	92	50

[a] All migrants.   [b] A few shared with one parent.
[c] Including some in institutions such as schools, rest houses and military barracks.
[d] Sharers only.
[e] Includes those still sharing with less than 1 year to date.

closest relative. There were cases of men with siblings or a parent in town who stayed with a more distant relative, possibly because the former was already overcrowded. Friends and institutions provided nearly a third of the accommodation. They were especially useful in Tema. Institutional accommodation includes schools and barracks, the help of the local tribal head and masters to whom young men were apprenticed. Quite a few migrants stayed with strangers met casually on the street or fellow townsmen who were unknown but to whom the migrant had been referred. One Kumasi migrant reported that he spent his first night with a man he didn't know 'because it was late in the night'. Not all migrants are so lucky. One man spent his first three weeks in Tema sleeping at the transport office and others found a place on someone's verandah or in the lorry park. Some of those who reported that they shared with friends did not make this arrangement until some time after their arrival.

Kumasi and rural migrants shared for a shorter time, on the average, than did those in the other cities. The short period of sharing among rural workers is due to the relative ease of making other arrangements. In Tema, at the other extreme, men hang on to their shared space as long as possible, since the alternative is moving out to Ashaiman.

Sharing is often terminated when the migrant's family arrives. Though there were cases of a wife or a sibling joining a migrant in shared accommodation, the imminent arrival of wife and children usually forces the migrant to find a room of his own. Setting up one's own household is often delayed by problems of finding a job and then waiting to be paid, since landlords may demand three months' rent in advance.

TABLE 6.5. *Housing density, single rooms, size of household and rent*

	Accra	Tema	Kumasi	Takoradi	Rural
Density (%)					
1–2.5 per room	63	66	45	62	73
2.6–3.5 per room	19	17	18	23	15
More than 3.5 per room	18	17	37	15	12
Total	100	100	100	100	100
Living in one room (%)	84	77	83	67	64
Mean size of household	3.28	3.39	4.03	3.65	3.54
Median monthly rent[a] (NC)	4.92	5.07	4.53	3.78	2.85
N	735	259	150	150	138

[a] Those who do not pay rent are omitted.

In a nationwide survey, Golding (1962:19,33) found that 26% of the households in large towns (15,000+ population) consisted of single individuals and that the mean size of household in large towns was 3.84, whereas the mean for Ghana as a whole was 4.68. His results are very close to ours (see table 6.5), indicating that the factory workers are probably typical of the population at large in their housing arrangements. The workers who were living alone (24%) represent two-fifths of those in non-crowded housing.

A household was considered overcrowded if there were more than 2.5 persons per room, counting children under five as half. Other housing surveys in Africa have used a somewhat lower base. Busia (1950:7) adopted the United Kingdom Census definition of more than two persons per room in assessing overcrowding in Takoradi. The United Nations Mission to Kenya on Housing (Bloomberg and Abrams 1964:15) reports the proportion of households with both two or more and three or more members by number of rooms. Half of all urban African households in Kenya had three or more persons per room and the proportion was higher for one-room units. As in Ghana, over half the households had only one room. (The proportion among the urban factory workers interviewed was 73%.) A higher number of persons per room can be sustained in Africa than in Europe because much of daily living takes place out of doors. A higher density is necessary because low wages limit the amount of housing a family can afford, regardless of its size.

The Kenya housing report makes several suggestions, especially in relation to the housing of industrial workers, which are also applicable to Ghana (Bloomberg and Abrams 1964:48–9). Employers are increasingly unwilling to invest potentially productive capital in housing for workers, yet it is to their interest that their workers are well housed fairly near the factory. Since employer-controlled housing may not be in the workers' best interests (because the room is lost when the job is lost and because the desire for housing may lead the worker to accept unduly low wages or unfavourable working conditions), there is a strong need for more government housing and loan schemes to enable workers to acquire their own homes. It should be added here that possession of a house in town is a powerful inducement to stay there on retirement, since it provides a sense of belonging which is otherwise lacking and also a source of income from the rent of rooms not used by the family.[1]

The report also recommends siting new industries near available housing if this can be done. Given the general shortage of housing in towns, this may not be possible, but it might be better to site 'rural' factories in small towns of between 5,000 and 10,000 population rather than in villages. Many houses in the former would have empty rooms due to outmigration and changing family size, whereas the latter provide too small a housing base for a factory of any size. Workers in one of the rural factories were scattered in thirteen villages, some more than 5 miles away.

Rents were considerably lower and there was less overcrowding in the rural households than in the urban ones. Though they included about the same number of people, rural households were more likely than urban ones to have more than one room. Workers in Kumasi had a lower average rent but more overcrowding than those in Accra or Tema. The men in Kumasi had the highest average household size and very few families there had more than one room.

The workers who live in Tema itself rather than in the 'free enterprise' suburbs such as Ashaiman pay high rents, but their houses are fitted with electricity, taps and waterborne sanitation, so they are better off than most workers elsewhere. The provision of housing for workers which is adequate by modern standards yet within the ability of workers to pay is a problem which causes considerable concern to planners. Housing projects for 'workers'

[1] The Belgian colonial government encouraged home ownership as a means of establishing a stable urban population (La Fontaine 1970:22).

often end up in the hands of middle-level civil servants and businessmen, since these earn enough to pay economic rents.

A recent household sample census in Tema found more overcrowding among the population generally than in the factory-worker sample; 26 % of the household sample had more than 3.5 people per room. Factory workers constitute a relatively young sector of the population and are therefore less often married. This is probably more true of Tema than of the other cities.

As might be expected, there is a direct relationship between age and over-crowding, though it is stronger in the provincial cities than in Accra because more workers in the former have their families with them. The majority of men in provincial cities over thirty years of age are living in overcrowded conditions. In Accra, the proportion does not pass 50 % except for men over forty-five. However, it is likely that overcrowding in all cities is greater than recorded on the schedules. A careful study of several houses in inner Accra (Hart 1969) found that households were far larger than reported on a pre-liminary census. A stranger who inquires might be told about the regular inhabitants of a room, but the listing is likely to stop when the interviewer seems satisfied, and casual visitors (who may stay for months) and sub-tenants who only sleep in the room are often omitted.

High rent provides no exemption from overcrowding. The proportion who are overcrowded is the same at all rent levels. Those living in family owned houses are more often severely overcrowded than are rent-payers; 28 % had more than 3.5 people per room compared to 19 % of the renters. Though there are many claimants to rooms in family homes (Marris 1961:13), a third of the workers' households in such houses had more than one room, compared to a quarter of those living in rented accommodation. Only 29 % of the workers who were sharing with a relative were in households with more than one room, which means that most sharers are living in the same room as their hosts.

Workers who are able to save enough to build their own houses often limit family use to one or two rooms. They rent the rest to provide an additional source of income. About half of the Accra workers who 'owned' their houses were Ga living in family houses very similar to those described by Marris for the Yoruba of Lagos. So far, the Ga have managed to resist redevelopment of central Accra where their property is located. A fifth of the house-owners were residents of the Zongo and nearby areas settled by the established 'stranger' community. The other third were scattered through the town. Whereas almost all house owners in the provincial cities had lived there at least ten years, house ownership in Accra was unrelated to time spent in town.

To find out about feelings toward overcrowding, workers in the provincial and rural factories were asked, 'If you could afford them, how many rooms do you think would be just right for yourself and your family (the people now living with you)?' Those with more than 4.5 persons per room were almost all dissatisfied. Most of these lived in one room and most specified that one additional room would be sufficient. A quarter of the people who were not overcrowded by the standard set said they would like to have more space. This was more often true of those with two or more rooms than of those with only one room, presumably because many of the latter were living alone. Provincial workers were more often satisfied with their housing than rural workers, whether they were overcrowded or not. This is a measure of their acceptance of one of the necessities of urban life. Rural workers maintained the expectation of being able to add an extra room as needed and were particularly dissatisfied at having to live in a single room. Some men living alone said they would prefer to have another room, which did not happen among urban workers.

Unskilled workers were more often satisfied with their accommodation than other workers, but they were least likely to be overcrowded. They may also have a lower standard of comfort. Clerical workers expressed the most dissatisfaction. Though the machine semiskilled workers were somewhat more often overcrowded than clerical workers, the latter seem to have higher aspirations in this respect. In Accra, higher clerical workers were most often severely overcrowded, but we do not have satisfaction data from them.

CONTACTS WITH FELLOW WORKERS

The migrant establishes contacts with others in his environment which vary in breadth and depth according to his background and orientation as well as according to his income and standard of living. The study of networks of interaction has been an important area of research on African migrants in recent years (Mitchell 1969, Pons 1969). It was not possible in a study of this type to go into these workers' friendship networks in detail, but some data were gathered on the possibility of kinsmen and townsmen working at the same factory and the choice of workmates as companions outside working hours. These are supplemented by the results of interviews with factory workers included in the Tema Network Survey, which was concerned with contacts with co-tenants, neighbours, relatives and friends in the Tema area.

When relatives are called on to find jobs for new arrivals, as many of them are, their first approach is probably to someone at their own workplace. This sometimes results in concentrations of workers from a given village among the workers at a given firm or government department. For job-seekers with low or no skills, such as northerners, the fact that one man has been hired means that this place has jobs for 'people like us', and new arrivals will try there first even if they have no direct contact with those who are already on the payroll. Another place gets the reputation of not hiring 'people like us' and this keeps away applicants (Hart 1969:183). Thus, many ethnic concentrations are a result of chance factors of original hiring and hometown networks rather than of deliberate policy.

TABLE 6.6. *Workers with relatives or townsmen in the same firm (percentages)*

	Urban	Rural
Relationship		
None	62	49
Sibling	7	17
Other kinsman	10	23
Fellow townsman	24	20
Total[a]	103	109
N	1,293	138
Contacts in the firm[b]		
Before employment	53	59
After own employment	32	29
Both	15	12
Total	100	100
N	469	68

[a] Totals are over 100% because of multiple responses.
[b] Of those with relatives or townsmen working at the firm.

Two-fifths of the urban workers and half of the rural workers had a relative or townsman working in the same firm (see table 6.6). Some had more than one. It was more common to have a townsman than a kinsman; less than half of the latter were siblings. It is more difficult to find places for new arrivals now than it used to be. Workers were more likely to have a contact at the firm when they arrived than to have a relative or townsman join the firm after they did. Both urban and rural samples showed this. It was thought that it would be easier to introduce new workers into small firms because procedures in such firms tend to be less bureaucratic and the management is closer to the workers. However, the largest firm in the sample had the highest proportion in Accra of workers with relatives or townsmen as workmates (45%) and in one of the smallest firms only a fifth of the workers had such contacts. Both of these firms had predominantly expatriate management.

It is possible that large firms have a higher proportion of workers brought by other workers because there are more places to be filled, but it is likely that management policy rather than size of firm or nationality of management is the important factor here. In the Tema firms, with their generally more bureaucratic organization, only a fifth of the workers had kinsmen or townsmen working at the same place, compared to 41% of Accra workers, 46% of Kumasi workers and 59% of those in Takoradi. In the Takoradi firm which preferred to hire people suggested by men on the payroll, only a quarter of the workers had no relatives or townsmen in the firm.

A rapidly expanding labour force is another factor encouraging workers to bring in their friends and relations. In one of the rural factories, workers were less likely than the workers in Accra to have such connections. In the other, which was growing rapidly and actively seeking workers all over the area, three-fifths of the workers had townsmen or kinsmen on the payroll.

Workers who have grown up locally are more likely than migrants to have townsmen among their fellow workers, but many local people do not think of all others who grew up in the same city as fellow townsmen. Unlike the man from a village, they probably had nothing to do with attracting local workers to the firm and they may not even know many of them. Loyalties of urban residents are necessarily circumscribed. The man who grew up in Osu (one of the oldest parts of Accra) will probably know other workers who are Osu men (in the sense of belonging to old Osu families), but he will know fewer of those from James Town (where the population is also predominantly old Ga families) and even fewer of the workers who grew up in Abose Okai or the Zongo (which are 'stranger' settlements). Similarly, a man thinks of himself as belonging to Asukwa or Ashanti New Town rather than to Kumasi, of which these are a part. Sekondi/Takoradi is even more divided than Accra and Kumasi, since there are several independent towns and villages within the Municipal Council area. Men who think of Kojokrom, Ketan or Ekuase as home would not consider each other or men from central Sekondi as 'townsmen'. In addition, many people who live all their lives in the cities maintain an allegiance to some other place as their hometown; 'townsmen' are people from this hometown, not their current residence.

Among the urban workers, those who had grown up in cities were no more likely than those with a rural background to say they had relatives or townsmen working at the same firm. Skilled and unskilled workers had these contacts more often than semiskilled or clerical workers and northerners are more likely than southerners to go where they know someone. Foremen are not more likely than other workers to bring kinsmen and townsmen into their firms, though the pressure to do so is probably greater than it is on other workers. Northerners are more likely than southerners to spend short periods of time in the cities. A man who wants to leave may arrange for a 'brother' to take his place on the job. A Voltaic labourer said, 'My brother asked me to come and take over his job because he wanted to go home.' Since names are often made up for the occasion (one firm had workers listed as Fulani Kordo No. 2 and Inusah Busanga No. 2), it is fairly easy for the change to be made without the employer's knowledge. The new man just appears, does the other man's work and uses his labour card. Labourers on the mines use this tactic to get around the ruling that a man will only be rehired after one trip home; if he goes home again he loses his chance of working at that mine. Two men working in tandem may keep a job long enough to earn the five-year gratuity.

Of course, not all workers who at one time had kinsmen or townsmen at their firms owed their jobs to these connections or were directly responsible for those who came later and many who had connections in their firms at one time did not have them at the time of interviewing. Also, the existence of such relationships need not imply that the workers associate with each other on or off the job. A further question was used to find out how many workers spent their spare time with their workmates: 'Do you ever meet men that you work with in the evenings or on weekends – to drink together, or go to football matches, or sit and talk?' Those who did were asked, 'Are they relatives of yours or do they come from the same town or the same tribe?' Two-thirds of the urban workers and a quarter of the rural workers said they had no contact with their fellows outside working hours. Of the rest, the majority said that the mates they saw away from work were 'just friends'.

Where workers are isolated from the rest of society because of the nature of their work or the hours involved (seamen, dock workers, printers) or concentrated residentially because of the monolithic dominance of their employer in the community (miners, lumberjacks) they usually spend much of their free time with their workmates. Since such occupations often run in families, workmates are often relatives. Where they are less isolated, manual workers usually spend most of their time with relatives and neighbours who have the same background as themselves, seeing little of workmates who do not live near them. They may even think it is a bad idea to have workmates as close friends, preferring to leave the job behind when they are looking for re-laxation (Goldthorpe *et al.* 1968:55–62). Lower-level clerical workers may be somewhat more open in their choice of spare-time associates, but kinship and propinquity are important for them as well (Goldthorpe *et al.* 1969:87–91).

Studies of African migrants indicate that most of their free time is spent with relatives, townsmen and tribesmen because the need for security draws relatives together and increases the pressure to join and be active in ethnic associations, because churches are usually ethnically homogeneous, and because the tendency of ethnic groups to concentrate in various parts of town ensures that most people will have neighbours of the same background as themselves.[1] It was expected that these factors would discourage factory workers from choosing to spend their free time with fellow workers even if they wanted to and that workers chosen as friends would usually be selected on ascriptive grounds – because they were also kinsmen or fellow tribesmen. However, it was thought that workers who were more stabilized on their jobs and more attuned to urban ways might be more universalistic in their choice of friends and thus more likely to see workmates away from the factory. This was confirmed to a certain extent, though the findings are rather ambiguous and require further study.

TABLE 6.7. *Percent of workers who see workmates away from the firm and relationship to these mates*

	Accra	Tema	Kumasi	Takoradi	Rural
Never	72	70	66	49	23
N	735	259	150	150	138
Relationship[a]					
Kinsman	14	0	28	32	23
Townsman, tribesman	34	24	35	27	32
Friend	60	78	57	61	58
Total[b]	108	102	120	120	113
N	208	79	51	77	106

[a] Of those who did see mates.
[b] Totals are over 100% because of multiple responses.

Relatively few Ghanaian industrial workers spend much time off the job with workmates (see table 6.7). Some maintained their traditional relationships with relatives and townsmen and spent all their free time with them. Although ethnic associations are much less important in Ghana than in Nigeria, so that they do not constitute a positive hindrance to making new friends with co-tenants, neighbours and workmates if one is so inclined, many migrants still spend much of their free time with their families or 'people from home'.

In the absence of adequate transportation, propinquity proved to be im-

[1] The syndrome of 'family-home localism' found among low-status, low-income American workers has been described by Wilensky (1960:351–2). Some of the factors in its development are similar to Ghanaian conditions, but the pattern is more common in developing countries than in the United States because recent migrants in the former tend to be more closely tied to their rural extended families. (But see Slotkin 1960.)

portant. Rural workers were more likely than urban workers to spend their free time with their fellows, and provincial workers more often reported meeting workmates in the evenings or on weekends than did those in Accra or Tema. (The data from Kumasi is ambiguous, since workers in one firm were much more likely than those at the other firm to see their mates away from work.) It seems likely that, in addition to dispersion of workers, the impersonal atmosphere of Accra and Tema adversely affects the possibility of making friends at work with whom one wishes to associate elsewhere.

The disinterest of Ghanaian workers in spending their spare time with workmates is also probably due to a lack of commitment to their present jobs, which at least some see only as a means of maintaining themselves in a hostile environment. The relatively short time spent on various jobs encourages workers to find their friends elsewhere (see Wilensky 1960:559). Jobs come and go and workmates come and go; one wants friends on whom one can rely in emergencies. This is, of course, a good reason for choosing friends on ascriptive grounds.

Nevertheless, many workers who saw their workmates outside of working hours said that these were 'just friends'. Some of them were probably townsmen or at least members of the same ethnic group, but the insistence that they were 'just friends' indicates that many workers who associate with workmates in their free time choose them on non-ascriptive grounds. There was no difference between rural and urban workers in the proportion who spent their free time with workmates who were neither relatives nor identified as fellow ethnics. A higher proportion of Tema workers than of workers elsewhere confine their contacts with workmates to 'friends'. This is due to the nature of Tema and of the sample. Workers there are likely to be educated, young and single and therefore have more time for recreation than workers elsewhere. They are also less concerned with traditional ties, which are largely lacking in Tema in any case.

Workers under thirty-five are more likely than those over thirty-five to see workmates off the job, but the older workers were as likely to see friends as the younger ones. Workers who see their mates away from the factory have not been on the job longer than other workers, but they are in occupational categories where we would expect a better integration into urban society and a higher level of adjustment to the expectations of an industrial work situation.[1]

[1] Amachree (1968:234–5) found that Nigerian semiskilled workers tended to choose their friends from among workmates who were not relatives; unskilled workers chose relatives who were not workmates and skilled workers chose workmates, some of whom were relatives. Non-kin workmates were chosen most often by semiskilled and unskilled workers of more than ten years seniority, while older skilled workers who were beginning to plan a return home chose relatives outside industry.

TABLE 6.8. *Choice of workmates as friends by occupation, urban male workers*

Occupation	Never saw mates		Those who saw mates	
	%	N	% Friends	N
Unskilled	66	(218)	40	(74)
Semiskilled				
Hand	66	(118)	62	(40)
Machine	64	(260)	70	(95)
Skilled	72	(385)	61	(109)
Lower clerical	58	(73)	81	(31)
Higher clerical	64	(58)	79	(19)
Foreman	68	(56)	81	(21)

Unskilled workers and northerners (the two overlap considerably) are farthest from this pattern (see table 6.8). Although they are average in the proportion who associate with workmates, most of their friends are chosen on ascriptive grounds. This is the group we would expect to show encapsulation (Mayer 1962) because of their evident cultural differences from southerners and unfamiliarity with urban ways. But linguistic differences also make a wide range of friendships difficult for northerners to achieve. Most southern Ghanaians can communicate with each other in one or more of the local languages or in English. Relatively few unskilled northerners know much English, and their knowledge of southern Ghanaian languages, while often adequate for the needs of daily living, is not usually sufficient for enjoyable relaxation. Although communication with fellow northerners of other ethnic groups is more frequent and less impeded than with southerners (cultural differences are also less of a barrier), apparently most northerners spend their free time with a few close friends, preferably kinsmen or men from the same local area and almost always of the same tribe. The additional tie of being workmates is useful but not necessary.

Skilled workers were even less likely than the unskilled to associate with their mates outside working hours and were higher than all but unskilled workers in the proportion whose friends were ascriptively chosen. Many skilled workers spend their free time on private jobs and thus have less time for relaxation than semiskilled or clerical workers. In addition, unskilled and skilled workers were more likely than the clerks or semiskilled to have kinsmen or townmen working at the same firm and thus more able to associate with workmates with whom they had other bonds.

It is the clerical workers, especially lower clerical workers, who are most likely to spend their spare time with workmates and to choose 'just friends' as associates. These are likely to be young southerners who feel themselves a part of urban society. Though the job may not live up to their expectations, many count themselves successful to have obtained such work. An additional factor which aids them in forming friendships is the amount of conversation which is possible on the job. Clerical workers are not as closely supervised as manual workers and it is not unusual to enter an office and find either general conversation or groups of two or three workers in conversation, which may or may not include business. Manual workers are more often separated from each other, noise interferes with conversation and work groups are kept at their tasks.

Women were less likely than men to see their workmates off the job. Since many of them were also running a home, they had less time than the men for visiting, but they were also less interested in their jobs, which were seen as marginal to their careers as wives and mothers.

CONTACTS IN THE COMMUNITY

To supplement the material reported above, we can use data from a household survey carried out in Tema and Ashaiman during the summer of 1968. The discussion here will deal with seventy-two factory workers included in this sample, twenty-three skilled workers and forty-nine operatives and drivers. The data show that factory workers are generally more sociable than other members of the community (perhaps because they are young and have relatively fewer family responsibilities) and that they usually have friends among their workmates.

Ethnic associations are not as popular in Ghana as seems to be the case in other African countries. Only a quarter of these workers belonged to an ethnic or any other mutual-aid association. Ewes and Nigerians are most often members of such associations. Very few of the men belonged to any church-related associations.

Interaction is usually on a casual, personal basis. Most workers know many of their neighbours well enough to greet them in the street and have a circle of friends whom they often see informally to share a meal or a drink or just sit and talk. Drinking is done with neighbours and/or co-tenants somewhat more often than with workmates or other friends. The group usually includes three to five people. Two-thirds of the workers claimed that they did not drink. Sharing a meal is more common; two-thirds of the workers eat with co-tenants, relatives or workmates, usually one to three times per week. Since cooking and eating are done out of doors and anyone who happens to be around may be invited to share the meal, this type of friendliness may well be more common than the figures indicate.

Trips to the cinema are usually made two or three times a month. Half never go and a fifth go alone. The rest go more often with a sibling or spouse than with a workmate or other friend. Very few of these men go to organized dances or concert parties, which are usually held at the Tema Community Centre, too far away for those living in Ashaiman and apparently of limited interest to, or too expensive for, the Tema residents. It is more congenial just to sit and talk; almost all the workers did this occasionally with workmates and many also whiled away evenings and weekends talking with co-tenants, neighbours, or other friends. Two-fifths had at least ten friends with whom they regularly relaxed in this way. A fifth said they knew workmates well enough to discuss problems with them. Listening to the radio provides recreation and companionship for many. Half of the workers owned a radio and about half of these let co-tenants listen to it. Many of those who do not own a radio themselves listen to one owned by a co-tenant or neighbour.

Factory workers are more likely than other members of the community to have relatives in the area. When these kinsmen live nearby, they are usually visited daily. Relatives who live in town but farther away are seen at least once a week. Thus, contacts are maintained, news is passed along, and the migrant remains part of an extended family even though most of its members live at a distance.

These workers reported considerably more friendship with workmates than was evident in the factory sample. Only 5% said they never sat and talked with their mates and 90% said they would invite workmates to a party such as the 'outdooring' of a new baby. (The comparable figures for the men in the sample as a whole were 24% and 76% respectively.) A possible source of the difference is the number and phrasing of the questions. The factory sample was asked one question which mentioned things workers do not do very often (drinking and attending football matches) before 'just talking' and specified that these activities must take place off the job. The people interviewed at home were asked a series of questions. Talking with workmates could be affirmed if it took place only during the lunch hour and the party question could be answered in ideal terms rather than reporting on actual practice. Another factor is the concentration on semiskilled and skilled workers. There were a small number of men in the household sample with unskilled and clerical occupations who worked in factories (seventeen of each). These had fewer contacts with their workmates than semiskilled and skilled workers. The difference was small in the case of clerical workers, but only half of the labourers reported any association with workmates. This is an area which requires further careful study.

REARING CHILDREN

Most factory workers are husbands and fathers. The size of their families and the practice of sending children to be reared at home will be discussed in the next chapter, but attitudes toward rearing children in town and toward educating children will be treated here because these provide information on feelings about urban living and the needs of modern society. Urban parents were asked, 'Would you say that bringing up children in — [this city] is easier, about the same, or harder than bringing up children in a small farming village? Why?'

There was general agreement by about four-fifths of the parents, regardless of occupation, ethnic group, number of children, monthly wage or the number of employed people in the household, that it is difficult to bring up children in a city. The rest were equally divided between those who said it was the same everywhere and those who thought child-rearing in town is easier than in a village. The proportion who preferred urban child-rearing was higher among semiskilled and clerical workers than among those in other occupations; among southerners than among northerners; and among non-migrants than among migrants. For non-migrants, home ownership and the presence of relatives probably helps, but a more complete adjustment to urban living is certainly a factor.

Most of those who said it was hard to bring up children in a city blamed this on the cost of living, pointing out that food is 'free' in a village. Those who said it was the same everywhere usually commented that there are many things which must be bought in both towns and villages. This is certainly true for southern Ghanaians, who have grown used to imported consumer goods such as milk, sugar, corned beef, etc. School fees are the same everywhere and children are usually clothed, though somewhat earlier in towns than in villages.

A carpenter who thought it was easier to bring up children in town said he would not have much work in a village, implying that it would be difficult to cover the expenses there even if these were smaller and that children should grow up under their parents' direction. A tailor had the same idea when he said, 'You can train them under your own eyes with methods developed in the city.' A Togolese printer who had grown up in Accra was not so sure. He thought rearing children would be easier in his home village: 'There will be people in my village to help me, but here I am alone. I even plan to send some back home.' He had two wives and eight children with him in Accra and had sent one daughter back to Togo.

Several parents mentioned the dangers of urban traffic; others worried about urban influences on their children. A printer was not sure his child would be best off in town: 'There is much food in the village; also they will concentrate on learning rather than running around cinema halls, etc.' Although women were more likely than men to see the benefits of bringing up children in town, one commented, 'It is easier but as a worker I don't get much time for them and they get out of control.' While many women take their young children to the market with them when they go to trade, older children, especially boys, may be left to play in the streets and get into trouble (Busia 1950:37).

Those who think rearing children in town is easier tend to emphasize the preparation this gives children for adult life (which they assume will be lived in town) and the amenities available in town. 'The children learn quickly from friends and soon become independent and civilized.' 'Once a house is obtained, everything (e.g. medical facilities, school etc.) is easy.' The word 'civilized' is used much less often in Ghana than in Liberia (Fraenkel 1964:67); it usually refers to the adoption of modern, urban ways.

Paradoxically, another reason for sending children home may be that it is easier to get them into school in a village than in town. A clerk in Accra said that he had trouble finding a school for his children. The Tema primary schools, which had space for many more children a few years ago, are now overcrowded. Taylor and Lehmann (1961:86) reported that Copperbelt workers complained if they were transferred because it was difficult to get their children into a new school. Cities grow so fast that services never catch up with the demand and, as an increasing proportion of migrants have their families with them, the schools are often more overcrowded in towns than in villages. At the same time, the economic situation has meant delays in the building of new schools. Competition for places often means that children must wait a year or two after the official starting age of six to begin their education. Parents may find that the best solution is to send their children home to attend the local primary school. Given the other advantages of sending children home, it is a measure of their desire to have their children with them that more parents have not done so. This will be discussed further in the next chapter.

All of the workers were asked, 'Do you think it is of great importance for boys to have as much education as possible or would a little or none at all be necessary? How about girl children, how much education is necessary for

178

them ?' Rural workers were also asked, 'How much education would you like your oldest son to have ?'

TABLE 6.9. *Amount of education desired for children (percentages)*

	Accra	Tema	Kumasi	Takoradi	Rural
Both as much as possible	70	85	69	44	55
Boys as much as possible, girls less	27	13	18	41	40
Other and don't know	3	2	13	15	5
Total	100	100	100	100	100
N	735	259	150	150	138

Except in Takoradi and one of the rural factories, a majority of the workers said that both boys and girls should have as much education as possible; most of the rest said that boys should have as much as possible, while girls could do with less. Very few said that either boys or girls could get along without education, even though they had not sent all of their own children to school. Of course, answers to questions of this type are often in line with what the man being interviewed thinks is expected of him. Education is known to be a good thing. Therefore, one must declare oneself in favour of it. Thus, the type of person who is less enthusiastic about education is more important than the proportion who give such an answer.

Women are more likely than men to say that both boys and girls should have an equal chance of an education. The proportion who give such a response increases with wage and the amount of education the worker has himself received. There is no difference between men in various occupations except that unskilled workers are less favourable to education, and those who have always held non-manual jobs more favourable. Those who grew up in villages are as likely to want a good education for all of their children as those who grew up in large towns, though non-migrants thought more highly of education for girls than did migrants. Togolese and Nigerians were only slightly less favourable than southern Ghanaians, but many northerners thought that education was not so important. Older workers were generally more conservative than the young. This is, of course, related to the lower educational level of the older men.

Half of the rural parents said they would like their oldest son to go to university and a third said he should attend secondary school.[1] Parents who said boys and girls should both have as much education as possible were equally likely to mean university or secondary school. Only one mentioned

[1] Only rural parents were asked to specify the level of education they had in mind.

any other type of schooling. Thus, the aim is an academic education, but 'as much as possible' may mean a relatively limited goal. Those who had attended at least middle school themselves were more likely than those with primary education or none at all to want their children to go on to university. Southern Ghanaians more often thought in terms of university for their sons than did non-Ghanaians. (There were no northern Ghanaians among rural workers.) But there was no difference between those who grew up in a city and those who grew up in a village on this. Other differences were in the expected direction but too small to be significant because this question was only asked of rural workers. We would expect that urban workers would have put more emphasis on going to the university than did the rural workers because university graduates as a reference group are more visible to them.

As shown in table 6.10, three-quarters of the workers with school-age children had all of their children in school and another 16% had sent some of them to school. The proportion who will send all of their children to school is probably higher, since some children who were six or seven had not yet started school. Nevertheless, an examination of the cases where all children over five years of age were not in school provides confirmation of the attitudes expressed on the previous question.

TABLE 6.10. *Percent of parents sending school-age children to school*

	Accra	Tema	Kumasi	Takoradi	Rural
All	86	92	64	58	70
Some	12	4	22	28	15
None	2	4	14	14	15
Total	100	100	100	100	100
N	205	48	91	71	54

In the first place, there are differences between cities and between the urban and rural workers. The order is as we would expect, with the highest participation in Tema and the lowest urban participation in Takoradi. Rural workers were as likely to send all their children to school as were provincial parents and they had the same proportion of parents who had sent none of their children to school. Very few Accra or Tema parents had not sent at least one child to school.

There are parents with all levels of education who have not sent all of their children to school, but most parents who neglected this had not attended school themselves. It is the father's education rather than the mother's which has the most influence here. Couples both of whom had been to school were not more likely than those where only the husband was educated to send all of their children to school. The decision as to when and whether to enrol a child and the payment of school fees belong to the father's role, though the mother sometimes supports the child when he asks to be sent.

As with other measures of modern attitudes, it is the unskilled worker, the Muslim or adherent of traditional religion, the northerner, who is least likely to send his children to school. (Muslim schools were included, though very few parents reported sending children to them.) Unskilled workers would face the greatest difficulty over school fees, but attitude is probably more important than income in this case, since the average unskilled worker had only one child. Older men tended to be more conservative; when they were younger, schooling was less important than it is today. Togolese and Nigerians were less likely to send their children to school than southern Ghanaians, but more likely than northerners. Addo (1967:26) showed from the 1960 Census that foreigners (children of non-Ghanaians, whether or not they had been born in Ghana) were less likely to attend school than Ghanaians and indicated that education rates for foreigners were closer to Ghanaian rates in the Capital District and the Western Region than elsewhere in the country. The difference in education rates between local people and migrants to these areas from elsewhere in Ghana is an additional factor which the census reports are not sufficiently detailed to show.

GOING HOME

Most African workers expect eventually to return to their hometowns. Twenty or thirty years ago, there were few migrants who stayed in town beyond the age of forty-five. Urban life was supposed to provide the necessities such as tax money and bridewealth and the extras to make rural life more pleasant – a bicycle, a radio, capital for a business. Whether or not one was able to save enough money, one should not stay in town too long. (See, for example, Mitchell 1961, Sofer and Sofer 1955:16–19, and, for Accra, Acquah 1958:39.) However, the proportion of older people in towns has always been higher in West than in East or Central Africa and there are indications that the proportion of migrants who remain in town for a long period has increased over time. Many will never return home even though they mean to do so (Caldwell 1969:186–90). A lengthened stay in town has been reported in the last fifteen years for workers in various parts of Africa. The present low proportion of old people in African towns, therefore, is more indicative of the death rate of an earlier era and of the present high birth rate than of the probability that few middle-aged men will remain in town when they retire.

There are, however, good reasons for going home when the time for retirement arrives. Living in a village is much cheaper than living in town and there are relatives at home to look after an old man or woman if they become ill. Many people look forward to an old age of supporting themselves with small farming and maintaining their sense of importance by being elders who can give advice to the young on the ways of living in a city.

One's hometown is usually the place of one's father's people or, in the case of matrilineal groups, the place of one's mother's people. Provincial and rural workers were asked to name their hometowns. While 64% had been born and reared in the towns they named, 15% had been born there but had grown up elsewhere, 4% had been born elsewhere but had grown up in their hometown or lived there at some time in their lives, and 17% had never lived there at any time.

Lack of contact with one's hometown is not always due to rural–urban migration and does not always result in failure to visit it when the individual reaches adulthood. Cocoa farmers who set up farming hamlets in new areas may only visit their homes once a year. Their children are often born in the new village, but retain an allegiance to their father's or mother's home village, which they may visit with their parents. Some children of migrants, on the other hand, lose touch with the home village and do not know anyone who lives there, though they may maintain an inactive allegiance to it as the home of their ancestors. That maintaining contact is more usually the case may be seen in that only 22% of the provincial workers who had never lived in their hometowns had never visited them and 20% visited at least bi-monthly.

Some children of immigrants grow up in Ghana and never visit their home country, though they speak their mother tongue (not always well) and maintain allegiance to the home village. They may even speak of retiring there in their old age, though it seems unlikely that they will do so.

Workers were asked about their plans to stay in town as a measure of their satisfaction with urban life, but of course the answers also reflect the age, income and prospects of the migrant and the strength of his family ties in the city and at home. The basic question was, 'When you stop working, will you stay in — [this city], go back to your hometown, or go somewhere else?' Some of the workers interpreted the question as asking what they would do when they left their present jobs. This was not realized until the Accra/Tema interviews were completed, but interviewers were given special instructions to help overcome the problem in later interviews. Further information was obtained by asking provincial and rural workers to explain their answers. It turned out that those who said they would go somewhere other than their hometowns were usually not thinking of the end of their working lives, but rather of going somewhere to find a new job, get further training, etc. They were usually young, recent arrivals and willing to move on if prospects looked better somewhere else.

Many men found it difficult to think of a time when they would stop working. It is still fairly common for men to die in middle age. On the basis of the United Nations model life tables, a Ghanaian man of thirty has a 65% chance of reaching sixty, the official retirement age. The question might have been better phrased 'When you are too old to work . . .', but even this would face the problem that many men cannot foresee a time when they will be too old to work. Retirement is more a question of health and opportunities than of age. One of the watchmen was in his seventies. Almost all of the workers who planned to stay in town said they would go on working.

Urban workers are used to being self-reliant and most do not seriously consider continuing to live in town after they stop working even if their children would contribute to their support and if housing were provided for them. They say, if asked, that any help children might give would go farther at home, as would any pension they might get. Nevertheless, the availability of housing is an important factor in the choice of a retirement residence. Plotnicov (1967) reports that several older men in Jos felt that they could not return home because they had not completed a house there. I found several older people in Ashaiman[1] and a few factory workers in Takoradi who planned to stay because they had built a house in which they could live and others who said they could not go home because they had no house there.

Two-thirds of the factory workers said they had land rights at home if they wanted to take up farming. Those with land rights were more often determined to go home than those without them, but there were many who said they had no land rights and yet planned to go home. Some skilled workers think they will be able to do enough business at home to support themselves, but others do not plan to go home while they are physically able to work.

Another factor encouraging migrants to stay in town is marriage. Women were more likely than men to plan to stay in town and those who had married in the city said they would stay more often than those married at home. Urban marriages often involve people of different ethnic groups or at least different hometowns. In this case, a wife who returns home with her husband must move in with strangers at an age when she is less adaptable than she would have been when first married. Studies elsewhere in Africa have found that some women remain in town with the children or go to their own hometowns when their husbands return home (Plotnicov 1967:98).

---

[1] The Tema Network Survey included a special sample of people over fifty years of age.

It might be expected that education would be directly related to a desire to stay in town on retirement. The more educated the man, the better chance he has of earning a good wage and being able to partake more fully of the amenities of urban life and the more likely that his attitudes and values are different from those of most people in his rural home. However, it was the workers who had attended middle school who most often said they planned to stay. Those who had continued their education beyond middle school were as likely as those who had no education or only primary schooling to plan to return home. It may be that those whom the family has supported in secondary or commercial school are more tied to their families through the process of repaying the debt and the increased prestige which their advanced education gives them at home than are middle-school leavers, for whom extra sacrifices have not been made. Also, since higher education leads to better-paying jobs, those who have gone beyond middle school are more able to build houses at home than are middle-school leavers.

There were no differences between workers in various occupations or from places of various sizes in the proportion who wanted to return home. Some people do not grow up in their hometowns but nevertheless want to end their days there, so a few men originating in towns look to a village for retirement. About two-thirds of the southerners from each region and about four-fifths of the northerners and non-Ghanaians planned to go home eventually. Caldwell (1969:195) suggests that southerners are more likely than northerners to go home when middle-aged, while northerners stay in town longer if they can remain in employment, but the census data indicate that northerners are more likely than southerners to have left Accra by the age of fifty-five.

It was thought that younger workers would most often say they planned to stay in town and older ones that they wanted to return home. Cities seem to offer great promise to the young, whereas older men have more often experienced the disappointment of their expectations and look forward to a less challenging life in a village. On the other hand, there is the attraction of familiarity. Newcomers are constantly faced with unexpected situations and are often plagued with unemployment. The proportion planning to go home increased with the length of initial unemployment, which presumably impresses newcomers with the insecurity of urban life. Established migrants, in addition to jobs, may have found many friends who would have to be left behind if they returned home. The age factor proved more important in Accra, where workers under thirty were more likely than older men to say they would stay. Among the provincial and rural workers, there was no difference between older and younger men, but recent migrants were most likely to plan to go home. It is much easier for a migrant to settle down in a small town or village than in a city, and if he stays many years and does some farming on the side there is less need for him than for a city dweller to return home in his old age.

TABLE 6.11. *Choice of location for retirement (percentages)*

Plans to:	Accra	Tema	Kumasi	Takoradi	Rural
Stay, this is my home	17	6	9	13	19
N	735	259	150	150	138
Those not in hometown					
Stay here	23	19	37	18	10
Go home	72	69	56	71	77
Go elsewhere	5	12	7	11	13
Total	100	100	100	100	100
N	604	238	135	126	112

The difference between Kumasi and the other cities is mostly due to life-long residents who want to stay in Kumasi even though it is not their home-town. If the proportion of non-migrants shown in table 5.1 (p. 128) is compared with the proportion who said they were living in their hometown in table 6.11, it is evident that the difference is greatest for the provincial towns, especially Kumasi. Not all of those who said they were living in their hometown were non-migrants. Many Ga living in villages regard Accra as their hometown. The reverse situation, where a person lives all his life in one town but considers another as home, is much more frequent. These people are less likely than migrants to leave town on retirement, whatever they may say about their intentions, because their ties are in the town.

SUMMARY

Attitudes toward living in town vary with the size of the town and one's education and occupation, which provide or deny status within the urban community. As both education and occupation are directly related to the level of development of a worker's place of origin, a north–south dichotomy can be observed on most measures of adjustment to urban life. Independent of this, a continuum based on the scale of the society can be seen on many variables, with workers in Accra and Tema expressing the most 'urban' attitudes, and those in Takoradi the least.

On most of the items studied, northerners show less adjustment to city life and less acceptance of urban values than southerners. This represents the different level of development reached by the two parts of the country and the resulting differences of primary socialization in these areas. Many aspects of urban living that are difficult for northerners have already become familiar to southerners in the process of growing up, regardless of whether this takes place in a small village or in Accra. Southerners often taste town life by visiting before they actually migrate and they can usually hear all about it when migrants return for weekends or festivals. Life in the city is strange at first, as in any new place, but it is not completely unrecognizable. This is why differences based on the size of place in which the migrant grew up and length of time he has spent in town are seldom significant.

Occupational differences are partly confounded by the north–south dichotomy, since most northerners are unskilled workers. But on many measures of modernity there is a continuum from unskilled, through skilled, to semiskilled, and finally clerical workers. Differences are often small, but almost always in the order given. The tendency in development literature is to look to skilled workers as the vanguard of the future, the most modern sector of the manual labour force, but here they are shown to be more conservative, more traditional than the semiskilled workers, who have less training and generally lower wages.

The answer lies, at least partly, in the educational background of different types of workers. Skilled workers are more often illiterate and of alien origin than semiskilled workers (see table 3.2, p. 50). This would be sufficient to explain their less enthusiastic attitude toward education. They find skilled work satisfying and, in Ghana, it does not require literacy. Although semi-skilled work does not require literacy either, many employers prefer school leavers for these jobs, and they have plenty of choice, since no training is required. Clerical work requires education, and quite a few clerical workers have gone beyond middle school. There are, of course, many other factors which influence the results, but it seems likely that increased education will have a more important effect on the development of modern attitudes than increasing the skill level of the labour force.

We have also seen that the size of town and its 'atmosphere' has an important effect on the reactions of residents. Though Tema is smaller than Accra or Kumasi, it is more 'urbanized' in a sociological sense because it is a new town created for industry where almost everyone is a stranger and where impersonalism is much stronger than in the more established cities. Comparatively few Tema residents have relatives in town. Young men looking for companionship can find many others of a similar background in their neighbourhoods or at their places of work without limiting their choice to fellow townsmen or even tribesmen. Since almost all of the factory workers there have completed middle school, language is less of a problem than elsewhere.

Accra is a much larger city than Tema, but more established in that many 'stranger' families have been there for more than a generation. The spread-out nature of the city and dispersion of workers for individual firms means that contacts with workmates are usually limited to the premises of the firm. The 'large city' atmosphere may also encourage an impersonal attitude toward casual contacts, though Ghanaian cities tend to be very friendly places.

Kumasi is in an intermediate situation – smaller than Accra and more paro-chial, yet larger and more compact than Takoradi. The results on the friend-ship questions are similar to those in Accra, while the attitudes of Kumasi workers toward their city are quite different from those of Accra workers. The men in Kumasi tended to be older and more established in the city than the workers in Accra and were evidently enjoying a lower cost of living. Most were quite satisfied, especially with the amenities available to them. The workers in Accra, on the other hand, were glad of work but felt strongly that the cost of living was too high to make work profitable. Although facilities are better in Accra than in Kumasi, few workers commented on them and these were mostly non-migrants.

Takoradi, though it is a city by Ghanaian standards, provides an example of a less urban point of view. The inclusion within the Municipal Council area of many small towns and villages serves to mediate the feeling of living in a city. Though workers are scattered as they are in the larger cities, they see more of their workmates and are more able to make arrangements for kins-men and townsmen to work with them. Housing density and rents are both lower than in Accra or Kumasi, and more workers in Takoradi are able to house their families in two rooms. Though dissatisfaction with the cost of living in Takoradi is high and almost no one considered it a good place from the amenity point of view, workers there liked the sense of living in a city, perhaps because this was less like a city and more like their hometowns than Accra or Kumasi would be.

Although the rural sample was small, differences between rural and urban workers are evident. Rural workers are more like those in traditional Euro-pean mining communities than are the urban workers, in that most rural workers spend their spare time with workmates and they frequently have relatives or townsmen working in the same firm. Though rural workers miss the facilities they might have in town, most are satisfied to remain where they are. In this, they appear to be a self-selected group. Factories established in rural areas are likely to attract people who prefer rural life without stemming the flow to the cities of people who prefer the wider opportunities which these offer.

Other findings in this chapter may be summarized briefly. As the reason for moving to town is primarily economic, so the strongest cause for dissatisfaction with urban living is also economic. Wages are low and wage increases are granted by the government only at long intervals, whereas the cost of living has moved upward much more rapidly. Widespread knowledge of the expense of living in town and the increased possibility of unemployment may be more effective in keeping potential migrants at home than any direct government action, though this will depend partly on keeping down the cost of living in rural areas.

On the positive side, migrants are glad to have come to a place where there is work, where schools and hospitals are available and where the things they want can be conveniently purchased. Some are prepared to enjoy the entertainment facilities of the town, but others would rather rest or talk with friends. The housing situation, with most households having only one room and about two-fifths overcrowded, means that most non-family contacts are out of doors.

The worker's desire to live as near his work as possible is tempered by the difficulty of finding a room at a rent he can afford to pay. Clustering of different types of people in various parts of town is due to income differentials as well as to tribalism. There is considerable ethnic mixing within houses and within neighbourhoods in Ghanaian cities, though the desire to associate with those of common language and culture means that close friends are usually chosen from within one's ethnic group.

Urban employment is said to contribute to the breakup of the extended family because each man works for a different employer away from home instead of them all working together on the farm or as artisans. The evidence from this study is that there is some drawing together of relatives and townsmen in some firms, though they may not actually work together if the firm is a large one. This happens because workers feel a responsibility to find jobs for relatives and townsmen rather than because they think kinsmen should work together. Relatives seeking jobs are likely to have much the same qualifications (or lack of qualifications) as oneself and therefore to want the same kind of work. The worker's influence and contacts are usually limited to the firm in which he is working, so it is a measure of the difficulty in making such arrangements that only three-fifths of the urban workers said they had a relative or townsman working in the same firm and that almost all of these had only one.

Many of the workers who had townsmen in their firms said they did not see them outside of working hours. Only a minority of workers reported spending any free time with their workmates. Those who did usually chose such friends on non-ascriptive grounds.

Attitudes toward education mirror the difference between cities discussed above. Northern workers are least well disposed toward education, but southerners in the provincial cities, especially Takoradi, are less interested in education for their children than southern parents in Accra and Tema. Provincial cities attract a less educated labour force, proportionately more rural in origin, than does Tema. The adjustment required of migrants to these cities is less severe and there is less pressure to change their values to conform to a new urban situation. Migrants to the provincial cities probably feel more at home there than do migrants in Accra or Tema, but this does not affect the decision of most of them to return eventually to their true homes. Cities, of whatever size, are still not considered the proper place for men whose working days are over. For this reason, if for no other, most men maintain their contacts with home.

CHAPTER 7

FAMILY TIES

A large part of the workers' time off the job is spent at home. This chapter is concerned with family relationships: the development of the nuclear family through marriage and the birth of children, household composition as reflecting limitations in family size and structure expected of urban-dwellers and contacts with the extended family through visits and the exchange of gifts, especially the sending of regular remittances to parents.

MARRIAGE

Because of the wide variety of forms of marriage acceptable in Ghana, all more or less permanent relationships defined as marriage by the workers were recorded as such. Table 7.1 shows that only a third of the workers under the age of twenty-five were married, compared to three-quarters of those between twenty-five and thirty-nine and nearly all of those over forty. Some of the older men who were not currently married were widowers or divorced. Data from the 1960 Census (Special Report E) shows that 39% of the urban African population over the age of fifteen and 41% of the adult male African population in the country as a whole were not currently married. Our figure of 33% is lower because the sample was concentrated in the years in which both spouses tend to be living and included few men under twenty, who are seldom married.

Workers in Tema and Takoradi were more likely to be living with women without benefit of ceremony (mutual consent marriages) than were workers elsewhere. Only one of the rural workers mentioned such an arrangement. Proportionally almost four times as many workers in Tema as in Accra had marriages by mutual consent. Most of these arrangements will be terminated either for another of the same type or, eventually, for a marriage according to customary law. Some men who already have a customary wife at home take a mutual consent wife in the city, or they may have customary wives in both places.

Most of the Muslims had gone through a Muslim marriage ceremony, but very few of the Christians had been married in church. A church marriage in Ghana is usually a very expensive social occasion and few outside the elite can afford it. Unless a man is seeking leadership in his church, there is little obvious benefit from a church marriage, since its function as a sacrament is seldom understood. Ordinance marriage (civil marriage in the Registry Office under the Marriage Ordinance) is likewise ignored by ordinary Ghanaians. None of the workers interviewed reported it. Church and ordinance marriage legally bind the parties to monogamy and many men who may not achieve polygamy do not want to rule it out. Most church marriages are preceded by traditional rites; some of those married by traditional rites later have their marriages blessed by the church rather than having a formal church marriage. This blessing provides religious recognition of the marriage without the necessity of a civil divorce if the marriage should break up.

TABLE 7.1. *Marriage by age (percentages)*

Type of marriage	18–24	25–39	40+	Total
None	66	22	7	33
Monogamous	33	73	71	59
Polygynous	1	5	22	8
Total	100	100	100	100
N	418	810	204	1,432

Only 8% of the married workers were polygynous, compared to 26% of the married males in the population generally (1960 Census Post Enumeration Survey). Polygyny is most widespread in the rural areas, where it is most functional, and least common in large towns, where the shortage and expense of housing make it difficult to maintain. The proportion of polygynous marriages was higher among the provincial and rural workers than among workers in Accra and Tema. Half of the rural workers over the age of forty, and a quarter of those in the provincial towns, were polygynous, compared to only 12% of the older men in Accra and Tema.

Supporting an extra wife is not much of a problem since most Ghanaian wives, in both urban and rural areas, support themselves. However, paying school fees and medical expenses and housing a large number of children in town are more than many men can afford. Wives of polygynists and wives of monogamists were equally likely to be earning money (usually as traders). Sometimes one wife may stay at home to take charge of the housekeeping and young children, or they may do this in turn.

The incidence of polygyny is directly related to age and wage. The older a man and the higher his wage, the more likely that he will be polygynous. Migrants were somewhat more likely to be polygynous than non-migrants and those with little or no education were more often polygynous than those who had at least attended middle school. Ewes were more often polygynous than married men from other ethnic groups. Although the Ewe area has been under mission influence for over two generations, the proportion of Ewes reported as Christians in the 1960 Census was lower than for other southern Ghanaians. Aryee argues (1967) that Christianity has made little headway against polygyny, but there are measurable differences in the amount of polygyny between Christians and non-Christians. In the present sample, a quarter of those who said they followed traditional religion or none at all were polygynous, compared to 10% of both Muslims and Christians. Since very few Ghanaians are really without religion, it is quite possible that those who say they have no religion are Christians who are polygynous and hence out of communion with their churches.

TABLE 7.2 *Inter-ethnic and polygynous marriage by location and ethnicity* (*percent of married workers*)

	Inter-ethnic[a]		Polygynous[b]	
	%	N	%	N
Location				
Accra	15	(350)	12	(433)
Tema	15	(117)	7	(148)
Kumasi	13	(118)	14	(118)
Takoradi	21	(112)	17	(112)
Rural	19	(85)	18	(85)
Ethnicity				
Ga	17	(93)	11	(101)
Fanti	11	(137)	9	(159)
Other Akan	21	(229)	10	(159)
Ewe[c]	8	(179)	20	(225)
Other Togo, Dahomey	14	(21)	9	(23)
Nigerian	18	(27)	15	(27)
Northern Ghanaian	12	(52)	12	(61)
Other	35	(48)	5	(58)
Total	16	(781)	12	(896)

[a] In Accra and Tema, ethnicity of wives was ascertained only for those living with their husbands.
[b] Males only.   [c] Includes a few Guan.

In this study, marriages between members of different subgroups (e.g Fantis who married Asantes or Akwapim who married Akim, all within the

Akan 'tribe') were counted as inter-ethnic. Most inter-ethnic marriages were of this type, or at least between southern Ghanaians. While a marriage between southerners who belong to matrilineal and patrilineal groups (the Akan and the Ewe, for example) would certainly pose problems, these would not be as great as on the rarer occasions when a northerner marries a southerner. Cultural differences certainly exist in the south, but these are decreasing with the spread of education, communications, a cash crop economy and extensive geographical mobility. Northerners have generally been less affected by these factors, and their attitudes, values and way of life are closer to traditional patterns, as has already been shown.

The interview schedules used in Accra and Tema did not ask for any details on wives who were not living in the same household as the worker, hence we do not know how many of the non-resident wives were of a different ethnic group from their husbands. However, since most of these wives were living in the worker's hometown and it can be presumed that in most such marriages the spouses were of the same ethnic group, the figures reported in Table 7.2 would be the maximum for inter-ethnic marriages. Only 16% of the married factory workers included in this study were married to women of other ethnic groups, including some polygynous husbands who also had a wife of their own group.

The amount of inter-ethnic marriage is partly a function of the availability of women from one's own group and partly, of the amount of social control exercised by one's home community and its local representatives. Non-Ghanaians were most likely to marry non-ethnics, and Ewes least likely. Southern Ghanaians living in Accra or Tema and Asante living in Kumasi have plenty of women of their own group living in town from which they can choose, or are close enough to their homes to make arrangements there. The Ewe have particularly strong urban associations to keep track of fellow villagers and see that they do not go astray. In addition, the Volta Region is close enough for Ewes to be able to go home for a partner, whereas men from countries to the north of Ghana can seldom afford a trip home. The sex ratio for these groups in southern Ghana is very high. Few women come to Ghana and most of these are already married. Northern Ghanaians have much less difficulty than foreigners in finding wives of their own ethnic group because many stay in the south for short periods and because they form a close-knit community in town where men can provide wives for their friends from among their sisters.

Social constraints are apparently less effective in the more isolated Takoradi and among workers at rural factories than in Accra. Busia reported (1950:29) that 31% of marriages in his survey of Sekondi/Takoradi were intertribal. It is difficult to estimate how representative Busia's sample was and the present sample represents only one sector of the population, but it seems likely that there has been a decrease in inter-ethnic marriage in Takoradi as the town has grown and more women from various subgroups have moved there. Inter-ethnic marriage in Takoradi was only slightly higher than in other towns studied. One-fifth of the married workers there had a wife of another ethnic group.

Women who marry outside their own ethnic group are unlikely to want to go home with their husbands when the latter retire. They prefer to return to their own homes or stay in town with the children. It is suspected that men with 'stranger' wives often delay their return home indefinitely because it would mean leaving their wives behind. This is probably more true of foreigners than of Ghanaians because the ties with home have been harder for the former to maintain.

TABLE 7.3. *Marriage homogeneity by region and size of place of origin (percentages)*

Origin of husband	Birthplace of worker and spouse			Total	N
	Same	Same region	Elsewhere		
Region/country					
Accra C.D., Eastern	58	20	22	100	219
Central, Western	50	31	19	100	180
Volta	57	28	15	100	78
Ashanti, Brong/Ahafo	46	31	23	100	104
North[a]	62	18	20	100	69
Togo, Nigeria	73	14	14	100	103
Size of place[b]					
City	62	14	24	100	180
Town[c]	53	25	22	100	171
Village	53	32	15	100	274
Total	57	24	19	100	753

[a] Includes northern Ghana, Upper Volta, Niger and Mali.
[b] Ghanaians only.   [c] 5,000–39,999 population.

Over half of the marriages on which we have information (where the wife was living with her husband) were between spouses of the same birthplace or hometown (see table 7.3). Only a fifth of the workers married someone born outside their home regions. Northerners and non-Ghanaians were more likely than southern Ghanaians to find spouses from their birthplace or hometown, perhaps because few women from their ethnic group are available locally, forcing them to send home for a wife if they want to marry intra-ethnically. Their close ties to townsmen also encourage them to send back for a wife or delay marriage until they can go home for the ceremonies. Southern Ghanaians can more easily meet people from different areas and from other towns or villages in their home region. Education and Christianity foster values favouring freedom of choice in marriage, but even educated Christians usually choose a spouse from within their own ethnic group.

Although the city-reared men married women from the same place more often than men from towns or villages, Ghanaians who grew up in cities married outside their ethnic group more often than those who grew up in smaller places. Villagers who do not marry someone from the same village usually find a spouse from their own region. Men originating in cities have a better chance of finding a spouse 'at home' than those from small villages, but families in the same city may easily be socially and even culturally more distant than families living in nearby villages.

Relatively few migrants married before leaving home for the first time. Some worked at home for a period between urban jobs and got married at that time. Others sent for a wife from home or went home briefly to marry the woman chosen for them by their parents. A quarter of the urban migrant workers married in the town. Sometimes this was to a woman they had met in town; others married someone from home who had come to town to work or, in the cases of workers from distant places, a bride who had been sent from home. Unmarried women who move to town usually marry within a year of their arrival.

Because of the lag in education for girls, which was much greater in the past than it is today, it was expected that few of these workers would have found educated wives, but a third of the wives living with their husbands had been to school. There were seven cases of illiterate husbands with wives who had attended school. In about half of the urban marriages for which we have information, the husband had attended school and the wife had not. In only 18% had neither been to school. The wives for whom we have no information (those living elsewhere, mainly at home) are less likely to be educated than the wives living in the city.

CHILDREN

Children are highly valued in Ghana and a marriage without children will not be considered successful. Most parents prefer to have the children with them in town, even though this may result in severe overcrowding of the one room in which the family lives.

As shown in table 7.4, the average worker has two children, but average

TABLE 7.4. *Mean number of living children of urban males by age and occupation*

Occupation	Age			Total
	18–24	25–34	35+	
Unskilled	0.15	0.90	2.50	1.24
Semiskilled	0.41	1.51	3.87	1.51
Skilled	0.52	1.75	4.07	2.28
Clerical, foreman	0.26	1.78	4.97	2.51
Total	0.37	1.55	3.85	1.88

completed family size will probably be between five and six (men over forty averaged 5.4 children). This is in line with Caldwell's findings (1967:97, 102) that the average Ghanaian woman has seven children, but that fertility is lower for urban than for rural women and when spouses are separated by migration. The mean number of children is lowest for unskilled workers in each age category. Clerical workers and foremen under twenty-five have fewer children than skilled or semiskilled workers of that age because the former have remained in school longer than the latter, which delays marriage. But the clerical workers and foremen over thirty-five tend to have larger families than other workers. The man with the largest family was a Tema store-keeper of fifty-two with nineteen children. He had only one wife at the time, but she was not his first. Four men in the cities had ten or eleven children and eleven had nine. The proportion of large families was higher among rural workers (6% had more than eight children compared to 1% of urban men) and the mean was 2.1, in spite of the higher proportion of rural workers who had no children at all (44%, compared to 37% of urban men).

Two factors which account for most of the fertility differentials are the infant death rate and the availability of wives. The death rate for children of clerical workers and foremen is probably somewhat lower than for children of other workers, because the parents' education has given them a greater awareness of steps to be taken if a child falls ill, and they are also better able to afford fees for medical treatment. Infant deaths are more frequent in the north, where many of the unskilled workers originate, and wives in the north are too far away for frequent visiting. Unskilled and semiskilled workers were less often married than other workers and those who were married were less likely to be living with their wives than other workers. Semiskilled workers make up for this to some extent because most of them are close enough to their hometowns to visit their wives regularly. The same is true for rural workers, who were not more likely than urban workers to be living with their wives but more often lived within a half-day's journey of their hometowns.

Fostering of children is fairly common in West Africa and is seen as the natural solution to many family problems which arise (Busia 1950:35; D. G. Mills-Odoi 1967:175; Goody 1966, 1970). Children may be sent to live with relatives because their natal family breaks up through death or divorce, in order that they may be taught skills not available at home (carpentry, sewing, drumming), to attend school, to help in a grandparent's home, or to cement family ties. Migrants' children may be sent home so they will learn their parents' language and know the people and customs of their ancestral home. If the child is staying with a relative while at school or living at the school, he may visit his parents on holidays or may stay with another relative who lives nearby or one who would like his help on the farm or on some other enterprise. It is thought that a child will be better disciplined by others than by his parents and hence the fostered child will grow into a better-trained adult. The incidence of growing up outside the parents' household was checked for both the workers and their children.

Four-fifths of the workers had been reared by both parents or by their father or mother alone, usually the father. (Where a marriage breaks up or spouses live separately, boys who are not fostered usually go to the father.) Rural workers had been reared by their fathers alone more often than urban workers. When it came to rearing by someone other than the parents, the mother's side of the family was used about twice as often as the father's (8% and 4% respectively). Only 3% had been reared by siblings or others of their own generation. Thirty-two had been brought up by non-relatives. These were usually family friends, but they included teachers, Anglican priests, a tribesman and 'a man who liked me'.

About two-fifths of the parents (39% of the men and 57% of the women) had children living outside their households. Of these, 56% of the men and 20% of the women also had children living with them; three-quarters of the workers' children were living with their parents. The women were more likely than the men to have only one child, but they more often found it inconvenient to have their children with them in town. Single and divorced women often place children with their parents or sisters if they find it difficult to care for them.

Half of the fathers with children living in other households had left them with their wives or ex-wives (see table 7.5). Most of the rest were with their parents, siblings, or other relatives. Less than one in ten had children living with any relative of their wives. There was no difference between

TABLE 7.5. *Guardianship, location and age of children not living with their fathers*

	Percent of	
	Fathers[a]	Children
Living with		
Wife	39	39
Ex-wife, child's mother	12	10
Parents of father	15	12
Siblings of father	9	7
Other kin of father	15	12
Wife's kinsmen	9	7
Non-kinsmen	3	3
Other[b]	9	10
Total	111	100
Location		
Hometown	53	53
This town[c]	11	10
Elsewhere	37	37
Total	101	100
Age		
0–5	61	42
6–15	47	41
16+	17	17
Total	125	100
N	297	608

[a] Fathers who have children living elsewhere. Totals are over 100 % because some have children in more than one category.
[b] Schools, spouse where child is married.
[c] Including cases where this town is hometown.

matrilineal and patrilineal peoples or between northerners, southerners and non-Ghanaians in the proportion who fostered children or the person chosen as guardian. Children not living with their mothers were most often living with their fathers' mothers. There were only sixteen cases of children staying with non-relatives. The practice of placing children with non-relatives may be more prevalent among farming parents than among those in non-traditional occupations; many 'housemaids' come from rural homes.

One in nine of these fathers had children living in the same town as himself but in a different household. About two-thirds of these men were living in their hometowns. Children living at home were most often with their father's mother, wife or siblings, while those living elsewhere were usually on their own, with non-relatives or with relatives of their mothers. Where a man had several children living elsewhere, those under sixteen were usually all in the same place, though they might be living in different households; e.g. a man might have two children living with his wife and another with his parents, but they would all be in his hometown.

TABLE 7.6. *Age and location of children not living with their fathers by guardian (percentages)*

Living with[a]	Age				Location				
	0–5	6–15	16+	Total	Home-town	This town[b]	Else-where	Total	N
Wife	55	42	3	100	67	7	26	100	237
Ex-wife	41	44	15	100	26	31	43	100	61
Parents	53	43	4	100	71	10	19	100	72
Siblings	20	62	18	100	67	9	24	100	45
Other kin	37	41	22	100	53	8	39	100	76
Wife's kin	45	50	5	100	32	5	63	100	40
Non-kin	31	63	6	100	19	6	75	100	16
Other[c]	0	5	95	100	20	10	70	100	61

[a] Relationship to father.
[b] Includes cases where this is hometown.
[c] Includes those at school, living alone, or with a spouse.

The high proportion of fathers with pre-school children is due to the nature of the sample rather than to selectivity in leaving young children at home. Many of the parents were young and had no children over the age of five. In fact, children under six were more likely than older children to be living in town with both of their parents. Only twelve men had children living with them but no wife in the household. These cases were often the result of divorce or the death of the wife. Where a wife stays at home when her husband migrates to town, the young children usually remain with her. As shown in table 7.6, most pre-school children living away from their fathers are with their mothers or with their father's parents; few have been placed with other relatives. Where spouses do not live together in traditional society, it is chiefly the older boys who go to live with their fathers, while young boys and girls of all ages remain with their mothers.

School-age children are often sent to siblings who supervise their education. The Post Enumeration Survey found that three-quarters of the relatives in households, other than siblings of the head or his spouse, were attending school. These were most often the children of siblings. Only half of the workers' children over the age of fifteen were living with their fathers. Half of the rest were married or living on their own. The others were more often living with a sibling or other relative of their fathers than with his wife. The higher proportion of children over age fifteen living with ex-wives than with wives is due to the older average age of ex-wives' children. Whereas many wives (especially of northerners) would be living in their husband's home-town with his relatives, ex-wives more often live elsewhere because they have returned to their hometowns or continued to live in the town which the ex-husband has since left.

HOUSEHOLD COMPOSITION

Workers were asked to list all of the people sharing their households and to give some basic information about each: relationship to the worker, sex, age, birthplace, year of arrival in the survey city and where they came from. Information on ethnic group, marital status, occupation and place of work was collected for all adults. The worker was allowed to make his own inter-pretation of the word 'household'. It usually means all the people who eat and sleep together, though a few used it to mean those sharing the same room within a family house or included people who either ate or slept elsewhere.

In traditional Ga families, the men and women live in separate houses or at least in separate parts of the house. The women bring food to their hus-bands or send the children with it, and join their husbands on occasion at night. This custom has been declining due to the influence of new ideas and the shortage of housing. Akan women may also live separately from their husbands, especially at certain periods during the marriage and if the hus-band is polygynous. Only 7% of the married workers had spouses living elsewhere in the same town. Table 7.7 provides information on household membership for various categories of workers.

The proportion of workers living alone is much higher in rural factories than in the urban ones, chiefly because of the unusual situation at firm Q. Nearly half of the workers there were single or had arrived recently and not yet sent for their wives. Living alone is most characteristic of young men and northerners. The older a man, the greater the chance he will be married and/or that some junior kinsman will have joined him.

The proportion of nuclear families (man and wife, usually with children) varied with the average age of the workers. Less than a fifth of the workers under twenty-five were living with a spouse, compared to over three-fifths of those between twenty-five and thirty-four and four-fifths of the older workers. This is not just a question of a low proportion of young men being married. Married young men were less likely to have their wives with them than married older men, perhaps because of the wives' desire for help with

TABLE 7.7. *Household composition by size of household and age and ethnicity of worker* (*percentages*)

| | | Household composition | | | | | |
	Single	Nuclear	Nuclear +kin	Worker +kin	Friends	Total	N
Household size							
1–2	59	14	0	20	7	100	591
3–4	0	79	7	9	5	100	446
5+	0	72	12	12	4	100	395
Worker's age							
18–24	36	18	3	33	10	100	418
25–34	22	57	8	9	4	100	640
35+	15	74	6	3	2	100	374
Worker's ethnicity							
Ga	18	53	3	23	3	100	191
Fanti	18	55	6	15	6	100	235
Other Akan[a]	21	49	8	15	7	100	397
Ewe	28	46	6	15	5	100	345
Northern[b]	36	46	3	7	8	100	194
Togolese, Nigerian	24	63	6	4	3	100	70
Total	24	50	6	14	6	100	1,432

[a] Includes a few Guan.
[b] Those originating in northern Ghana or countries to the north.

their babies, which is most easily arranged at home. In addition, there is often a delay before women join their husbands in town.

Most of the large households were due to the presence of children rather than to relatives. About one couple in ten had relatives living with them. The true proportion was probably higher than this because of incomplete listing of household members, but it would still be considerably lower than the picture which is usually presented. Pfeffermann (1968:169) reported that the average size of Dakar workers' families included in his sample was 9.63 persons (including the worker). There was seldom more than one wage-earner in the Dakar households. Among the Ghanaian workers, the average household had three or four members and few households with more than one adult had to depend on only one source of income. Although relatives living in the household may contribute little or nothing to household finances, wives often make a considerable contribution. The large number of women in Ghana who support themselves and their children through petty trading or as bakers, seamstresses etc. is an important factor in the Ghanaian economy. Just under three-quarters of both urban and rural wives living with their husbands were working, usually as petty traders. The proportion rose to

84% in Kumasi, where households were largest and where there was more often a child old enough to look after the younger ones.

Many young workers live with relatives when they first come to town, as described in chapter 6. Young men or women prefer to move in with siblings, who may be living alone or with a spouse and children. There were a few cases of two or three generations living together (an uncle with his nephews, a grandparent living with a son and his children), but more often the relatives were of the same generation even if they were not full siblings.

Given the general level of overcrowding discussed in chapter 6, a young man often moves into a room of his own when he is earning enough to be able to afford it. A very small number of workers (thirty-two, mostly in Accra and the rural factories) were living with their parents. Sometimes they shared a single room with a three-generation family. In another thirty-five cases the worker and his sibling or wife had a separate room in his parents' house or the parent had come to live with the worker and his wife and children. Parents sometimes join their children in town for a time in order to obtain medical treatment.

More men were living with friends or townsmen in Accra and Tema than in the other locations. There were none at all in the Takoradi sample, only three in Kumasi and one at each of the rural factories. Housing in both Accra and Tema is expensive and hard to find, which encourages men to double up. Such arrangements are usually made by young southern men who have recently moved to town, though there are cases of older men and non-migrants living with friends. Tema workers were more likely than others to be living with friends or siblings. They were, on the average, younger than workers in Accra and likely to have relatives with whom to share.

Groups of friends tend to be of the same tribe. In one case, a Wangara from Mali said 'over one hundred' men had jointly rented 'a large room' for which they each paid NC1 per month. Another Wangara reported that twenty tribesmen had rented a six-room house. He said that it was the fact that they were all fellow tribesmen which made the arrangement work smoothly. In two-thirds of the cases in Accra, friends all came from the same place. In Tema such groups were more heterogeneous; in only three-quarters of the Tema groups were all of the friends from the same region. Educational background was not the same for all group members in about one-third of the cases, and occupations of members showed considerable variation. In several cases at least one of the friends was unemployed. Such arrangements are particularly prevalent in times of unemployment, when several men without families in town band together and pool their earnings from temporary work to pay expenses.

Almost all of the workers staying with relatives or friends were under thirty. Those in Accra or Tema who had relatives living with them tended to be in their early thirties (the relatives came before the household was crowded with children). In the provincial cities, those over forty were most likely to have relatives living with them.

Men were more likely than women to be living with their spouses or with friends. Women were more often living with relatives or had relatives living with them. They were equally likely to be living alone. Most of the women in Tema (82%) were single; over half (58%) of the married women in Accra were not sharing a household with their husbands. Many of these women were following the Ga customary pattern of single-sex households. Other women had remained behind when their husbands had been transferred to another town. The relatively lower emotional involvement in many Ghanaian marriages may make long-term separation of spouses less of a problem than it would be for European couples.

VISITS OF RELATIVES

Very few migrants cut themselves off from their relatives and townsmen. They usually go to a town where they know someone and spend their early weeks or months there with these contacts. As they get settled, relatives will come to visit them, bringing produce from the farm. They will be expected to give small gifts in return. If their home is not too far away, they will probably go home frequently, or at least for special occasions such as Christmas, Easter and the yam festival. Most migrants expect to return home permanently when they retire. Workers were asked several questions about visits to and from relatives and on the sending and receiving of money and goods.

Caldwell (1969:82) reports that most rural–urban migrants visit the towns before they migrate. Many villagers within fifty miles of an urban centre visit at least once a year and most urban visitors have relatives living in town. Visitors come to get some idea of what city life is like or to enjoy it for a while, to solicit aid and to contribute to the exchange of information and gifts that maintains close ties between migrants and their rural extended families. They may stay only a few hours or a day or two, but some stay several months and a few who come as visitors find work and settle permanently. Thus, it is difficult to draw the line between visitors and temporary migrants.

About half of the workers (55% of the migrants and 40% of the non-migrants) reported that they had been visited by some relative from out of town during the previous year. To this could be added those who frequently saw relatives who lived in town but had not had any out-of-town visitors. Others may have forgotten visits of several months before. It was not realized until too late that 'relatives' was not understood by the workers to include wives and children. Men with young children at home who have not gone there in several years are obviously being visited by their wives occasionally. Only four of over 100 men whose wives were living elsewhere said she had visited. Some wives come for a fairly long stay, perhaps for several months or even half a year. They then return home for the farming season or the birth of a child. The most frequently reported visitors were siblings, though some of these were probably siblings only in the classificatory sense in which the term is used in Ghana.

TABLE 7.8. *Visits by relatives (percentages)*[a]

Visited by	Accra	Tema	Kumasi	Takoradi	Rural
No one	52	37	47	50	49
Siblings	25	36	33	30	33
Parents	14	27	9	11	13
Other kin	17	18	11	17	13
Total	108	118	100	108	108
N	735	259	150	150	138

[a] Some totals are over 100% because of multiple responses.

Workers in Tema were more likely to be visited than those in other cities or in the rural factories. There was little difference between the other cities in this respect (see table 7.8). The youth of Tema workers may account for the high proportion whose parents visited them. We expected workers in Accra and Kumasi to have the most visitors, because these cities are central to the transportation network and many people visit them to buy or sell or on government business. However, it may be that some workers did not mention the visits of relatives who did not stay overnight, or that many casual commuters do not call on relatives when they come to town but wait to see them in the more relaxed atmosphere of a visit home. It is also likely that visitors to these cities have several relatives there and may see only one of them, whereas most would have only a single relative in Tema and would go there specifically to see him.

The number of visits to ordinary workers and their character may be quite different from visits to elite relatives, since the former are much more limited in the aid they can give. The elite pattern was most closely approached by the higher clerical workers in Accra. Three-quarters of them had visitors, compared to 34% of the unskilled workers.

Low-paid, unskilled workers and those from the greatest distance (northern Ghana and outside Ghana) were least likely to have visitors, as might be expected. There are cases such as the father coming down from Upper Volta to see his son who is a labourer in Takoradi and returning with NC 40, but few relatives can afford such a trip. Northerners in Kumasi were less likely to have had visitors than those in the cities farther south (81% and 63% respectively had no visitors). The opposite was true of southerners in Accra, Tema and Takoradi. Northerners in Kumasi tended to be long-term migrants (half had been there at least five years) who had more or less lost touch with their relatives at home. Those in Accra were similar in making few or no visits home, but most had been gone for a shorter period.

Northerners more easily lose touch with their relatives at home if they stay for an extended period because communication is more difficult for them than for southerners. Post offices are rare and the migrant and his family are illiterate. There may be no travellers going near the family compound. (Only 8% of the northern population lives in places of over 5,000 population.) 'Losing touch' does not mean losing interest. Long-term migrants who have had no contact with their families for years are just as firm as those who stay only a year or two in their intention to return home, and they expect to be welcomed whenever they choose to go. They cannot qualify for a post in the traditional hierarchy until they are at least middle-aged and migration does not adversely affect their chances of getting such a post. Insofar as money is needed for gifts to higher office-holders, migration may be advantageous.[1]

A less-expected finding was that workers who came from nearby were not more likely to be visited by relatives than those from other parts of southern Ghana. Workers in Accra who came from the Volta Region were more likely to have been visited than those who came from the nearby Eastern Region or from elsewhere in southern Ghana. In the provincial cities, intraregional and interregional migrants were equally likely to have visitors. Workers from villages were more often visited by parents or siblings than those who had grown up in towns or cities.

Young, single workers and those who had spent a year or less in town and were living with relatives or friends were less often visited than those who were married, older and/or had been there longer. The proportion receiving visitors rises steadily with time spent in town until fifteen years, then drops. Older men who have been in town for some time are more likely to have

---

[1] E. Goody, personal communication.

visitors than new arrivals. Married men who had relatives living with them were especially likely to have visitors. Courtesy requires that a visitor greets the oldest kinsman in town first, even though there is a closer relative living there. The oldest representative of the family will be most able to help when help is needed and he is also a centre of communications who can provide information on the whereabouts of other family members and will pass on messages to everyone who should know. Younger men are not expected to perform these functions, since they are just getting established. Men who were living with relatives tended not to mention visitors because these were guests of the head of the household.[1]

The polygynous were more likely to have visitors than the monogamous. In both categories, those married inter-ethnically were more often visited and were considerably more generous to their guests than those with ethnically homogeneous marriages. Evidently, inter-ethnic marriage does not lead to cutting ties with kin.

A question added to the schedules used in provincial and rural factories asked whether the worker had given his visitors money or anything else. Only 14% of those who had been visited had given their guests nothing. Gifts ranged from a few beers or the palm wine required by hospitality to over NC20. Almost all involved cash, usually in small amounts. Eleven percent of those who had visitors gave a cedi or two (to cover the lorry fare) and 15% gave more than NC10. Most visits seem to have been primarily social calls rather than pleas for aid, but the majority of workers do not have much ready cash which they could give a visitor. Within a few days of payday, many are back on credit (Hart 1969:221). Rural workers were much less likely to give large gifts than the provincial workers, possibly because relatives of the former lived nearby and visited more often. A total figure for these casual gifts was not asked for, as it was unlikely that an accurate answer could be given.

Those whose relatives lived a short distance away and whose jobs were fairly good tended to pay out the most. Three-fifths of the provincial skilled workers who had visitors said they gave out more than NC5, compared to half of the unskilled workers (when someone did come, they were obliged to be as generous as they could manage) and 42% of the clerical workers. The unmarried were more likely than the married to give nothing at all, though they should have been more able to afford gifts.

Whether the visitor was a parent, a sibling or other kinsman made no difference to the gift. A visitor is often representing someone else; e.g. a brother who comes with a message from a parent. Visitors were usually

---

[1] P. Leyland, personal communication.

from the worker's hometown, though occasionally siblings or others came from nearby towns.

Visitors do not just receive gifts; most of them bring a gift for their hosts. Nearly three-quarters (71 %) of those who had been visited said they had received something, usually food, from their guests. Neither does money always travel in one direction. Twenty-one workers had been given money and twelve were given cloth or clothing. Gifts were sent also to workers. Nearly a quarter of all workers (mostly those who had also had visitors) were sent gifts from home, either through a townsman who was travelling, a lorry driver or, less often, through the post. Again, the emphasis was on gifts of food, but eight men were sent money and sixteen cloth or clothing. A relative brought one young man a book; another was sent gunpowder and a third received medicine.

SENDING MONEY HOME

Giving money to visitors is not a substitute for sending money home regularly or taking gifts when one visits home. Workers who send money regularly also usually give something to visitors. Nearly three-quarters of the workers sent money home. Over a quarter said they sent or gave money monthly to one or both parents. The chief limits on sending money are one's ability to save and, for non-Ghanaians, the prohibition on remittances to other countries. This prohibition is either more easily circumvented in Accra than elsewhere or has become better enforced with time. While 58 % of the workers in Accra and Tema from Togo, Dahomey and Nigeria sent money home, only 11 % of those in Takoradi and Kumasi (interviewed a year later) reported doing so, and many complained that they were unable to get money out.

The purpose of the prohibition is to save on foreign exchange. Caldwell (1967:120) estimates that if all the foreign-born people in Ghana sent home £4 per month, the country would lose about £32 million a year in foreign exchange. While the average amount sent or taken home by international migrants was probably considerably less than this before exchange controls were imposed,[1] even a much smaller total is felt to be an impossible situation given current economic problems. The constraint on remittances also discourages immigration in a way that is more acceptable to other African governments than outright prohibition.

[1] The only available data on this is Rouch (1954:46–9), who estimated that 30–50% sent from £1.15s. (£1.75) (wage-earners) to £12 (traders) yearly. They took back goods and money valued at £30–200, much of which was lost to customs.

Family ties

As unemployment has increased in Ghana in recent years, there has been a growth of feeling that jobs should be saved for local people. This resulted in the wholesale deportation of African aliens without residence permits in December 1969 and January 1970. Though foreigners often do jobs which are not wanted by Ghanaians, the greater competition for employment of any kind has broadened the willingness of local people to undertake work which was formerly scorned.

TABLE 7.9. *Relatives to whom money was sent and amount sent (percentages)*[a]

Sends money to	Accra	Tema	Kumasi	Takoradi	Rural
Parents[b]	57	56	44	44	56
Siblings	6	8	15	7	2
Wife	5	3	4	0	8
Other kinsmen	5	4	5	5	9
Receiver unknown	1	4	4	2	0
No one	28	27	39	43	27
Total	102	102	111	101	102
N	735	259	150	150	138
Median amount sent last year (NC)	32.44	24.83	35.00	40.50	37.50

[a] Totals are over 100% because of multiple responses.
[b] Includes those living at home who gave money to their parents.

As shown in table 7.9, there is a distinct difference in the proportion of workers sending money home between those in Accra, Tema and the rural factories (73%) and the provincial workers (60%). One reason for this difference is that workers in the provincial factories were, on the average, older than those in Accra, Tema, or the rural firms and thus less likely to have parents alive. Most of those who send money home send it to their parents. The proportion who send to parents decreases and the proportion who send to others increases with time spent away from home, which is directly related to age. Provincial workers who did send money home tended to send somewhat more than those in Accra or, especially, than the Tema workers, who were making about the same wages but had fewer dependents to support.

Remittances ranged from a few shillings to NC360, but relatively few had sent more than NC50 in the previous year (about NC4 or £2 per month).[1] Most of those who did not remit money monthly sent it only two or four times per year. Workers who send money monthly usually pay larger amounts

[1] Urban household heads interviewed by Caldwell (1969:169) claimed to send about twice this much, an average of £43 per year. He does not give occupation or income data on his sample, and this may represent remittances of more than one wage-earner in the household.

over a year than those who send less often. Whereas 80 % of the remittances of monthly senders totaled more than NC 33, 80 % of the remittances of less-frequent senders totaled less than this. The monthly remittances are more likely to be supporting parents, whereas the other workers' remittances more often go to siblings (frequently for school fees) or more distant relatives (usually on the maternal side).

One-quarter of the monthly contributors (half of the rural ones) were living with their parents and gave them part (in two cases, all) of their monthly paycheck for room and board. Few of the workers living with other relatives indicated what contribution they made to expenses, since they were only asked what they paid toward the rent. Those living in their hometowns, with relatively high wages, inter-ethnic marriages and/or living with relatives were most likely to give or send money monthly.

The relationship between father's occupation and his chances of receiving money from sons is in an unexpected direction. Workers in Accra whose father was in skilled, clerical or professional work were somewhat more likely to send their parents money than those whose father had another occupation (usually farmer). Among the provincial workers, more of those whose father was a clerical worker or professional (usually a teacher) and fewer of those whose father was a trader sent him money than those whose fathers were in the more common occupations. Sons of skilled, clerical and professional workers are more likely than sons of farmers, unskilled or semiskilled workers to have relatively well-paying jobs and thus to have more money to send home. Also, they may feel obliged to help retired parents maintain a relatively high standard of living. Oppong (personal communication) found the same pattern of more support for parents with non-manual occupations among her elite couples. Where the parents are relatively well off, money sent home is often in the nature of investment. It is spent on house building, land, money lending, or other rural enterprises with the income being reinvested for the sender.

The median sent to parents was NC 34 per year, whereas the median sent to others, including wives and children, was NC 30. Only 4 % of the workers in Accra, Tema, Kumasi and one of the rural factories said they sent money to their wives (about a quarter of those who had wives living elsewhere). None of the Takoradi workers reported sending money to their wives, but 11 % of those at the newest rural factory did so. Most of these had arrived within the previous six months and planned to send for their wives when they got established. The question asked about money sent home, so money sent to wives who were not living at home may well have been missed. Also, they may have taken 'home' to mean their extended family rather than the family they were establishing. In many cases, no doubt, the money sent to parents helped support the wife, who was living as a dependent in the parental household. On the other hand, one reason for leaving the wife and children at home is that they can support themselves there by farming and/or trading (with some help from members of the extended family) while the husband saves what he can in town for major purchases.

The relationship between age and amount sent per year varies with the location. In Accra and Tema, half of those under twenty sent nothing. For those over twenty, age and amount sent were unrelated. In the provincial cities, where there were a larger proportion of older men and only one under twenty, two-thirds of the men of thirty-five or older sent NC 17 or less; half sent nothing. But 57% of the younger men sent more than this. One reason for this difference may be that in Accra the young men are unskilled or semiskilled workers, whereas older men hold the skilled and clerical jobs which pay better wages. In the provincial cities, it is the young men who hold the clerical jobs, and older men the unskilled and semiskilled ones.

Relatives expect clerical workers to send more than if they were unskilled and most do. The average amount sent is more directly related to occupation than to wage, except for those in the highest wage category. The average unskilled worker sends less than NC 10 per year, compared to NC 30 sent by the average clerical worker. However, the averages are closer together when only the senders are considered, as shown in table 7.10. While two-fifths of the unskilled workers sent nothing (some of these were non-Ghanaians and unable to send money if they had wanted to), about a quarter of the skilled and clerical workers failed to send anything to their families at home.

TABLE 7.10. *Median amount sent and proportion sending money home by occupation and wage*[a]

	Median sent per year (NC)		Percent send-ing nothing	N
	All workers	Senders		
Occupation				
Unskilled	9.08	25.51	39	239
Semiskilled	17.62	31.75	31	509
Skilled	23.53	36.64	28	449
Clerical	30.00	41.32	24	139
Wage (NC per month)				
Under 21	12.43	28.18	34	413
21–33	17.74	32.71	30	423
34–45	19.82	32.38	31	263
46+	43.66	54.70	21	111

[a] Workers away from home less than one year omitted.

Although those making the minimum wage do send less and are less likely to send anything than workers who make more, the differences between the first three wage categories are small. It is those making more than NC45 per month (8 % of the workers interviewed) who are able to send home really large sums as a norm. These are often cases where the migrant is merely investing his money at home rather than using it to improve his relatives' standard of living. While as many workers making between NC21 and NC33 per month as those making more than NC45 reported sending home over NC100 in the previous year, these were a very small proportion of the workers in the lower wage category and were balanced by a large number of workers who sent very small sums. The proportion of workers sending nothing home is also very similar for the lower three wage categories, about a third of the workers in each. It is only in the highest wage category that the proportion who send nothing drops to a fifth.

Pfeffermann's report on Dakar workers (1968:166) shows them as less likely than Ghanaian workers to send money home, but those who did send remitted larger amounts than the typical Ghanaian worker. About a third of the Dakar workers interviewed sent money regularly. The proportion sending irregularly was not reported. They averaged about £3 per month, whereas Ghanaian senders averaged little more than NC2 (£1) per month. Wages appear to be considerably higher in Dakar than in Ghana (over half the workers in Pfeffermann's sample were earning over £25 per month), so those who are not supporting urban relatives should have more surplus cash to send home.

Most urban workers get requests for money from time to time to pay for special expenses at home, especially for funerals or medical expenses, including the birth of children. Workers who cannot afford to send money regularly usually try to meet such requests, and others contribute in addition to their normal remittances. Emergencies get many into debt, because their relatives do not understand that they have no extra funds. At one of the rural factories we added the question, 'Have you sent any money recently for emergencies, school fees etc. ?' About a fifth of the workers had sent money for such an emergency, usually for funeral expenses. The money sent ranged from less than a cedi to NC80; half of the remittances were of NC5 or less. These remittances were added to their yearly total.

The relationship of these data to actual fact is hard to assess. A check on accuracy was attempted by asking several related questions: 'How often do you send money home?' 'How much do you send each time?' 'During the last year, how much have you sent home?' While some people probably reported that they sent money when in fact they only wanted to and others may have inflated the amount sent, there were probably many who sent money for special occasions and did not report this because the questions concerned regular remittances. The amount sent each time was multiplied by times sent per year. In the few cases where these totals differed, the lower amount was taken as more likely to be correct. Thus, the amounts mentioned here can be taken as the probable minimum of the contributions sent home by workers.

Though the amount sent by one individual is small, the total accruing to a village could make a considerable difference in the standard of living. The total sent home by these 1,432 workers in one year comes to over NC 34,000, certainly a substantial contribution. At this rate, 25,000 factory workers would give their families (mostly in villages and small towns) nearly NC 575,000 in a year. Caldwell (1969:169) estimates that £5 million (NC 10 million) leaves Accra each year in gifts and savings. It can be assumed that rural Ghanaians benefit from most of this.

HOMETOWN VISITS

The frequency of sending money home is directly related to the frequency of visits home. Those who send money monthly are two or three times as likely as those who send money less often to visit home at least bimonthly and five or six times as likely to visit frequently as those who never send money. Or, to put it the other way, those who often visit their homes tend to be the most regular senders of remittances. In addition, those who go home often usually take food or provisions or a small amount of money with them.

Of those who visited their homes, 23% took nothing. Nearly two-fifths (38%) took money; 29% took food or provisions such as soap, cigarettes, sweets, matches or kerosene; and 19% took cloth or clothing. Some brought money and either food or clothing and a few brought all three. Other items taken home include a cutlass, medicines, perfume (sold at lorry parks), a watch and 'all I have'. For all that has been written about migrants who bring home bicycles, only one of these workers said he had taken a bicycle home. Southern Ghanaians tend to consider bicycles beneath their dignity and northerners probably include them only when making the final return home, since a bicycle would be intended for their own use.

As the trips home become less frequent, the proportion who take nothing increases and fewer take food or provisions. Infrequent visitors are often the poorest workers and those from farthest away. Many can save only the cost of the journey and, for those who can afford more than this, money is more conveniently carried than food. Workers in the provincial and rural factories less often take food, provisions, or cloth with them than do workers in Accra and Tema, but they more often take money. It is often possible to buy goods in Accra which are not available elsewhere.

While about 30% of the Accra workers take money when they go home, regardless of how often they go, the proportion of the provincial workers who take money increases with the frequency of visits. Half of those who go at least bimonthly take money along. Provincial workers who take money take larger sums, on the average, than rural workers,[1] but more rural workers visit their homes at least three times a year, so large gifts would be a considerable drain on their resources.

Of those who brought money with them when visiting home, half took less than NC10, a third took between NC10 and NC20 and only 14% took more than this. However, it should be remembered that money brought home usually supplements rather than substitutes for money sent regularly. Those who go home weekly or monthly usually take a cedi or two; about half of those who brought more than NC20 went home less than once a year. Two-fifths of these infrequent returnees were from northern Ghana or were immigrants, who used visits to present the money they were unable to send.

TABLE 7.11. *Frequency of visits home by location of firm and of home, workers not living in their hometowns (percentages)*

Location of	Never	Under 1 per year	1 per year	2–5 per year	More	Total	N
Firm							
Accra	14	30	21	24	11	100	595
Tema	6	18	27	38	11	100	232
Kumasi	15	32	23	12	18	100	137
Takoradi	23	24	20	21	12	100	126
Rural	10	18	31	32	9	100	98
Home							
Same region[a]	7	18	21	30	24	100	416
Other southern Ghana	5	22	28	35	10	100	478
North and outside Ghana	35	43	16	5	1	100	294

[a] Accra Capital District counted as part of Eastern Region.

As with visitors, distance from home is undoubtedly the deciding factor in the frequency of visits home. Having been reared by one's parents, having

[1] Accra/Tema workers were not asked this question.

land rights at home, or having been born and/or grown up in one's hometown have no apparent effect on the frequency of visits. None of the northerners or non-Ghanaians in the provincial cities or Tema went home more than once a year and very few went that often. Three northerners and a few Togolese in Accra said they went home more than once a year. Since the journey to Lomé takes no longer than a trip to Kumasi, Togolese might go more often if it were easier to take money and/or goods across the border.[1] The fact that few Tema workers go home less than once a year (see table 7.11) is related to the prevalence of southern Ghanaians there. The provincial workers are not notably different from those in Accra in the frequency of visits home.

Few workers living outside their home regions go home bimonthly or more often. The proportion of southern Ghanaians who never go home is about the same for those living in their home regions and elsewhere; it is very low in either case. In contrast, a third of the workers from northern Ghana and from other countries had not gone home at all and only 22% went at least once a year.

The length of visits home is governed by the time which workers are allowed to be away from their jobs. Extended visits usually require quitting one's job and finding another on return to town. For those who want to keep their jobs, there are usually four days available at Christmas and Easter. Some firms grant two weeks annual leave as well. Three-quarters of all home visits lasted less than a week and only 6% lasted more than a month. Those who must travel a long distance most often quit their jobs and take a 'rest' at home; some of the work histories show periods of a year or two farming while on visits home. At the other extreme, the man whose home is nearby and who visits frequently may only stay a few hours, going and returning on the same day.

Apparently, a pattern of visits is established in the first few years away which is then maintained or only slightly decreased as long as the migrant remains in the same place. Age seems to have no effect on the frequency of visits. Workers living with a wife and children or with friends or relatives were more likely to visit home regularly than men living alone. This is not just because men living alone tended to be long-distance migrants. The differences were small but consistent for southerners, northerners and non-Ghanaians. In each case, workers living with their wives were similar in their visiting patterns to those living with relatives or friends; having one's wife in town does not decrease one's propensity to visit relatives at home.

---

[1] The border was officially closed for long periods in the years immediately preceding the study, but those who wanted to cross could usually do so.

Those who had been away from home less than five years were more likely to visit home more than once a year and those who had been away a longer time to visit less often, but there was no difference in the proportion who never visited. More migrants who grew up in cities than who grew up in smaller places had never visited their hometowns. Some of these were foreigners who grew up in Ghanaian cities and consider the ancestral home as their hometown even though they have never visited it. This may also be taken as evidence that second-generation city-dwellers (the children of migrants) who do not go home regularly with their parents during their childhood will lose all but a vague emotional attachment to 'home' since they have been effectively cut off from village life.

Although many long-distance migrants and unskilled workers (often the same people) were able to afford few, if any, visits home and seldom had visitors, they had not necessarily cut themselves off from their relatives and townsmen. It is usually possible to send messages from time to time with people who are travelling. More of those who had never gone home since they first migrated than of those who had gone said they planned to retire to their hometowns, whereas those who went often were more likely to say they planned to stay in town indefinitely. While the infrequent visitors miss their relatives and often cut short their stay in town to return home, the frequent visitors can enjoy both the companionship of their relatives and the urban amenities and income.

Some workers who never go to their hometowns visit relatives and/or townsmen in nearby towns. Some have school friends living nearby whom they visit occasionally. Provincial and rural workers were asked a series of questions about these visits: 'What place outside — [his hometown] do you visit most often?' 'How often do you go there?' 'Whom do you visit?' About three-fifths of the workers questioned, including most of the northerners, never travelled except to go home. Of the rest, most went to towns in other regions. Rural workers mostly went to Accra. Nearly three-quarters of the visits were to relatives. Although casual visits were usually at the rate of one or two per year, workers who had parents living away from their hometowns visited them more often than they went home. Rural workers were much more likely than urban workers to visit other places, perhaps to make up for the lack of contacts in the village where they were living or to enjoy city life from time to time. Only 19 % of the rural workers (compared to 74 % of the provincial workers) made no visits except to their hometowns. Rural workers who visited other places were half again as likely as the provincial workers to visit rural places.

Family ties

SUMMARY

As most factory workers plan to spend their working lives in town, they prefer to have their wives and children living with them. Workers over twenty-five are usually married; over half had a wife in town and most of these also had children. Most of the workers are married by traditional or Muslim rites. Church and ordinance marriages are very infrequent at this level of society because of the expense involved and because these types of marriage rule out polygyny. Though only a small minority of factory workers have two wives at once and very few of these have both wives with them in town, polygyny remains an aspiration for quite a few. Inter-ethnic marriage occurs more often. One man in six or seven who is married has a wife of a different ethnic group, though at least half of these are marriages between people of closely allied groups and cases of northerners marrying southerners are rare.

Workers do not appear to respond to the high cost of living by limiting family size. Large families are still the ideal and the average of two children is due to the relative youth of workers in the sample. The government has recently decided to promote smaller families, but it seems unlikely that the average completed family size for this group of workers will be less than five. Large families are possible because the extended family system allows urban parents to send some of their children home to be brought up by relatives. Where the wife is living at home, the children usually stay with her. Such wives usually have food farms and are self-supporting, so the husband is able to save more for his eventual retirement than he could if the whole family lived in town. Nevertheless, parents prefer to have most of their children with them in town, especially the younger children, so that they can supervise them personally.

Households tended to be relatively small. Three-quarters of the households everywhere except Tema consisted of a single individual or man and wife with no extended family members. Workers were asked to list all the people living with them. Certainly there were some who neglected to mention long-term visitors, new arrivals etc., but other studies carried out in Ghana confirm the impression that relatively few urban households are overburdened with relatives. The level of income of these men allows many of them to have a room of their own if they are single and the rapid growth of their families after marriage (there are quite a few with three or four children under five) means that there is little space available for long-term guests. If they earned enough to pay for a second or third room, they would probably have to house more relatives than they do at present.

216

    Contacts with relatives are chiefly governed by the distance a worker has migrated, though his income is also a factor. Workers whose hometowns are nearby are often visited by relatives and go home fairly frequently. Those from farther away have few visitors and seldom get home more than once a year. Visitors often bring gifts, usually foodstuffs, and usually receive a small cash gift in return. Food is sent or brought to urban workers, but probably too seldom for it to be economically important to them. The regular remittances of large numbers of urban workers are an important factor in equalizing rural and urban incomes and in maintaining contact with home.

CHAPTER 8

GHANAIAN FACTORY WORKERS AND MODERNITY

The origins, occupational background and attitudes, migration patterns, adjustment to urban life and family relations of the workers studied have been discussed in considerable detail. In concluding, I shall assess the place of factory workers in the wider society, the factors promoting and inhibiting modernity among them and the implications of this study for the 'industrial man' hypothesis.

FACTORY WORKERS AND THEIR SOCIETY

Factory workers constitute only a small proportion of the Ghanaian population. It has been shown that they are by no means homogeneous in their background, attitudes, or behaviour. They range from illiterate labourers of northern origin who are only very partially committed to urban employment and spend all of their spare time with townsmen or tribesmen to men who completed middle school in Accra, are fully committed to spending the rest of their lives working in the city and whose friends are chosen for compatibility rather than by tribe, religion, or occupation. Young school leavers are attracted to factory work, but many others who are neither young nor educated find work in factories. In fact, if clerical workers are included (as they have been in this study), there are factory workers who are typical of almost all sectors of the urban population except the elite.

Factory workers may be differentiated from the general public in some ways because of the nature of their jobs. They work regular hours for an employer, in a country where the majority of people work irregular hours in self-employment. Their jobs are specific, rather than diffuse, and usually involve training, though this is seldom very extensive. Their work frequently requires the use of machines and impersonal contacts with a large number of workmates, whereas most of their countrymen have only simple hand tools and work alone or with a few members of their family. Because the jobs are there, factory workers usually live in cities and prefer to do so. They may thus develop a somewhat greater awareness of time than characterizes the average Ghanaian, a set of norms for dealing with individuals one does not know well but interacts with daily and some ideas about the functioning of machines and the need for maintenance.

Workers do not all acquire these attitudes to the same extent. They are affected by the nature of their specific job, the size of their factory and the nature of its management, the length of time they have remained at the same post and the nature of their ties to kinsmen and townsmen inside and outside the factory. The man who works in a small firm of little more complexity than a roadside workshop finds it easier to continue to operate on the basis of personal relationships and to work at his own pace than the man who spends his life working in a large factory where he must clock in, where records are kept of his daily production and where he never sees his employer face to face. The man who has a succession of short jobs (a frequent occurrence in Ghana), who is in and out of self-employment and unemployment, may maintain his traditional norms because he is not on a job long enough to develop new norms even if the job were effective in doing this.

Shift work in particular sets some factory workers off from other people in the society. Only a small number of workers are as yet on shift work, but it is sufficiently widespread in Tema for the results to be evident. Workers on shifts are free at times when other people are working and are employed when most others are free. The difference is magnified when they have their day off during the week rather than at the weekend. They must try to sleep in the daytime, when there is considerable noise in the neighbourhood and/or the heat makes their room least comfortable. Many spend endless hours playing cards or other games with friends on the same shift. They often see relatives and other friends only every third week, when they are free in the evenings. They seldom belong to any associations, because they cannot attend meetings often enough to make it worth while. Of necessity, work plays a much more important part in the life of a shift worker than of others in industrial or non-industrial employment. This applies less to the employee in a factory with two shifts than to one working three shifts, since the former can sleep at night and have more evenings and weekends to maintain contacts with relatives and friends.

However, where they are not working unusual hours, there is little to distinguish factory workers from other men in their urban neighbourhoods. The factory workers are somewhat younger, somewhat more educated than the majority of urban workers, but society appears to have a greater effect on their behaviour than does their industrial employment. Structural transformation of Ghanaian society is proceeding rather slowly, and the workers appear to be well adjusted to the society as it is today rather than anticipating the modern, industrial society which may one day appear. Early socialization and contacts outside the workplace are more important in shaping attitudes and behaviour than is work experience.

This is true because so many workers maintain close ties with people in non-industrial employment, both in the cities and in the rural areas and because of the frequency of moves into and out of industrial employment. While many have deliberately moved from their villages to the cities to improve their standard of living (implying that they have goals which cannot be fulfilled within the traditional society; see Imoagene 1967: 378, 384), they by no means turn their backs on that society. Even those who are cut off for long periods usually value home ties and plan to return home on retirement. Changes in behaviour resulting from the demands of employers or the requirements of urban living are often made without changing other areas of life not so affected. Behaviour on and off the job, in town and at home, can be kept separate (Mitchell 1966), so that the effects of industrial employment are minimized and long-established patterns are maintained.

The work experience was more important in the development of attitudes among workers in countries which industrialized early than it is today because of the nature of the work and of the communities in which the workers lived. The best example of this is mining. Mine work is dangerous, forcing the workers to rely on each other for aid, and mines are usually isolated so that the workers' companions on and off the job are necessarily the same people. Thus, a strong sense of community usually develops among miners.

Much early industry was also in small towns (e.g. the mill towns of Lancashire and New England) where the work dominated men's lives. But industries in today's developing countries are usually in cities where workers in many factories and in non-industrial employment are all living together. Choice of employment and of companions is far wider than was the case a hundred years ago. In addition, men taking up factory work in developing countries can usually return to a farm if they are not satisfied, which was not the case during the early period of industrialization. Thus, new workers are not tied to industrial work and work is less important as a socializing factor.

Factory workers are a reference group chiefly for schoolboys who aspire to this occupation. Rural schoolboys in particular think of factory work as the modern thing to do. Other people, who might be expected to know more about the conditions and wages of factory workers than do rural schoolboys, rate factory work high among manual occupations but give no evidence that men with such jobs are particularly admired. For the average member of

Ghanaian society, factories are probably seen in terms of the employment they may provide for oneself or one's relatives rather than as examples of advanced technology. Certainly, visitors are impressed by the machinery, but the jobs done by the workers seem (and usually are) simple enough. The repetition and the steady work needed to keep up with the machines are not valued, but the wages are seen as adequate compensation for these disadvantages. Thus, factory work is considered similar to other urban employment. The vital point is to be in employment, not the level of technology which this employment involves.

Given the current economic climate and level of unemployment, men with middle-school education or less value the ability to find and keep a job but do not place much emphasis on the type of job except insofar as the prospects for its continuance are good or bad. Job mobility among manual workers is high and is frequently accompanied by occupational mobility, so workers without trade training tend to be identified by background factors rather than by occupation: 'He is an Ewe' or 'from Bawku' rather than 'He is a polisher at Pioneer Plastics.' A man may not even know the specific job of one of his good friends, or a wife of her husband, though they usually know the name of the firm at which he works. Thus, factory workers are young men in employment, perhaps working unusual hours, but not noticeably different in behaviour or attitudes from others of similar age and background.

The government attitude toward factory workers tends to be expressed in pronouncements urging higher productivity and the avoidance of strikes. The government is generally more concerned with management than with the workers, since the former are important to its development policy. There is no need for government efforts to build up the factory labour force, since the demand for such jobs is well in excess of the supply. From an official point of view, factory workers are important to the economy and a symbol of the industrialization which the country is seeking. They should therefore be loyal and hardworking.

THE CONCEPT OF MODERNITY

Modernity, as applied to individuals, has been defined as 'a set of attitudes, values and ways of feeling and acting, presumably of the sort either generated by or required for effective participation in a modern society' (Smith and Inkeles 1966:353). There have been many attempts to give meaning to this concept by developing scales of modernity. Most of these have been limited to the community or country in which they were developed, but three scales developed recently have been tested in more than one country. These provide a picture of the values expected to become more widespread as a country modernizes. The findings of these studies will be summarized briefly as a prelude to the discussion of the level of modernization among Ghanaian factory workers.

Inkeles (1966) found various 'themes' which are characteristic of a modern man: an openness to new experiences, knowledge and opinions on a wide variety of topics, an orientation toward the present and future rather than the past, a belief in planning and organizing one's life and in science as a means of dominating one's environment, trust in and respect for other people, and acceptance of rewards based on achievement rather than ascription. As a result of his studies in India and Pakistan, Chile and Argentina, Nigeria and Israel, these themes took the form of the OM Scale (Smith and Inkeles 1966). The short form of this scale measures the responses to questions on political activism and identification, perception and valuation of change, planning for the future (including family planning), awareness of and interest in the opinions of others, use of and interest in the mass media, religious orientation and membership in voluntary associations.

Kahl's study of modernism in Brazil and Mexico (1968) was carried out at about the same time as Inkeles'. Fourteen unidimensional scales were developed, each measuring a single value on a traditional/modern continuum. These were tested on large samples of men in small and large towns and in various occupations, whereas Inkeles limited his samples to peasants, factory workers and urban non-industrial workers, carefully selected so that background variables would be represented in equal proportions in each country. Kahl measured many of the same values as Inkeles, but some of those accepted by Inkeles have been rejected by Kahl. He found seven values which constituted a 'core of modernism' (1968:30–37): the ability to plan and work for the future, a willingness to be separated from relatives and to trust non-kinsmen, a preference for urban life even though it is impersonal, acceptance of the possibility of making friends on various social levels and of upward mobility. He rejected, as not sufficiently correlated with the other scales, measures of attitudes toward large companies, risk taking, the primacy of occupation, manual work, family planning, religiosity and mass communications. The last three were included in Inkeles' scale and the first three appear to be cornerstones of an industrial society.

Doob's scales (1967) are based on studies in East Africa. They measure orientation toward and optimism about the future, loyalty to the government and the country, trust in other people and in science, and rejection of tribalism. They contain many more political questions than the scales previously discussed. Doob claims this is the way modernity is seen in East

Africa. This may be because most of his samples were of secondary or university students, who expected to spend their lives in government employment.

In using these results to assess the modernity of Ghanaian factory workers, it is necessary to determine the extent to which these values are culture- and class-bound. One cannot help but be struck by the relationship between many of the attitudes characteristic of modernity and attitudes considered typical of the middle class in industrialized Western countries. The authors presumably expected modernity to vary separately from social class, but they appear to be closely connected. Kahl reported that modernism as tested by his scales was more closely related to socio-economic position than to location. Those with good jobs (who were usually also well educated) were more modern in their attitudes than the unskilled, regardless of whether they lived in metropolitan areas or in the provinces. It is probably quite true that elites and sub-elites in developing countries have been more exposed to modern values than the ordinary people, but these values are also likely to be more functional for them than for the average employee or farmer.

The typical workingman in many 'advanced' countries would probably show less modernity than his middle-class fellow citizen in terms of these scales. Goldthorpe and his colleagues (1968, 1969) were concerned with demonstrating that a few workers in Britain have moved away from traditional values, implying that most have not, in the country where the industrial revolution began.

If modernity is essentially incorporation in a Euro-American middle class, then it is not likely to become widespread in developing countries for a long time. Many workers in these countries face difficulties which prevent the development of modern values or make them disfunctional. Attitudes suitable for a modern society may be irrelevant, meaningless, or merely not of much use to ordinary members of societies which are not yet modern. This can be shown in relation to the values of efficacy and optimism about the future, relations with kinsmen and use of mass communications. Other values such as trust and individualism and behaviour in planning fertility and membership in associations seem to vary considerably between societies at the same level of development as well as with social class.

Efficacy is defined as the belief 'that man can learn, in substantial degree, to dominate his environment in order to advance his own purposes and goals, rather than being dominated entirely by that environment' (Inkeles 1966: 143). It is considered central to modernity. It includes some understanding of the basic principles of science and an interest in planning for the future with the expectation that the plans will come to fruition.

But the ordinary worker, especially in a developing country, is faced by many situations he cannot control and which his government, doctors, employers and other specialists seemingly cannot control either. He may suddenly be laid off because a machine breaks down and cannot be repaired, or because bad planning on the part of management puts the firm out of business. His wife or child may die of a disease for which treatment is either unknown, too late, or too expensive, or they may be healed by a traditional or religious healer when modern medicine has failed or is not available. A demand for cash from his extended family may leave him in debt to the money-lenders. The government talks about economy, but inflation steadily erodes his earnings and government services depending on modern technology (such as water and electricity supplies) frequently break down. In none of these cases would faith in science or planning for the future have been of much use to him. Thus, it may be more rational to maintain ties with the past and live in the present, letting the future take care of itself.

People who do not show much optimism about the future and their chances of rising in socio-economic status may be equally realistic. Opportunities for long-distance upward mobility may well have declined in recent years. In any case, the possibilities for moving up are greatest for those who are still in school and those who have already achieved some mobility early in their occupational careers. Those who are over twenty-five, with little education and in low-status jobs have little chance of upward mobility. There are large numbers of school leavers in many developing countries who believe in the efficacy of hard work to get ahead but cannot find any work to do. Their parents, who tend to think that getting ahead depends on whom you know, may be less modern or merely more aware of the realities of a culture still only partly modernized. After all, hard work does not inevitably produce upward mobility even in the United States.

Planning for the future among Ghanaian workers takes two forms, depending on age group. Young men who have just left school sometimes start correspondence courses or sign up for classes at the local Workers' College. The proportion finishing such courses is small and the proportion who pass the appropriate examinations is still smaller. Nevertheless, this indicates hopes for the future and a belief in the possibility of rising through one's own efforts. However, many of the young men who undertake these studies would be better advised to try some other way of improving themselves. The excessive self-confidence of many students who take examinations over and over though they have no chance of passing is certainly misplaced. If the equivalent amount of time and effort were spent learning other skills, it might be more profitable to the individuals concerned and to the country.

Older men's plans for the future are based on traditional goals. To secure a prestigious return to their hometowns, they put aside what money they can to buy farm land (in areas where this is necessary) and to build a house. This is planning, but it is not modern behaviour, because it looks to a return to traditional ways and involves turning away from urban life. Yet, these are the workers who should be the most modern, because they have lived longest in the cities and worked longest in the factories. At the present stage of development, returning home on retirement is still likely to be the most rational decision for people of limited resources and also for many who have done well. The few men who remain in town during their old age must not only contrive to remain independent, but must forgo the prestige they would have at home, the security of aid when it is needed and the positive functions they might fulfil at home.

Perhaps the few who stay in town are the truly modern men, in that they have organized their resources well enough to have something on which to live in retirement (usually a house) and who feel sufficiently at home in town to be willing to stay there when most of their friends have gone. But this cannot be assumed without further research. There is certainly a need for more study of these people, but a distinction must be made between those who stay in town because they were unable to organize their future and hence cannot afford to go home and those who stay because they prefer to do so. When the data from the 1970 round of censuses is available, we will at least know whether the proportion of old people in towns is increasing and be able to investigate whether such an increase is related to increases in the level of education or industrial employment among the migrants.

Another characteristic of the modern man is a willingness to substitute new relationships with non-relatives for the security and all-embracing concern of the extended family. Predictions of the rise of the conjugal family are familiar enough and are partly confirmed by data from a wide variety of places. But a distinction must be made between housing arrangements and relationships. Cities are inimical to extended families living together, but conditions may favour the continuance of close ties between kinsmen who live near each other. These ties are maintained whenever possible by a majority of Ghanaians at all levels of society. Workingmen use them as a hedge against misfortune, but also for the pleasure they provide. Studies in various industrialized countries have confirmed the importance of kinship among workingmen. Relatives will support one in an emergency. One can go to them for advice on marital and other problems, and can relax best with them because of shared background and experiences. It is the inability of relatives to reciprocate aid and especially to share their experiences which leads some people gradually to cut their ties with their relatives as they rise in the society. Thus modernity, defined as cutting family ties, tends to be related to position in the social hierarchy.

Willingness to trust others is closely related to one's relationships with kinsmen. Very few Ghanaians would take a serious matter to an outsider if a kinsman were available. Cases where this occurs are likely to concern members of the elite who feel that the situation is not one their relatives would understand. The modern response would probably be to discuss the problem with one's wife rather than with an elder kinsman. But trust also depends on the milieu. Anthropologists have found that impersonal trust is far more prevalent in some societies than in others. Trust is related to the norms of the society, which regulate the conditions of trust and the sanctions for breaking it. Kahl (1968:143) found trust in outsiders much more widespread in Brazil than in Mexico.

Access to mass communications is also related to wealth and hence to social class. Radios are more often owned by the rich than by the poor and the former are less likely to have their radios stolen than the latter. Illiterates are limited to radio broadcasts of news in local languages, which are very brief; the radio is used by them chiefly as a source of popular music. Members of the elite may read several papers daily, but many ordinary citizens in developing countries cannot afford to buy a daily paper even if they are able to read. Lack of interest in the mass media may be fostered by the felt distance of the government from the people. The elites are more likely to be affected by government decisions and other local events (which form most of the content of local media) than are ordinary citizens. The latter get news of interest to them by word of mouth rather than from the mass media. Insofar as interest in international news is a sign of modernity, working-class people in most advanced countries are not very modern either. There are many large city newspapers in America which devote far less space to news of Africa than African papers give to news about America, and many of their readers would not notice if there were no news except of sports.

Attitudes toward fertility are associated with social class in most societies. Although the upper class may favour large families (being able to afford them), middle-class families are consistently of smaller average size than lower class families. Since this is so, and since there is still resistance to family planning among lower-class families in industrialized countries (where many of the men concerned work in factories and should therefore be imbued with modern values), it is difficult to see why a positive attitude toward family planning should be regarded as a necessary aspect of individual modernity, regardless of its alleged necessity for economic development of the country in which the individual is living. It should be noted that Kahl (1968:142) found that Brazilians wanted fewer children than Mexicans, even when socio-economic status and geographic location were controlled.

There are evidently cultural factors involved here which are not overcome by urban residence or modern occupation. Studies of fertility attitudes in Ghana have shown that most people at all levels of society still want large families. It seems likely that urban workers may eventually adopt family planning more seriously than elite couples because of their limited income, but there is as yet no indication that widespread acceptance of the small family in the modern sense (two or three children) will occur in any sector of the population in the near future. In this case, the traditional culture remains strong.

An aspect of urban life which has a large place in the literature on urban Africa but has been almost ignored in this book is associations. Membership in associations was included in Inkeles' scale of modernity, but it varies greatly between countries, even for people of similar education and occupation (Inkeles 1969: 219). In developed countries, multiple memberships are not common among lower-class people. For various reasons, associations appear to be less important in Ghana than in other African countries about which we are fairly well informed. Measuring modernity by the number of memberships or the types of associations may thus be very misleading.[1]

Almost all employees in Ghana must belong to a trade union, but these unions are important to very few workers who are not officers except in rare industries such as the railroads. Nkrumah subordinated the Trades Union Congress to the Convention People's Party so that it became an agent for promoting government policy rather than worker demands. Its loss of credibility was partially redeemed after the 1966 *coup*, but the majority of workers pay little or no attention to their unions. Very few mention a union when asked about associations to which they belong, because it is not voluntary or because it is meaningless to them. Using membership in a union as evidence of modernity in such a case is merely giving a man an extra point for being in closed-shop employment.

While unions might be considered a modern affiliation, membership in ethnic or community improvement associations is usually regarded as a sign of traditional orientation. But, in Ghana, place of origin seems to have more influence on such membership than education or orientation. Akans seldom have such associations. Where they exist, they tend to be 'scholars' unions', where migrants who have been to school (especially secondary school or university) meet once a year, at home, to plan for their town's future and

[1] Inkeles noted the number of memberships, not the type of association the individual belonged to.

enjoy social activities to enliven the holidays. Ewes are much more likely to have associations and to belong to them, but participation varies greatly from one hometown to another. Where there is someone to organize, literates and illiterates will join together in regular meetings. Where there is no organizer, the association usually dies out temporarily.[1] Ga associations tend to be composed of illiterate women who join together for mutual aid. The Ga live near enough to their hometowns to visit regularly and apparently have less need for improvement societies than the Ewe. Northerners may have associations, but more often group themselves under a headman or obtain what help they need from relatives and townsmen without formalizing the situation by creating an organization.

Factory workers are like the rest of the urban population in that few of them have any meaningful relationships of this type. Relaxation with members of the family or small groups of friends is preferred. This is true even for many members of the elite, though quite a few of these do belong to one or more professional or recreational associations.

Individualism is another attribute of modernity which appears to vary with cultural background. Kahl (1968:143) found Brazilians generally more individualistic than Mexicans. LeVine (1966) showed how the cultural background of Ibos makes them more individualistic than the Yoruba or Hausa in spite of their lack of urbanity. Among the Ghanaian workers studied, individualism was more evident among skilled workers than among the semiskilled or clerical workers, who appeared generally to be more modern in their attitudes than the skilled workers. It would seem in this case that the tendency to independent thinking is fostered by the ability to support oneself. It is certainly not encouraged by the school system as it exists in Ghana today, or by the civil service emphasis on conformity and maintenance of the *status quo*.

Although Ghana has become more modern in the years since independence, in the sense of becoming more urbanized, industrialized and educated, political activism has decreased. A general election still evokes considerable enthusiasm, but the ordinary citizen does not otherwise feel that there is much he can do to affect government action. Significantly, the government is referred to as 'they'. It is thought of as a tool of the 'big men' which is not very concerned about the inhabitants of the slums, the small farmers, and the unemployed. Many Ghanaians welcomed the military takeover because it brought a diminution of corruption. Enthusiasm for the return to democracy is tempered by a 'wait and see' attitude. Hence, political activism tends to be limited to those who have something to gain by being noticeably loyal to the

---

[1] P. Leyland, personal communication.

party in power. If one favours the opposition, rationality may dictate political passivism.

The same tendency to passivism carries over to all dealings with authorities. People in Tema[1] were asked if they had ever complained to the Tema Development Corporation or to the police. Four-fifths had never made a complaint about their houses to the T.D.C. The police often appeal to the public for help in tracing criminals, but there is considerable reluctance to become involved and a strong feeling that it would be a waste of energy.

The connection between modern attitudes and social class has seldom been mentioned.[2] The expectation that modernity would vary with education, urban experience and type of occupation has been generally confirmed, though these do not account for all of the variance in modernity scores (Stephenson 1969:155). However, there is the danger that emphasis on cross-cultural comparisons of industrial workers will hide the very real ethnic differences within countries and the gap which exists between accepting the means to modernity and accepting the goals of Euro-American society. Clignet and Sween (1969) use data on polygyny in Ivory Coast to demonstrate the importance of these factors in understanding the process of modernization.

Polygyny is still a widely held ideal in Africa. The expectation that it would die away with the spread of education, urbanization and Christianity has been shown to be incorrect. Certainly, there is less polygyny in the cities than in the countryside, but there is more polygyny in parts of Abidjan where a high proportion of the population have been to school and are in non-manual occupations than in areas where this is not the case. Education is being used to obtain a high-status occupation, but the income from this occupation is being used to finance a traditional goal – an extra wife. In addition, ethnic groups which traditionally favoured polygyny have been much slower to modernize in this respect than groups in which polygyny was relatively rare. Thus, involvement in modern society may have relatively little effect in changing a strong cultural norm. Modern behaviour (monogamy) and the expression of modern attitudes in this respect may have more to do with the lack of means than with the acceptance of a new norm.

Measures of attitudinal modernity should therefore be treated with considerable reserve. The development of modern attitudes in some aspects of life is quite compatible with the maintenance of traditional attitudes in other areas. There have also been cases, most notably in connection with independence movements, where elites consciously returned to traditional ways. The desire to become modern without becoming Western remains

[1] In the Tema Network Survey.
[2] An exception is Stephenson 1969.

strong in many countries, and is expressed by adherence to traditional ways in spite of their apparent incompatibility with an urban, industrial social structure. The modernity which results may place little emphasis on one or more of the attitudes currently included in the scales.

THE MODERNITY OF GHANAIAN FACTORY WORKERS

Although efforts have been made to develop theoretically satisfactory measures of modernity which could be used in all countries, the evidence available so far indicates that individuals identified as modern in one country may be quite different from those characterized as modern in another country in at least some of their attitudes and in their behaviour. Each society comes to modernization from a particular cultural background and structural transformation of the society is necessarily building on this cultural foundation, so the results differ from one country to another even when a modern industrial society has developed. This is more evident at the level of individuals than at the societal level.

Inkeles accommodated his scale to national differences by dichotomizing the answers to each question at the mean for each country separately. Differences between countries were considerable. For example, of the highly educated Nigerians in his sample, 86% of those with a low modernity score belonged to two or more organizations, compared to 97% of those with a high modernity score. The proportions for East Pakistanis were 0% and 6% respectively. While half the Pakistanis (irrespective of modernity score) were able to cite three or more city problems, only 1% of the Indian sample could do so (Inkeles 1969b:218, 215). Thus, modernity does not have the same characteristics in every country.

Ghanaian workers were not measured on these scales, and it should be evident that I would question the use of some of these measures in assessing them. Still, it may be helpful to summarize the information we have on their level of modernity and try to analyze the reasons why they appear to be less modern than industrial workers in some of the other countries where these scales have been used. Some of the factors militating against modernity as these scales measure it have been mentioned in the previous section. The discussion here will be based on measures of job stability and satisfaction and contacts with workmates off the job. Insofar as modernity is closely related to education and occupation, evidence has been presented throughout the book. Occupation will feature more largely in the present analysis because the industrial man hypothesis makes it the primary factor of change, though I do not think this is the case in Ghana.

Various studies have shown that most people are fairly well satisfied with their jobs, though people in more prestigious occupations are more satisfied than those in humbler occupations. As Blauner (1960:341) sums it up:

In a given plant, the proportion satisfied is higher among clerical workers than among factory workers, just as in general labour force samples it is higher among middle class than among manual working class occupations. Within the manual working class, job satisfaction is highest among skilled workers, lowest among unskilled labourers and workers on assembly lines.

The Ghanaian workers depart from this pattern in that skilled workers were considerably more satisfied with their jobs than the lower-level clerical workers and there was little to choose between unskilled and semiskilled workers (who were not on assembly-line-type jobs) in the proportion who were dissatisfied. The Ghanaians also showed lower satisfaction than the workers in developed or developing countries studied by Form (1969). The assumption of a fairly rapid adjustment to industrial work and relatively general satisfaction seems to fall down in this case.

The level of development of the country has something to do with these differences. None of the parents of the Ghanaian workers had been employed in a factory. The industrially or technologically based norms claimed to be present in modern societies are largely absent in Ghana and there are, instead, other norms to which workers are expected to respond. As two examples, take the importance of having a job and the sense of time. A Ghanaian worker may leave his job because he has inherited a traditional position, because a parent or relative is ill or has died and his services are needed at home, because he has inherited a farm, or because his relatives think he should be doing some other type of work or be working in some other town. The norms of the society dictate that one should not owe allegiance to any particular job, and the worker is usually well advised to follow them. A sense of time is basic to industrial experience, yet people at all levels of society, including factory workers, do not take time very seriously. This has already been discussed in chapter 4, but it can be added here that industrial development in Africa (and perhaps in Latin America as well) may not produce societies as dedicated to the clock as are Northern Europe and North America.

Inkeles has described the constraints of the modern factory which produce industrial men (1966:149):

Certain features of the modern factory are relatively invariant, and they communicate the same message, no matter what the cultural setting in which they may be installed. In them there is always an intense concentration of physical and mechanical power brought to bear on the transformation of raw materials; orderly

Q

and routine procedures to govern the flow of work are essential; time is a powerful influence in guiding the work process; power and authority generally rest on technological competence. In addition, a factory guided by modern management and personnel policies will set its workers an example of rational behavior, emotional balance, open communication, and respect for the opinions, the feelings, and the dignity of the worker which can be a powerful example of the principles and practice of modern living.

This description may apply to factories in Europe or America, but a visitor to Ghanaian factories might describe many of them in quite different terms. There may be little mechanical power in evidence; the flow of work may be subject to constant interruption; authority figures may have been appointed because they were related to the managers rather than for their technical competence; the rationality of personnel policies may not be at all evident to the average worker; and emotional balance, open communication and respect for the worker's dignity may be missing. In these circumstances, it is not surprising that workers learn more about modern living from education and adjustment to the city than they do from their employment in a factory.

Industrial workers score consistently higher than peasants on modernity scales, but there appears to be a relatively low correlation between modernization score and time spent in industrial employment (Inkeles 1969b:213). There is some increase in political and geographical information among the more experienced workers (holding education constant), but this might have been related to the length of time spent in a city. In any case, the difference is not significant in Nigeria, the only African country included in the study. To prove that industrial work makes one more aware of and interested in national and international news, or more modern in other ways, it would be necessary to compare industrial workers with other people of similar age, education and length of urban residence. At the time of writing this, such a comparison was not yet available.

Among Ghanaian workers, time on the job appears to have relatively little effect on job satisfaction. Workers who had been on the job at least five years were more satisfied with their foremen than newer workers, and the preference of semiskilled workers for their own jobs was also greater for those who had been employed at least five years, but the unskilled were least satisfied, and the skilled most satisfied, in each time period. Choice of a future job did not vary with the length of time the worker had held his present job except that long-term (and older) unskilled workers (especially those from northern Ghana) were most likely to be thinking of going into farming.

Job satisfaction varies by occupation because of the different wage levels for different jobs and the intrinsic rewards of practicing a skill. Nevertheless, there are various aspects of satisfaction as expressed in intended stability and preference for one's own type of work where age, origin and education are important factors regardless of occupation.

Though the generally low economic position of aliens shows up in complaints about pay, non-Ghanaians are generally more satisfied with their jobs and more interested in remaining in them than are Ghanaians. This applies to all occupational categories. It is not unrelated to the distance foreigners have had to travel and the fact that they cannot retire to a nearby farm if temporarily out of work. Stability on the job and satisfaction with the job generally increase with age. This may be a sign of adjustment or of resignation, with workers who originally hoped to better themselves deciding in their late twenties or early thirties that their chances of further mobility are low. Older unskilled and semiskilled workers who are illiterate are often looking forward to farming on retirement; those who hope to go into trade in future tend to be non-Ghanaians or clerical workers of city origin. Small businesses started by the latter would be quite different from the petty trading in which the former have specialized.

Workers of rural origin were particularly interested in changing to clerical work and achieving non-manual occupations for their children. If this is seen in terms of aspirations for upward mobility, workers of rural background would be more modern than those who grew up in the cities. However, this may be a desire for the prestige held by the clerk in colonial society and may spring from a lack of knowledge about the society which is developing. Generally, the less education a man has the more likely he is to want his children to work in a factory or learn a skill. Differences were small but consistent for various age and educational categories. This interest in skills seems to be a sign of greater modernity of orientation among the uneducated.

Middle-school leavers were generally less satisfied than other workers. In theory, they should find it easier to settle down to industrial employment than men who have not been to school, but the values of the society still strongly favour non-manual over manual occupations and many middle-school leavers inevitably find it hard to see themselves in the latter category, regardless of the favourable pay and conditions of their jobs relative to unskilled clerical work. This dissatisfaction is far less evident among middle-school leavers in skilled work than among those in unskilled and semiskilled jobs. This is one case where socialization on the job is evident. Many of the younger semiskilled workers hoped to become clerical or skilled workers, but older ones had evidently settled down; most said they preferred semiskilled work.

Support for the hypothesis that early socialization and societal development are more important than occupation comes with the finding that
northern Ghanaians are consistently different from southerners in the same
occupation in their stability and satisfaction with their jobs, in their aspirations for their own and their children's future and in their relations with
kinsmen and workmates off the job. While there are some differences between
southerners originating in the Capital District, Volta Region and other areas,
they are often remarkably similar in their responses. This is an indication of
the spread of social change in this area, so that migrants from villages to the
cities have already been exposed to new ideas and urban ways to an extent
still uncommon in the north. Even northerners who get an education and
training in a skill are strongly influenced by their primary socialization and
regular contacts with their less advanced fellows.

Two reasons for the lack of importance of occupation in the development
of modern attitudes in Ghana are that occupation is easily changed (as noted
in the discussion of occupational mobility) and that the average worker spends
little of his time off the job with workmates, so that his social life is effectively
dissociated from his working life. The people with whom he interacts off the
job may well counter the norms developed at work, rather than reinforcing
them. Well over half of the workers reported no contacts with workmates
outside of working hours and many of those who did see workmates limited
these to kinsmen and townsmen who happened to work at the same firm. It
was noted earlier (chapter 6) that more workers probably see mates off the
job than reported doing so, but it is apparent that many do not make friends
at work.

Although industrial workers in developed countries often find their
friends among non-workmates (Goldthorpe *et al.* 1969), this can be regarded
as a sign of lack of modernity in the Ghanaian case, since the alternative is
often spending time with relatives and townsmen. We would expect a
development of common interest through common employment to promote
some association of this type, especially since so many of the workers share a
common background. Workers were not expected to limit their friendships
to workmates, but to have at least one friend at work. That the association
with non-related workmates is a sign of modernity can be demonstrated in
the differences between men who said they spent time with workmates off
the job and those who did not.

Occupation is more important than place of origin in this case, probably
because it is easier to make friends in some types of work than in others.
Socializing with workmates who are neither kinsmen nor townsmen is most
prevalent among clerical workers and decreases progressively among semi-

skilled, unskilled and skilled workers. The younger unskilled and skilled workers have more non-ascriptive friends than the older ones, but age and time on the job have no affect among semiskilled and clerical workers, who are consistently more social. Illiterate unskilled workers, northerners and non-Ghanaians are more likely than others to associate only with workmates who are kinsmen or from their hometowns. Those who have been to school, however, are as unlikely as southerners and those in other jobs to choose friends on an ascriptive basis.

Workers over twenty-four who had attended middle school associated less with workmates to whom they were related and more with 'just friends' than those who had not been to school, but there was no difference among younger workers. This may be due to the spread of urban values into the countryside, whereby young men find it easier than older men to make friends in town, regardless of whether they have been to school.

To a certain extent, one can predict the modernity of a Ghanaian from his occupation. Clerical and semiskilled workers are more exposed to the paraphernalia of modernity – rational bureaucracy and complex machinery – than skilled and unskilled workers. However, it seems likely that their attitudes are influenced at least as much by the fact that they have been through ten years of schooling and come from an area where urban ideas are widespread as by the occupation they have attained. The gradual modernization of Ghanaian society will probably effect change in workers' values rather than (or to a greater extent than) the values which they develop on the job affect the modernization of the society. In this process, traditional values which the society maintains will remain strong among the workers in spite of conflicting values promoted by their industrial employment. The factories of the late 1960s were not, on the average, sufficiently modern to be strong promoters of new values among their employees.

VARIETIES OF 'INDUSTRIAL MAN'

Unless, and until it can be shown that these value orientations derive from the industrial system and are influenced significantly by the three kinds of changes, scale, organization and efficiency . . . it is not valid to hold that industrial societies will converge as a result of the immanent developments in the structure and function of enterprise. Such convergences as occur might better be explained by culture contact or diffusion . . . There is as yet insufficient sociological knowledge in this field to make valid predictions about convergence or divergence possible [Banks 1964:58].

There are three possible explanations why Ghanaian workers have different norms and values than those characterizing workers in industrialized countries:

(1) The 'industrial man' hypothesis is wrong. The experience of working in large, technologically advanced, bureaucratic organizations does not form men everywhere to the same mold.

(2) The hypothesis is not wrong, but Ghanaian factories have not yet developed sufficiently to require this type of adaptation from the workers. When the factories are larger and more complex and the workers are employed in them for longer periods, the expected changes will occur.

(3) The hypothesis is partly wrong. Advanced technological society does demand adjustment from members of the population, whether they live in the cities and work in the factories or merely participate in the relatively high standard of living which such a society makes possible. However, the cultural background of each country impresses itself on society at all stages of its development, so that the result differs from one country to another. There are some basic similarities associated with urban, industrial society, but each country contributes something unique to its modernity. I am inclined to accept this last view.

The 'industrial man' hypothesis has gone through two stages so far. The first, exemplified by Inkeles' pioneering essay (1960) and the work of Kerr and his associates (1962), was based on published material, mainly reports of studies carried out in advanced nations. Comparability of the results was often a problem, since different questions were asked in various countries and the user of secondary data has no control over the sample or techniques of data collection. Blumer (1960) proposed an alternate explanation of the observed phenomena, but this appears to have received little attention.

In the second stage, individuals or teams of sociologists have carried out identical surveys in two or more countries. The aim of their studies has been to provide comparability and control while testing hypotheses under rigorous conditions. The chief factor inhibiting a thorough understanding of the data collected is the difficulty in being well versed in the intricacies of more than two societies, including one's own. (This is partially handled by having local specialists on the team, but there is seldom one individual who is fully equipped to make the comparisons.) Cross-cultural researchers are usually looking for similarities, and usually find them. The differences, which are sometimes small, are much more difficult to explain than the similarities and are often ignored.

The third stage of research in this area will have to involve attempts to explain these differences, which are just as important as the similarities for a full understanding of modernity. Why are Indian and American automobile workers more favourable to agricultural work than Italians or Argentinians? (Form *et al.* 1970:7.) Why are Brazilians more concerned about personal relations on the job than Mexicans? (Kahl 1968:124.) Why are Nigerians so much more likely to belong to organizations than Pakistanis? (Inkeles 1969b:218.) Unless attention is paid to these differences, the qualities of modernity which differ from one country to another will be missed.

Studies of Japan have shown that some cultural autonomy can be compatible with industrialization, that nations can become modern without becoming thoroughly Western or European. This is more difficult for African nations to achieve than it was for Japan because such a large part of African industry is under European (including American) management, and because these societies are constantly influenced by advice and other material and non-material imports from the advanced Western nations, especially their former colonial masters.

Bendix (1970:293) points out that all industrializing countries have necessarily been influenced by the first ones, since these provide a model for change. Recent developments in transportation, mass communications and international politics have strengthened this process and made the relative isolation which accompanied Japanese industrialization impossible for today's developing nations. Nevertheless, Bendix argues that societies in transition must be studied from the standpoint of their pre-industrial structure, since this inevitably affects the end result.

The growth of private, locally owned and managed enterprise in Africa is an encouraging sign of social as well as economic independence. Europeans who study these entrepreneurs (and managers of state enterprises) may shake their heads over what they regard as inefficiency, but the experience has so far been too brief to indicate the direction of development. These firms, mostly small, often operate in a way that requires less adjustment of their workers than is the case in foreign-run firms. This, and the general feeling of being understood, results in considerable worker satisfaction. If these firms are allowed to develop in their own way, it is possible that a form of industrial life compatible with local values will gradually take shape. Workers in such firms are likely to be similar to industrial workers elsewhere in some of their attitudes, but in others they will remain uniquely African (Ghanaian, Senegalese, Tanzanian etc., as the case may be).

The Ghanaian factory worker is becoming modern while maintaining many aspects of his traditional culture. In the process, a new variety of 'industrial man' is developing. Recording this development should be a rewarding task for African industrial sociologists of the next twenty years.

THE INTERVIEW SCHEDULE[1]

No...................

Firm...............

1. A. What language do you speak most of the time? (ONE)
   B. What language do you speak mostly at work? (ONE)
   C. What other languages do you speak?
2. A. Are you a Christian, a Muslim, or do you believe in traditional religion or have you no religion at all? 8. Traditional[2] 9. None

   (IF CHRISTIAN) What Christian church do you belong to?
   3. Catholic   4. Presbyterian
   5. Methodist   6. Apostolic
   7. Other (SPECIFY):

   (IF MUSLIM) Which Muslim group do you belong to? o. Orthodox
   1. Ahmmadiya   2. Other:

3. A. What is your job here? (BE SPECIFIC)
   B. Have you always done the same work since you started here or have you done different jobs? (SPECIFY ALL JOBS) [A, P]
   C. Have you ever taken a trade test? [A]   1. Yes, passed in:
      o. No, never tried   2. Yes, but failed in:
   D. Are any of your relatives or men from your hometown working here?
      o. No.   1. Yes: Who?

      (ii) Were they working here before you came or have they come since?   1. Before
                                                                             2. Since
                                                                             3. Both
   E. How many weeks or months were you unemployed between your last job and this one? (IF FIRST JOB, BETWEEN LEAVING SCHOOL AND THIS ONE):
   F. What did you do during that time?
   G. How did you go about finding this job?
   H. Have you ever paid a dash to get a job? [P, R]
   I. How long did it take you to learn the job you are doing now?
   J. What is there about this job that you like?
   K. What is there about this job that you do not like?   (PROBE)   What things would you like changed or improved?

[1] A, P, or R indicates that the question was asked only in Accra/Tema, Provincial, or Rural interviews. Instructions to the interviewers are in small capitals. Extra forms for all tables were provided, though they have not been duplicated here.

[2] Where alternative answers are listed, the interviewer circled the number before the appropriate one.

4. A. How do you get to work? o. Walk 1. Bus 2. Lorry 3. Car (THE ONE HE DOES MOST) 4. Combination of:
   B. How long does it take you from the time you leave home until you arrive at work? o. Under 10 minutes. 1. 11–30 min. 2. 31–59 min. 3. 60+ min.
   C. How much does it cost you each day? (BOTH WAYS) .... np.
   D. Do you eat before starting work – either at home or on the way? [A, P] o. No 1. At home 2. Chop bar 3. Street seller X. sometimes (CIRCLE WHERE)

5. A. Do you ever meet men that you work with in the evenings or on weekends – to drink together, or go to football matches, or sit and talk?
   o. No 1. Yes: Are they relatives of yours or do they come from the same town or the same tribe? (SPECIFY):
   (CHECK THAT THESE ARE LISTED IN 3 D)

6. A. Where did you live most of the time when you were growing up?
   Place: Region or Country:
   B. Did you grow up in your own father's or mother's household? o. Both 1. Father 2. Mother 3. No: By whom were you reared?
   C. What was your father's occupation while you were growing up?
   (IF MORE THAN ONE, INDICATE ONE HE SPENT MOST TIME ON AS PRIMARY AND OTHERS AS SECONDARY) 2nd:
   D. (IF R IS OF A NON-GHANAIAN TRIBE) Did your father ever live in Ghana? 9. NA o. No 1. Yes: For how long?
   Where?   , R.

7. We would like to know about all the jobs you have had and all the places where you have lived.
   A. Did you work full time as a farmer or at some other job while you lived in ——? 1. Yes o. No, moved to: , R.
   B. What was the first work you did full time? (RECORD ON TABLE BELOW)

TABLE I

	First Job	2	3
1. What was the next job you had?			
2. How long were you without work between this and the previous job?			
3. A. Did you visit your home between jobs? (IF YES) How long did you stay?			
B. Did you farm or do some other work while you were at home? What?			
4. What year did you begin this job?			
5. Were you working for yourself, the government, or someone else? (SELF, GOVT, KIN, PRIV)			

239

Appendix

6. Where were you living?
   Place:
   Region or Country:

7. How old were you when you started
   this job?

8. (IF A SKILL) A. Did you have an
   apprenticeship before you became
   a — or did you just learn from
   another ——?
   (ON JOB, PRIV MASTER, KIN)
   B. How long was the apprenticeship
   (training)?
   C. Where were you living?
      Place:
      Region or Country:

9. How long did you work on this job?

10. Why did you leave? [R]

RETURN TO I UNTIL YOU COMPLETE TABLE INCLUDING PRESENT JOB.
NO PERIOD OF 3 OR MORE MONTHS SHOULD BE UNACCOUNTED FOR.

    C. Did you ever live anyplace else – somewhere you went to look for work or
to stay with a relative? (IF YES) Where?   ,   R.
How long did you stay there? .... months. (IF WORKED THERE,
INCLUDE ON THE TABLE)

8. A. How long do you think you will stay on this job? (PROBE) Do you think you
might leave in less than a year, or stay for 2 or 3 years, or 5 or 10 years?
0. Under 1 yr. 1. 1–3 yrs. 2. 4–5 yrs. 3. 6–10 yrs. 4. 11–15 yrs.
5. over 15 yrs. 6. until pension 7. other:
   B. What kind of job would you like to have after you leave here?
   C. How often in one day does the foreman or charge hand supervise your
   work (tell you what to do)?   1. At least once/hour
   2. sometimes (at least 2/day)   3. Rarely (less than 2/day)
   D. Generally, how well does your foreman get along with the workers?
   (COMMENTS)
   E. If you could have any job in this firm, which one would you choose?
               F. Why?
   G. If a young man asked your advice on what is the best work to do, what
   would you tell him: (i) If he was educated?
   (BE SPECIFIC)   (ii) If he had no education?
(IF HE GREW UP HERE, SKIP QUESTION 10)

9. You moved here in 19...
   A. Why did you decide to move to — instead of going someplace else?
   B. Why did you decide to come to — *just at that time*?
   C. Did you know anyone who was already living in —? (SPECIFY)
   D. Did you come to — alone at first, or did you move here with your family?

1. Nuclear family came together
2. Extended family came together
3. Came with wife, has no children
9. NA, no family (lives alone)
6. Met wife here

4. Came alone, others later————
5. Some with him, others later ————
E. How long after you moved to — did your — join you here?
     .... months

F. Did you find a place for yourself right away or did you share (eat and sleep) with someone else for a while? 1. Had own place
2. Shared: With whom did you stay? (BE SPECIFIC)
(ii) How long did you stay with them? .... months

G. When you first came to —, how long did it take you to find a job? [P, R]

10. A. What do you like best about living in —?
    B. What do you like least about living in —?
    C. Have you ever thought of moving to Accra? [R] What would be the advantages and disadvantages of such a move?

11. A. When you stop working, will you stay in —, go back to your hometown, or go somewhere else? 0. This is my hometown 1. Stay 2. Hometown
                              3. Other: ,   R.
    B. Why? [P, R]
    C. Do you have any land rights, so that you could take up farming if you wanted to? [A, P] 0. No 1. Yes

12. A. We would like to know something about your housing. Do you own your own house or do you rent? 0. Own 1. Rent: How much is the rent per month? NC . or £ .   . 2. Other:
    B. How many rooms are there in the whole house?
    C. How many rooms do you and your family use?
    D. If you could afford them, how many rooms do you think would be just right for yourself and your family (the people now living with you)? [P, R]
    E. How many people are living in your household (counting yourself)?

TABLE 2

	R	2	3
1. Relation to R (S, D, Wi, Br, Si, Mr, Friend)	Resp.		
2. Do they all usually eat and sleep there? [A, P]			
3. Sex (M or F)			
4. Age			
5. Education (None, lit, Musl, Pr, Mid, In-Pr, In-Sec, etc.)			
6. Birth: Place: Region/Country:			

7. Year moved here:
8. Former residence:
   Place:
   Region/Country:

ALL THOSE OVER 14:
9. Tribe
10. Single, wid., sep., or type of mar-
    riage: (Church, cust, Musl, ord,
    mutual consent)
11. Occupation   × × × ×
12. Place of work   × × × ×

F. (IF R WENT TO SCHOOL) How long after you left school did you start to
work full time? .... months 9. NA, no school
13. A. Do you have a wife (husband) who is not living in the same house with you?
   Number .... Where living? Place   ,   R. Tribe:
   B. (IF NOW MARRIED) For how long have you been married (to your present,
   chief wife? .... years [A, P]
14. Do you have any children who are not living in the same household with you?
   o. No 1. Yes: How many? (COMPLETE TABLE 3)

TABLE 3

	1	2	3	4
1. What ages are they?				
2. Which are boys and which are girls?				
3. Where are they? Place: Region:				
4. Who are they living with? (GIVE RELATIONSHIP TO RESPONDENT)				
5. Are they in school? (COMPLETED OR IN–)				

(IF HAS NO CHILDREN AT ALL, GO ON TO QUESTION 17.)
15. (IF HAS CHILDREN) Would you say that bringing up children in — is easier,
    about the same, or harder than bringing up children in a small farming village?
    o. Same   1. Easier   Why?
                  2. Harder
16. A. (IF HAS CHILDREN) Would you like your children to work in a factory or
    would you rather they did something else? o. Factory 2. Other:
    B. Why?
17. A. Do you think it is of great importance for boys to have as much education
    as possible or would a little or none at all be necessary?

1. As much as possible   2. Only a little   3. None necessary
4. Doesn't matter   9. Don't know
  B. How about girl children, how much education is necessary for them?
     1. As much as possible   2. A little   3. None   4. Doesn't matter   5. DK
  C. Have you ever studied by correspondence or at the Worker's College or
     part time at the Polytechnic? [A, P]   1. Yes: Subject:
     0. No   For how long?
  D. How much education would you like your oldest son to have? [R]
18. A. (IF R BELONGS TO NON-GHANAIAN TRIBE AND HAS LIVED IN GHANA
       FOR AT LEAST 5 YEARS): You have lived in Ghana for — years (OR You
       were born in Ghana); do you consider yourself a Ghanaian or a —?
       [A, P]
    B. (IF A WAS ASKED AND CHILDREN ARE IN GHANA) Are your children
       Ghanaians or —? [A, P]
19. How many brothers and sisters do you have, same father, same mother?
    .... brothers   .... sisters   .... total (NOT COUNTING SELF)

TABLE 4

	1	2	3	4	5
1. Brother or sister?					
2. Education					
3. Occupation					
4. Where living?					
Region:					

20. A. During the last year, how many times have relatives from outside — come
       to visit you? .... times
       0. None   B. Who was it? (SPECIFIC)
                   C. Where did they come from?   ,   R.
                   D. Did they bring you any gifts? What?
                   E. Did you give them any money or other things? How
                      much? [P, R]

(IF LIVING AT HOME, GO TO 21F)
21. A. Has anyone at home sent you any food or other gifts during the last year?
       0. No   1. Yes: What?
    B. About how often do you send money home?   .... times per year
    C. Who do you send it to? (SPECIFIC)
    D. How much do you send each time? NC   .   or £   . .
    F. (IF LIVES AT HOME) Do you give any money to your parents when you get
       paid?   0. No   1. Yes: How much each month? NC   .
22. A. What place do you consider your hometown? [P, R]   ,   R.
       (IF LIVING IN HOMETOWN, GO ON TO 23)
    B. When was the last time you visited your hometown? (Month)   , 19...

Appendix

C. How long did you stay? .... (IF OVER 2 MONTHS, IT SHOULD BE ON TABLE I)

D. How often did you visit your home since you left? .... times in .... years

E. How long do you usually stay? (IF OVER 2 MOS., LIST ON TABLE I)

F. Do you usually take gifts or money along? (HOW MUCH MONEY?)

23. A. What place outside — do you visit most often? [P, R] , R.

B. How often do you go there? [P, R]

C. Whom do you visit? [P, R]

24. A. How many times were you absent in the last month?
   0. None 1. .... times: What is the chief reason why you stay away from work?

B. How much did you earn in the last month — the amount you took home after taxes, pension, etc. had been taken out (but counting the advance)? NC .

Thank you very much. (CHECK THAT EVERY QUESTION HAS BEEN ANSWERED.)

AFTER THE INTERVIEW: Interviewee No.: Interviewer:

1. Language of interview: 1. Ewe 2. Akan 3. Ga 4. Hausa 5. other:
   6. English   7. Mixture of English and:
                     8. Mixture of vernaculars: and

2. Would you say he is generally satisfied with his job? Why or why not?
   0. No 1. Yes 2. Yes, except pay

BIBLIOGRAPHY

Abbey, J. L. F. 1970 'The National Service Corps', *Legon Observer*, IV (13 February), 5–7.

Acquah, I. 1958 *Accra Survey*. London: University of London Press.

Addo, N. O. 1967 'Assimilation and absorption of African immigrants in Ghana', *Ghana Journal of Sociology*, III: 17–32.

Amachree, I. T. D. 1968 'Reference group and worker satisfaction: studies among some Nigerian factory workers', *Nigerian Journal of Economic and Social Studies*, X: 229–38.

Ampene, E. 1967 'Obuasi and its miners', *Ghana Journal of Sociology*, III: 73–80.

Aryee, A. F. 1967 'Christianity and polygamy in Ghana: the role of the Church as an instrument of social change', *Ghana Journal of Sociology*, III: 98–105.

Baldamus, W. 1961 *Efficiency and effort*. London: Tavistock Publications.

Banks, J. A. 1964 'The structure of industrial enterprise in industrial society', in P. Halmos (ed.), *The Sociological Review Monograph*, no. 8. Keele, Staffs.: University of Keele.

Bell, E. M. 1961 *Polygons: A survey of the African personnel of a Rhodesian Factory*. Occasional Paper no. 2. Salisbury: Department of African Studies, University College of Rhodesia.

  1963 *Polygons, Part 2: a study of labour turnover*. Occasional Paper no. 3. Salisbury: Department of African Studies, University College of Rhodesia.

Bendix, R. 1970 *Embattled reason: essays on social knowledge*. New York: Oxford University Press.

Bissmann, K. 1969 'Industrial workers in East Africa', *International Journal of Comparative Sociology*, X: 22–30.

Blauner, R. 1960 'Work satisfaction and industrial trends in modern society', in W. Galenson and S. M. Lipset (eds.), *Labour and trade unionism*. New York: John Wiley and Sons.

  1964 *Alienation and freedom: the factory worker and his industry*. Chicago: University of Chicago Press.

Bloomberg, L. N. and Abrams, C. 1964 *United Nations mission to Kenya on Housing*. Nairobi: United Nations Department of Economic and Social Affairs.

Blumer, H. 1960 'Early industrialization and the labouring class', *The Sociological Quarterly*, I: 5–14.

Boateng, E. A. 1966 *A geography of Ghana*, 2nd ed. Cambridge University Press.

Bibliography

Busia, K. A. 1950 *Social survey of Sekondi–Takoradi*. London: Crown Agents for the Colonies.

Caldwell, J. C. 1967 'Population; general characteristics' and 'Migration and urbanization', in W. Birmingham *et al.* (eds.), *A study of contemporary Ghana: some aspects of social structure*. London: George Allen and Unwin, Ltd.

1968 'Determinants of rural–urban migration in Ghana', *Population Studies*, XXII: 361–77.

1969 *African rural–urban migration: the movement to Ghana's towns*. Canberra: Australian National University Press.

Carter, M. 1966 *Into work*. Harmondsworth: Penguin Books.

Census 1960 *Population Census of Ghana*. Accra: Central Bureau of Statistics.

Vol. II. *Statistics of localities and enumeration areas*. 1962.

Vol. IV. *Economic characteristics of local authorities, regions and total country*. 1964.

Vol. VI. *The Post Enumeration Survey*. Forthcoming.

Special Report A. *Statistics of large towns*. 1964.

Special Report E. *Tribes in Ghana*. 1964.

Central Bureau of Statistics 1962 *Statistical Reports*, series VII. Accra: Government Printer.

1963 *Directory of industrial enterprises and establishments*. Accra: Government Printer.

1966 *Quarterly digest of statistics*, XV (December 1966).

1967a *Industrial statistics 1965–66* Accra: Government Printer.

1967b *Statistical handbook 1967* Accra: Government Printer.

1967c *Quarterly digest of statistics*, XVI (March 1967).

1968 *Quarterly digest of statistics*, XVII (March 1968).

Chinoy, E. 1952 'The tradition of opportunity and the aspirations of automobile workers', *American Journal of Sociology*, LVII: 453–59.

Clignet, R. and Foster, P. 1966 *The fortunate few*. Evanston, Ill.: Northwestern University Press.

Clignet, R. and Sween, J. 1969 'Social change and type of marriage', *American Journal of Sociology*, LXXV: 123–45.

Davison, R. B. 1955 'African labour: studies of migrancy and industrial relations in a factory in the Gold Coast', unpublished Ph.D. thesis for London University.

1956 'The story of the Gold Coast railway', *West Africa*, pp. 515, 587, 607, 633, 657, 681.

Deniel, R. 1968 *De la savane à la ville*. Paris: Aubier-Montaigne.

Diop, A. B. 1965 *Société Toucouleur et migration*. Dakar: IFAN.

Doob, L. W. 1967 'Scales for assaying psychological modernization in Africa', *Public Opinion Quarterly*, XXXI: 414–21.

Duodu, C. 1967 *The gab boys*. London: Andre Deutsch.

Elkan, W. 1956 *An African labour force*. Kampala, Uganda: East African Institute of Social Research.

Fage, J. D. 1969 *A history of West Africa*, 4th ed. Cambridge University Press.

Feldman, A. and Hurn, C. 1966 'The experience of modernization', *Sociometry*, XIX: 378–95.

Form, W. H. 1969 'Occupational and social integration of automobile workers in four countries: a comparative study', *International Journal of Comparative Sociology*, X: 95–116.

Form, W. H. and Geschwender, J. A. 1962 'Social reference basis of job satisfaction', *American Sociological Review*, XXVII: 228–37.

Form, W. H., *et al.* 1970 'The accommodation of rural and urban workers to industrial discipline and urban living: a four nation study', in *Proceedings of the Seventh World Congress of Sociology*, Varna, Bulgaria.

Fortes, M., Steel, R. W. and Ady, P. 1947 'Ashanti Survey, 1945–46: an experiment in social research', *Geographical Journal*, CX: 149–79.

Foster, P. J. 1965 *Education and social change in Ghana*. London: Routledge and Kegan Paul.

Fraenkel, M. 1964 *Tribe and class in Monrovia*. London: Oxford University Press.

Gamble, D. P. 1966 'Occupational prestige in an urban community (Lunsar) in Sierra Leone', *Sierra Leone Studies*, new series no. 19, pp. 98–108.

Garlick, P. C. 1959 *African traders in Kumasi*. Accra: Economic Research Division, University College of Ghana.

Golding, P. T. F. 1962 'An enquiry into household expenditure and consumption and sale of household produce in Ghana', *The Economic Bulletin of Ghana*, VI, no. 4, pp. 11–33.

Goldthorpe, J. H., *et al.* 1968 *The affluent worker: industrial attitudes and behaviour*. Cambridge University Press.

1969. *The affluent worker in the class structure*. Cambridge University Press.

Goody, E. 1966 'The fostering of children in Ghana: a preliminary report', *Ghana Journal of Sociology*, II: 26–33.

1970 'Kinship fostering in Gonja', in P. Mayer (ed.), *Socialization: the approach of social anthropology*. A.S.A. Monographs no. 8. London: Tavistock Publications.

Gulliver, P. 1957 *Labour migration in a rural economy*. East African Studies no. 6. Kampala, Uganda: East African Institute of Social Research.

Hart, J. K. 1969 'Entrepreneurs and migrants: a study of modernization among the Frafras of Ghana.' unpublished Ph.D. thesis for Cambridge University.

Hauser, A. 1961 'L'Absentisme et la mobilité des travailleurs des industries manufacturières de la région de Dakar.' Dakar, Senegal: IFAN. Mimeographed.

1965 *Rapport d'enquête sur les travailleurs des industries manufacturières de la région de Dakar*. Dakar, Senegal: IFAN.

1968a *Les ouvriers de Dakar: étude psychosociologique*. Paris: ORSTOM.

1968b 'Les problèmes du travail', in M. Sankale *et al.* (eds.), *Dakar en devenir*. Paris: Présence Africaine.

Hutton, C. 1972 *Reluctant farmers: some aspects of the balance of unemployment and rural development in Uganda*.

Imoagene, S. O. 1967 'Psycho-social factors in rural–urban migration', *Nigerian Journal of Economic and Social Studies*, IX: 375–86.

Inkeles, A. 1960. 'Industrial man: the relation of status to experience, perception, and value', *American Journal of Sociology*, LXVI: 1–31.

1966 'The modernization of man', in M. Weiner (ed.), *Modernization: the dynamics of growth*. New York: Basic Books.

R

Bibliography

1969a. 'Comments on John Stephenson's "Is everyone going modern?"',
American Journal of Sociology, LXXV: 146–51.

1969b 'Making men modern: on the causes and consequences of individual
change in six developing countries', *American Journal of Sociology*, LXXV:
208–25.

Kahl, J. A. 1968 *The measurement of modernism: A study of values in Brazil and
Mexico*. Latin American Monographs no. 12. Austin: University of Texas
Press.

Kerr, C., *et al.* 1962 *Industrialism and industrial man*. London: Heinemann.

Kilby, P. 1961 'African productivity reconsidered', *The Economic Journal*,
LXXI: 273–91.

1965 *African enterprise: the Nigerian bread industry*. Stanford, Calif.: Stanford
University, The Hoover Institution on War, Revolution and Peace.

Killick, T. 1966 'Labour: a general survey', 'Labour: industrial productivity'
and 'Manufacturing and construction', in W. Birmingham *et al.* (eds.), *A
study of contemporary Ghana: the economy of Ghana*. London. George Allen
and Unwin.

Kimble, D. 1963 *A political history of Ghana*. Oxford: Clarendon Press.

Klein, L. 1964 *Multiproducts Ltd*. London: HMSO.

La Fontaine, J. S. 1970 *City politics: a study of Leopoldville, 1962–63*. Cambridge
University Press.

Lambert, R. D. 1963 *Workers, factories, and social change in India*. Princeton,
N.J.: Princeton University Press.

Lawson, R. M. 1966 'Inflation in the consumer market in Ghana', *The Economic
Bulletin of Ghana*, X: 36–51.

1967 'Innovation and growth in traditional agriculture of the Lower Volta,
Ghana', *Journal of Development Studies*, IV: 138–73.

Leslie, J. A. K. 1963 *A survey of Dar es Salaam*. London: Oxford University
Press.

LeVine, R. A. 1966 *Dreams and deeds: achievement motivation in Nigeria*.
Chicago: University of Chicago Press.

Lewis, W. A. 1953 *Industrialisation and the Gold Coast*. Accra: Government
Printer.

Lloyd, P. C. 1967 'The elite', in P. C. Lloyd *et al.* (eds.), *The city of Ibadan*.
Cambridge University Press.

Lupton, T. 1963 *On the shop floor*. Oxford: Pergamon Press.

Mabogunje, A. L. 1968 *Urbanization in Nigeria*. London: University of London
Press.

Macmillan, A. 1920 *The red book of West Africa*. London: W. H. & L. Collingridge.

Marris, P. 1961 *Family and social change in an African city*. London: Routledge
and Kegan Paul.

Mayer, P. 1962 'Migrancy and the study of Africans in towns', *American
Anthropologist*, LXIV: 576–92.

Mills-Odoi, D. G. 1967 'The La family and social change', unpublished M.A.
thesis for the Institute of African Studies, University of Ghana, Legon.

Mills-Odoi, G. C. 1967 *Report of the Commission on the Structure and Remuneration of the Public Services in Ghana*. Accra: Government Printer.

Ministry of Education 1970 *Primary school enrolment by local authorities and Middle school enrolment by local authorities.* Accra: mimeographed.

Ministry of Lands, Town and Country Planning Division 1965 *National Physical Development Plan 1963–70.* Accra: Government Printer.

Mitchell, J. C. 1951 'A note on the urbanization of Africans on the Copperbelt', *Rhodes–Livingstone Journal*, no. 12, pp. 20–7.

1961 *Sociological background to African labour.* Salisbury, Rhodesia: Ensign Publishers.

1966 'Theoretical orientations in African urban studies', in M. Banton (ed.), *The social anthropology of complex societies.* A.S.A. Monographs, no. 4. London: Tavistock Publications.

1969 *Social networks in urban situations.* Manchester University Press.

Mitchell, J. C. and Epstein, A. L. 1959 'Occupational prestige and social status among urban Africans in Northern Rhodesia', *Africa*, XXIX: 22–40.

Morris, M. D. 1960 'The recruitment of an industrial labour force in India, with British and American comparisons', *Comparative Studies in Society and History*, II: 305–28.

Oppong, C. 1966 'The Dagomba response to the introduction of state schools', *Ghana Journal of Sociology*, II: 17–25.

Peil, M. 1966 'Factory management and workers in the Accra Capital District', *The Economic Bulletin of Ghana*, X: 23–35.

1967 'The household heads', in A. K. Quarcoo *et al.*, *The Madina Survey*. Legon: Institute of African Studies, University of Ghana.

1968a 'Aspirations and social structure: a West African example', *Africa*, XXXVIII: 71–8.

1968b 'Migration of middle school leavers in Ghana', paper presented at symposium on Population and Socioeconomic Development at the University of Ghana. (Mimeographed.)

1968c 'Reactions to housing: a survey of Tema', *Ghana Journal of Sociology*, IV: 1–18.

1969 'Unemployment in Tema: the plight of the skilled worker', *Canadian Journal of African Studies*, III: 409–20.

1970 'The apprenticeship system in Accra', *Africa*, XL: 137–50.

Pfeffermann, G. 1968 *Industrial labor in the Republic of Senegal.* New York: Frederick A. Praeger.

Plotnicov, L. 1967 *Strangers to the city.* Pittsburgh, Pa.: Pittsburgh University Press.

Pons, V. 1969 *Stanleyville.* London: Oxford University Press.

Rimmer, D. 1970 'Wage politics in West Africa.' Birmingham University: Faculty of Commerce and Social Sciences, Occasional Paper no. 12. Mimeographed.

Rouch, J. 1954 *Migration in the Gold Coast.* Accra. (Mimeographed.)

Scott, C. 1967 *Survey of Ghana middle schools, 1966.* Accra: Statistical Training Centre. (Mimeographed.)

Seibel, H. D. 1968 *Industriearbeit und Kulturwandel in Nigeria.* Köln und Opladen: Westdeutscher Verlag.

Sheth, N. R. 1968 *The social framework of an Indian factory.* Manchester University Press.

Bibliography

Skinner, E. P. 1960 'Labour migration and its relationship to socio-cultural change in Mossi society', *Africa*, XXX: 375–401.

Slotkin, J. S. 1960 *From field to factory: new industrial employees*. Glencoe, Ill.: The Free Press.

Smelser, N. J. 1959 *Social change in the Industrial Revolution*. London: Routledge and Kegan Paul.

1968 *Essays in sociological explanation*. Englewood Cliffs, N.J.: Prentice Hall.

Smith, D. H. and Inkeles, A. 1966 'The OM Scale: a comparative socio-psychological measure of individual modernity', *Sociometry*, XXIX: 353–77.

Sofer, C. and Sofer, R. 1955 *Jinja transformed: a social survey of a multi-racial township*. Kampala, Uganda: East African Institute of Social Research.

Stephenson, J. 1968 'Is everyone going modern? A critique and a suggestion for measuring modernism', *American Journal of Sociology*, LXXIV: 265–75.

1969 'The author replies', *American Journal of Sociology*, LXXV: 151–6.

Taylor, J. V. and Lehmann, D. A. 1961 *Christians of the Copperbelt*. London: SCM Press.

Turner, A. N. 1955 'Interaction and sentiment in the foreman–worker relationship', *Human Organization*, XIV, no. 1, pp. 10–16.

University of Natal 1950 *Dunlops: the African factory worker*. Cape Town: Oxford University Press.

Van der Horst, S. 1964 *African workers in town*. Cape Town: Oxford University Press.

Wells, F. A. and Warmington, W. A. 1962 *Studies in industrialization: Nigeria and the Cameroons*. London: Oxford University Press for the Nigerian Institute of Social and Economic Research.

Wilensky, H. L. 1960 'Work, careers and social integration', *International Social Science Journal*, XII: 543–74.

Wober, M. 1967 'Individualism, home life and work efficiency among a group of Nigerian workers', *Occupational Psychology*, XLI: 183–92.

Xydias, N. 1956 'Prestige of occupations', in D. Forde (ed.), *Social implications of industrialization and urbanization in Africa south of the Sahara*. Paris: UNESCO.

Yaukey, D. 1955 'A metric measurement of occupational status', *Sociology and Social Research*, XXXIX: 317–23.

Zweig, F. 1952 *The British worker*. Harmondsworth: Penguin Books.

INDEX

Index